The
Acts of the Apostles

R.H.Horton
Author of *An Introduction to the Bible*

E.O.N. Aghaegbuna
Head, Bible Knowledge Department,
Uwani Secondary School, Enugu

with
"Palestine and its People"
by Dr. J.A. Ilori,
President, NABKTN

Edward Arnold
in association with the
**National Association of Bible Knowledge Teachers
of Nigeria**
and
African Universities Press

© R. H. Horton and E. O. N. Aghaegbuna
First published 1982
by Edward Arnold (Publishers) Ltd
41 Bedford Square, London WC1B 3DQ
© 1982 Dr. J. A. Ilori, "Palestine and its People"

Reprinted 1982

ISBN 0 7131 8084 6

Acknowledgement

The Bible text in this publication is from the Revised Standard Version of the Bible, copyrighted 1946, 1952, © 1971, 1973 by the Division of Christian Education of the National Council of the Churches of Christ in the U.S.A. and used by permission.

The publishers would also like to thank Thomas Nelson & Sons U.K. Ltd. for permission to redraw a diagram from A. S. Peake: *Commentary on the Bible* ed. Black, Matthew and Rowley.

Illustrated by Peter Jamieson

Set IBM 11pt Journal & Univers by 𝍄\Tek-Art, Croydon, Surrey
Printed and bound in Great Britain at
The Camelot Press Ltd, Southampton

To our wives

R.H.H.
and
E.O.N.A.

Contents

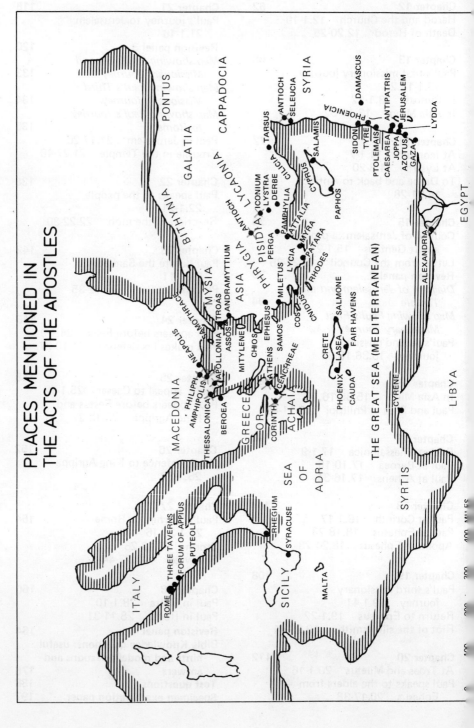

PLACES MENTIONED IN
THE ACTS OF THE APOSTLES

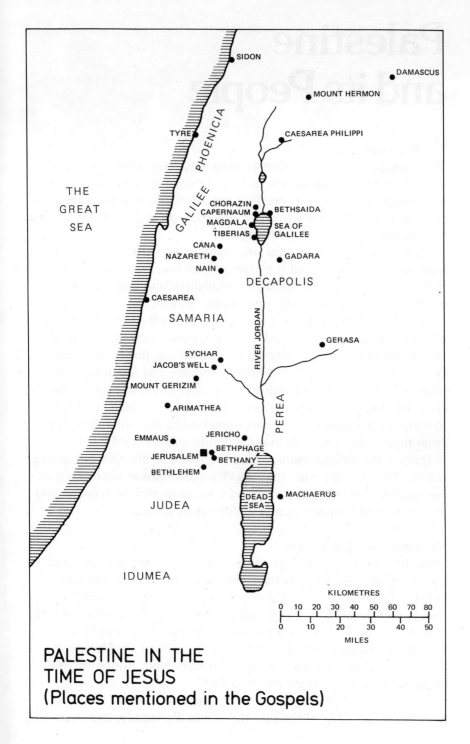

PALESTINE IN THE
TIME OF JESUS
(Places mentioned in the Gospels)

Palestine
and its People

The Pharisees

These were probably so called because they advocated a policy of
separation and independence, both in national affairs and in matters
of ceremonial cleanliness. Another explanation is that the name was
given to them after the separation or expulsion at one period of their
representatives from the Sanhedrin.

Their guiding principle was strict obedience to the letter of the
Law, and the Tradition of the Elders which had accumulated around
it. Politically, they were strongly nationalistic and opposed
submission to Rome or any other foreign power.

During the early years of their history they effected a great reform
of the religious life of their countrymen, making the synagogue a
real centre of prayer and instruction in the Law. But by the time of
Our Lord the extremists of the party, followers of Shammai, seem to
have held the reins, and Phariseeism degenerated into more of an
outward observance of prescribed rules and formulae. This led them
to adopt an attitude of intolerance and hypocrisy, which brought
upon them Jesus' condemnation as 'white-washed tombs'.

Despite the unfavourable picture presented in the New Testament,
it should not be forgotten that the Pharisees represented much that
was good in Judaism and performed a valuable service in protecting
the worship of Yahweh against idolatrous innovations.

The Sadducees (Zaddikim)

These probably derived their name from Zadok, the high priest of
David's reign. Like the Pharisees, they accepted the written Law
(Torah), but denied the authority of the prophetic books and
rejected the whole of the oral tradition. No doctrine or practice was
regarded as binding unless based on the written Law, and for this
reason they could not accept the prophetic idea of the Messiah as
"the son of David". They also denied resurrection, future life, the
existence of angels and spirits (Acts 23.8).

They were the aristocratic, wealthy party which held the high
priesthood and most of the priestly offices. Politically, they were

not opposed to foreign rule, and being in possession of the best financial positions, they readily acquiesced to the Roman domination of Palestine. The primary goal of the Sadducees was the continuation of the Temple services under the supervision of the authorized clergy. To attain this goal, they were sometimes more willing to collaborate with foreign rulers than stricter Jews thought they should be.

They were regarded, and also regarded themselves, as strict and conservative because they insisted on taking only the written Law or Torah as their rule of faith.

The Sanhedrin

This probably had its origin in the council of 'seventy men of the Elders of Israel', appointed by divine command to assist Moses to bear the burden of the people in the wilderness (Numbers 11.16). The high priest was president, and the seventy members consisted of representatives from the three ruling classes: chief priests, scribes and elders, the last-named being men chosen for their integrity and breadth of experience. No money-lender or proselyte was eligible for membership.

The duty of the Sanhedrin was to administer the law in all its fullness, and it formed a final court of appeal in matters criminal, civil and religious, to which all the more serious cases from the local councils were referred. The Sanhedrin alone could impose a capital sentence.

The court met daily (except on the sabbath and feast days), usually in the Temple, but on some special occasions in the house of the high priest.

The Scribes

They were the interpreters and teachers of the Jewish Law and did not form a religious sect, but were mostly drawn from that of the Pharisees. They were well represented in the Sanhedrin, where their legal knowledge was of great service, as were their commentaries on the judicial decrees of the Sanhedrin.

The Publicans

The collection of the taxes from the provincial subjects of the Roman Empire was in the hands of the publicans, who formed the wealthy capitalist class of the Imperial City. Many of them were unjust and extortionate in their demands, though Zacchaeus of Jericho seems to have been a notable exception.

St. John the Baptist exhorts them to 'collect no more than is appointed you'. When mentioned in the Gospels they are almost invariably classed with sinners.

The Zealots

The Zealots, so called because of their fiery nationalistic zeal, saw the future of Judaism in terms of an independent Jewish state, and jumped at the slightest opportunity to revolt against their overlords, fully trusting that Yahweh would come to their aid.

Unfortunately, their zeal outdistanced their realism and eventually gave rise to rebellions (in A.D. 66 – 70 and A.D. 132 – 135) that led to the destruction of Jerusalem and the dissolution of the Jewish state. This party continued to exist until the siege of Jerusalem, when they again opposed the might of Rome and were the last survivors of the defending forces.

One of their members, Simon the Zealot, was called to be an Apostle of Our Lord.

The Synagogue

The synagogue originated during the captivity in Babylon. This form of worship continued after the return, and synagogues sprang up in large numbers. In Christ's time, synagogues appeared in every town and village, and it is said that at the time of the destruction of Jerusalem by Titus there were 480 such buildings in the city.

The synagogue was used not only as the place of worship on the sabbaths and fast days, but also during the week as a school for the instruction of the young, and as a local tribunal in which the court of Elders administered justice and dealt with petty offences, inflicting punishment in the form of fines, scourging, imprisonment and excommunication. The chief official was the ruler of the synagogue, who was responsible for the appointment of readers and for the general conduct of the services.

The Tradition of the Elders

This tradition claimed that, along with the written law given to Moses, there were a number of oral instructions of equal or greater importance, and these, together with the written law formed a complete guidance for all the affairs of life.

This oral tradition consisted mainly of the scribes' interpretation of the case law and contained a mass of trivial ceremonial details, such as the ceremony of washing hands before eating.

Introduction

This Book of the New Testament, written by the author of St. Luke's Gospel, is a sequel to his story of Jesus. It is the first written history of the early days of the Christian Church. The opening words refer to the preface to the Gospel (Luke 1.1-4), and the story of the Church begins with Jesus' Ascension.

We read about the disciples — now the Apostles — and how they continue Jesus' mission. The first twelve chapters tell of Peter, John and Philip, of the life and work of the disciples in Jerusalem, and of the spread of the mission from that city to other parts of Palestine. The remaining sixteen chapters are concerned with the life and work of the great missionary Paul and his friends, much of whose preaching was carried out in distant places, such as Europe and Asia Minor.

In his writing Luke describes in detail the attacks made on the Early Church by its various enemies. He tries to show that the Christian faith is really a part of Judaism, a natural development of the Jewish religion, and brought about by the long-awaited Messiah, Jesus Christ: a concept which the Jewish authorities of the time are unable either to understand or accept.

Luke's aim is to show that the Gospel is for everyone, Jew or Gentile, who believes Jesus to be the Messiah through whose death, Resurrection and Ascension — all part of God's great purpose — the Kingdom of God will be brought about. So he tells from the beginning the story of the spread of the Gospel to the Jews, Samaritans and Gentiles, the conversions and the baptisms, the coming of the Holy Spirit, and the miracles done by the Apostles in the Name of Jesus.

As the introduction (1.1-5) may suggest, the book is aimed especially at Roman readers, describing for them the nature of the Early Christian Church, its growth and its effect upon both Jewish and Roman authorities.

The end of the book is sudden; no details are given of Paul's trial in Rome. Some believe that it was Luke's intention to write a third book: this may have been the case, for if he were writing later than about A.D. 65 he would have had to include the fate of Paul. The fact that Luke used Mark's Gospel in writing his own sets the date of Luke's Gospel as later than A.D. 64-65, and it has been suggested that this second book, Acts, belongs to A.D. 80 or even later.

An interesting feature of the Acts is what we call the 'we passages', which imply strongly that the author was himself present during parts of Paul's journeys; these passages are indicated in the notes.

Preface

This series has been written with the specific needs of the WASC Bible Knowledge student in mind. In this volume the full text of the Acts of the Apostles in the Revised Standard Version is combined with clear, concise notes in such a way that the reader can follow both simultaneously, with ease: the double-page format enables the student or teacher of Bible Knowledge to refer at a glance to the verse of Scripture and its accompanying commentary, saving valuable time and preserving concentration during class or periods of private study.

Each section ends with a revision panel which gives a detailed overview of the material and identifies the key points within it. This information is intended both to complement the briefer notes and to indicate those areas of the Bible text which require particular attention for examination purposes.

Useful advice is also included on dealing with the different types of question, together with model answers and a complete specimen examination paper.

For those, particularly teachers, requiring knowledge of a more specialized nature, we list the following works of reference:

Peake's Commentary on the Bible
Chronology of the New Testament G.Ogg
The Theology of the New Testament John Marsh
The Apostolic Age and the Life of Paul W.D. Davies
Acts G.W.H. Lampe (Nelson)
Torch Bible Paperbacks
Acts of the Apostles R.R. Williams (S.C.M. Press)
New Clarendon Bible
The Acts in the R.S.V. R.P.C. Hanson (Oxford University Press)

R.H.H.
E.O.N.A.

The
Acts of the Apostles

LINK WITH THE GOSPEL   1.1-5

1 In the first book, O The-oph'ilus, I have dealt with all that Jesus began to do and teach, ²until the day when he was taken up, after he had given commandment through the Holy Spirit to the apostles whom he had chosen. ³To them he presented himself alive after his passion by many proofs, appearing to them during forty days, and speaking of the kingdom of God. ⁴And while staying*a* with them he charged them not to depart from Jerusalem, but to wait for the promise of the Father, which, he said, "you heard from me, ⁵for John baptized with water, but before many days you shall be baptized with the Holy Spirit."

THE ASCENSION   1.6-14

⁶So when they had come together, they asked him, "Lord, will you at this time restore the kingdom to Israel?" ⁷He said to them, "It is not for you to know times or seasons which the Father has fixed by his own authority. ⁸But you shall receive power when the Holy Spirit has come upon you; and you shall be my witnesses in Jerusalem and in all Judea and Samar'ia and to the end of the earth." ⁹And when he had said this, as they were looking on, he was lifted

a   Or 'eating'

Link with the Gospel   1.1-5

A summary of the end of Luke's Gospel and events of the 'forty days' (v.3) between the Resurrection and the Ascension of Jesus.

1   Links with Luke 1.1-4 and what his Gospel is about: 'all that Jesus began to do and teach'. Theophilus is not known, and the name may not be the real name of any person; perhaps he is a Roman who holds some important post.

2   'The day when he was taken up' is the end of the Gospel (24.49-51). 'The Holy Spirit' (and v.5) is an important feature of Luke's Gospel and the Acts.

3   Jesus' appearances to His disciples: Matthew 28.9, 16-18; Mark 16.9-10, 12, 14-19; Luke 24.13-31, 34, 36, 50-51; John 20.14-17, 19, 26; 21.1-24. 'Forty days' is not an exact number, but simply many days: cf. the Flood (Genesis 7.17); the Spies in Canaan (Numbers 13.25); Moses on Sinai (Exodus 24.18); Elijah's journey to Horeb (I Kings 19.8); Jesus in the wilderness (Matthew 4.2; Mark 1.13; Luke 4.2).

4   'The promise' of Luke 24.49.

5   'Baptized with the Holy Spirit' as foretold by John the Baptist (Matthew 3.11; Mark 1.8; Luke 3.16).

The Ascension   1.6-14

6   The Apostles await the coming of the Spirit to bring in God's Kingdom. 'Restore the kingdom to Israel' suggests that some may still be thinking of an earthly kingdom.

7   Jesus tells them not to worry about how or when.

8   In Acts, the Holy Spirit is the source of the Christians' strength. With the Spirit's help they are to be missionaries: their work begins in Jerusalem (chapters 1-7) but will spread to Judea and Samaria (chapters 8-9) and beyond (chapters 10ff). 'To the end of the earth' — it is hard to understand that some were later reluctant to admit Gentiles (non-Jews).

9   The 'cloud' is supernatural and recalls the Transfiguration (Matthew 17.5; Mark 9.7; Luke 9.34-35). The scene recalls the taking up of Elijah (2 Kings 2.9-12).

up, and a cloud took him out of their sight. [10] And while they were gazing into heaven as he went, behold, two men stood by them in white robes, [11] and said, "Men of Galilee, why do you stand looking into heaven? This Jesus, who was taken up from you into heaven, will come in the same way as you saw him go into heaven."

[12] Then they returned to Jerusalem from the mount called Olivet, which is near Jerusalem, a sabbath day's journey away; [13] and when they had entered, they went up to the upper room, where they were staying, Peter and John and James and Andrew, Philip and Thomas, Bartholomew and Matthew, James the son of Alphaeus and Simon the Zealot and Judas the son of James. [14] All these with one accord devoted themselves to prayer, together with the women and Mary the mother of Jesus, and with his brothers.

AN APOSTLE TO REPLACE JUDAS   1.15-26

[15] In those days Peter stood up among the brethren (the company of persons was in all about a hundred and twenty), and said, [16] "Brethren, the scripture had to be fulfilled, which the Holy Spirit spoke beforehand by the mouth of David, concerning Judas who was guide to those who arrested Jesus. [17] For he was numbered among us, and was allotted his share in this ministry. [18] (Now this man bought a field with the reward of his wickedness; and falling headlong*b* he burst open in the middle and all his bowels gushed out. [19] And it became known to all the inhabitants of Jerusalem, so that the field was called in their language Akel'dama, that is, Field of Blood.) [20] For it is written in the book of Psalms,

'Let his habitation become desolate,
and let there be no one to live in it';
and
'His office let another take.'

[21] So one of the men who have accompanied us during all the time that the Lord Jesus went in and out among us, [22] beginning from the baptism of John until the day when he was taken up from us — one of these men must become with us a witness to his resurrection." [23] And they put forward two, Joseph called Barsabbas, who was

b Or 'swelling up'

4

10-11   'White robes' suggests heavenly beings (cf. Luke 24.4). Jesus
        will come again as 'the Son of man coming in a cloud with
        power and great glory' (Luke 21.27): this is the Parousia
        (Second Coming), and early Christians believe this will be
        soon. They must not 'stand looking into heaven' — it is not
        to happen yet.
12   'Olivet' — according to Zechariah (14.4) this is the scene of
        the coming of the Lord. 'A sabbath day's journey' is the
        distance the Law allows a Jew to travel on the sabbath, six
        furlongs or two thousand cubits (nearly one thousand metres).
13   'The upper room' may well be the scene of the Last Supper,
        in the house of John Mark's mother (12.12).
14   'The women' are probably their wives. Jesus' mother and
        brothers join (cf. Mark 3.31; John 7.5). 'His brothers' seem
        to be sons of Mary and Joseph born after Jesus, but those
        who object to this suggest that the word means cousins:
        they are named by Mark (6.3). They do not believe in Jesus
        during His ministry and are not mentioned again in Acts,
        except for James (12.17; 15.13; 21.18).

An Apostle to replace Judas   1.15-26
15   The number of disciples is growing: Peter is leader (cf.
        Matthew 16.18).
16-17   Peter recalls events, all part of God's plan. The early
        Christian Church believes all the Psalms to be the work of
        David: by means of them the Holy Spirit speaks of the
        coming Messiah.
18-19   'A field' — a smallholding. This story differs from Matthew's
        (Matthew 27.5-8): the name of the field is the same, and in
        each case Judas dies violently: the way in which he dies and
        the buying of the field are different.
20   The words of the Psalms (69.25 and 109.8) are used to refer
        to Judas and what becomes of his smallholding and 'his
        office' as apostle.
21-22   The one chosen must have been present at all events from the
        Baptism of Jesus to His Ascension: an Apostle must be 'a
        witness to his resurrection'.
23   'They' — probably all present.

surnamed Justus, and Matthi'as. ²⁴And they prayed and said, "Lord, who knowest the hearts of all men, show which one of these two thou hast chosen ²⁵to take the place in this ministry and apostleship from which Judas turned aside, to go to his own place." ²⁶And they cast lots for them, and the lot fell on Matthi'as; and he was enrolled with the eleven apostles.

THE DAY OF PENTECOST 2.1-47

2 When the day of Pentecost had come, they were all together in one place. ²And suddenly a sound came from heaven like the rush of a mighty wind, and it filled all the house where they were sitting. ³And there appeared to them tongues as of fire, distributed and resting on each one of them. ⁴And they were all filled with the Holy Spirit and began to speak in other tongues, as the Spirit gave them utterance.

⁵Now there were dwelling in Jerusalem Jews, devout men from every nation under heaven. ⁶And at this sound the multitude came together, and they were bewildered, because each one heard them speaking in his own language. ⁷And they were amazed and wondered, saying, "Are not all these who are speaking Galileans? ⁸And how is it that we hear, each of us in his own native language? ⁹Par'thians and Medes and E'lamites and residents of Mesopota'mia, Judea and Cappado'cia, Pontus and Asia, ¹⁰Phryg'ia and Pamphyl'ia, Egypt and the parts of Libya belonging to Cyre'ne, and visitors from Rome, both Jews and proselytes, ¹¹Cretans and Arabians, we hear them telling in our own tongues the mighty works of God." ¹²And all were amazed and perplexed, saying to one another, "What does this mean?" ¹³But others mocking said, "They are filled with new wine."

¹⁴But Peter, standing with the eleven, lifted up his voice and addressed them, "Men of Judea and all who dwell in Jerusalem, let

24-25 Luke often mentions the importance of prayer. The Lord alone chooses apostles (v.2): now He is to guide the choice through 'lots'. Decisions are often made in this way (cf. Mark 15.24) and Jews and Christians believe the decision is made by God.

26 Matthias is chosen to take Judas's place in 'ministry and apostleship' (v.25). Nothing more is known of him or of Barsabbas.

The Day of Pentecost   2.1-13

1 Pentecost, fifty days after Passover, marks the beginning of harvest: it is also known as the Feast of Weeks (Exodus 34.22), the Feast of Ingathering (Exodus 23.16) and the Day of First Fruits (Numbers 28.26). By Luke's time it also commemorates the giving of the Law on Sinai (Exodus 19.1). 'All together' may mean the 'hundred and twenty' (1.15), but v.14 suggests the Twelve.

2-3 'Wind' and 'fire' often mark the presence of God or the Holy Spirit (cf. Luke 3.16): this is what John the Baptist foretells.

4 'Other tongues' are not needed for the apostles to speak: their hearers understand Greek or Aramaic. This may mean the flow of strange words under the influence of the Holy Spirit, the promise of the prophet Joel (Joel 2.28-32 and Acts 2.16-21). This still happens and is known as 'glossolalia': such speaking explains v.13.

5 There are Jews living in many countries and a great number are in the city.

9-11 Places are named, generally speaking, from east to west.

10 'Proselytes' are converts to Judaism who have accepted circumcision and other Jewish rites. (There are also God-fearers, attracted to the Jewish religion but not fully converted.) 'Visitors from Rome' may simply mean Roman citizens.

12-13 The zeal of the Apostles astounds their hearers. 'New wine' is unfermented.

Peter speaks to the people   2.14-36

This is Luke's account of what he has heard from others: Peter's speech was probably a great deal longer. There are similar speeches in Acts 3.12-26; 4.8-12; 10.34-43.

this be known to you, and give ear to my words. [15] For these men are not drunk, as you suppose, since it is only the third hour of the day; [16] but this is what was spoken by the prophet Joel:

[17] 'And in the last days it shall be, God declares,
that I will pour out my Spirit upon all flesh,
and your sons and your daughters shall prophesy,
and your young men shall see visions,
and your old men shall dream dreams;
[18] yea, and on my menservants and my maidservants in
those days
I will pour out my Spirit; and they shall prophesy.
[19] And I will show wonders in the heaven above
and signs on the earth beneath,
blood, and fire, and vapor of smoke;
[20] the sun shall be turned into darkness
and the moon into blood,
before the day of the Lord comes,
the great and manifest day.
[21] And it shall be that whoever calls on the name of the Lord
shall be saved.'

[22] "Men of Israel, hear these words: Jesus of Nazareth, a man attested to you by God with mighty works and wonders and signs which God did through him in your midst, as you yourselves know — [23] this Jesus, delivered up according to the definite plan and foreknowledge of God, you crucified and killed by the hands of lawless men. [24] But God raised him up, having loosed the pangs of death, because it was not possible for him to be held by it. [25] For David says concerning him,

'I saw the Lord always before me,
for he is at my right hand that I may not be shaken;
[26] therefore my heart was glad, and my tongue rejoiced;
moreover my flesh will dwell in hope.
[27] For thou wilt not abandon my soul to Hades,
nor let thy Holy One see corruption.
[28] Thou hast made known to me the ways of life;
thou wilt make me full of gladness with thy presence.'

[29] "Brethren, I may say to you confidently of the patriarch David that he both died and was buried, and his tomb is with us to this day. [30] Being therefore a prophet, and knowing that God had sworn with an oath to him that he would set one of his descendants upon his throne, [31] he foresaw and spoke of the

15	Peter replies to the accusation of drunkenness (v.13): nine in the morning is too early for such drinking.
16	See note on v.4.
17	'In the last days' — the days of judgement have begun with the death and Resurrection of Jesus.
18	'They shall prophesy' — the voice of prophecy is believed to be the Holy Spirit speaking through men: many years have passed since the days of the prophets, but prophecy will come again 'in the last days'.
19-20	Even Nature points to the last days.
21	In Joel 'the Lord' is God: here it means Jesus.
22-23	The life and death of Jesus is all part of God's will. 'Lawless men' are Gentiles who do not follow Jewish Law: the Romans 'crucified and killed' Jesus.
24	Again, God's will is done.
25	Once more we have the view that David wrote the Psalms (cf. 1.16), and Early Christians think of this as a Messianic prophecy (Psalm 16.8-11).
27	'Hades' means death in this case.
29-31	The fact of David's tomb shows that he is not speaking about himself: he speaks of the Resurrection of the Messiah.

resurrection of the Christ, that he was not abandoned to Hades, nor did his flesh see corruption. [32] This Jesus God raised up, and of that we all are witnesses. [33] Being therefore exalted at the right hand of God, and having received from the Father the promise of the Holy Spirit, he has poured out this which you see and hear. [34] For David did not ascend into the heavens; but he himself says,

'The Lord said to my lord, Sit at my right hand,
[35] till I make thy enemies a stool for thy feet.'

[36] Let all the house of Israel therefore know assuredly that God has made him both Lord and Christ, this Jesus whom you crucified."

[37] Now when they heard this they were cut to the heart, and said to Peter and the rest of the apostles, "Brethren, what shall we do?" [38] And Peter said to them, "Repent, and be baptized every one of you in the name of Jesus Christ for the forgiveness of your sins; and you shall receive the gift of the Holy Spirit. [39] For the promise is to you and to your children and to all that are far off, every one whom the Lord our God calls to him." [40] And he testified with many other words and exhorted them, saying, "Save yourselves from this crooked generation." [41] So those who received his word were baptized, and there were added that day about three thousand souls. [42] And they devoted themselves to the apostles' teaching and fellowship, to the breaking of bread and the prayers.

[43] And fear came upon every soul; and many wonders and signs were done through the apostles. [44] And all who believed were together and had all things in common; [45] and they sold their possessions and goods and distributed them to all, as any had need. [46] And day by day, attending the temple together and breaking bread in their homes, they partook of food with glad and generous hearts, [47] praising God and having favor with all the people. And the Lord added to their number day by day those who were being saved.

A LAME MAN HEALED   3.1-26

3 Now Peter and John were going up to the temple at the hour of prayer, the ninth hour. [2] And a man lame from birth was being carried, whom they laid daily at that gate of the temple which is called Beautiful to ask alms of those who entered the temple. [3] Seeing Peter and John about to go into the temple, he asked for alms. [4] And Peter directed his gaze at him, with John, and said, "Look at us." [5] And he fixed his attention upon them, expecting to receive something from them. [6] But Peter said, "I have no silver and gold, but I give you what I have; in the name of Jesus Christ of Nazareth, walk." [7] And he took him by the right hand and raised him up; and immediately

34-35   Psalm 110.1 is quoted often (cf. Mark 12.35ff, 14.62;
        1 Corinthians 15.25; Hebrews 1.13).
36   David's prophecy is fulfilled by the Messiahship, Resurrection,
        Ascension and Lordship of Jesus.

The Early Christian Church in Jerusalem   2.37-47

37-38   Many are affected by Peter's words. Those who believe and
        repent are baptized 'in the name of Jesus Christ' and are
        made ready for the coming of the Holy Spirit: baptism and
        the gift of the Holy Spirit often go together.
39   'All that are far off' — the Gospel to the Gentiles.
        N.B. Verses 42-47 describe the Early Christian Church: the
        Apostles' teaching, common sharing, breaking of bread,
        prayers (in the Temple and synagogue as well as in Christian
        houses), wonders and signs as in the days of Jesus Himself,
        and the daily growth of the Church.
42   The Apostles' teaching, fellowship, breaking bread, prayers.
        Jewish meals begin with breaking bread and thanksgiving,
        but 'the breaking of bread' can mean not only the Eucharist
        but also a meal shared with other Christians, or the
        breaking of bread during such a meal.
43   'Wonders and signs'.
44   Common sharing.
45   Almsgiving.
46   As Jews, they still keep Jewish customs but meet together
        also in Christian homes.
47   Daily growth of the new Church — those who are 'being
        saved' (cf. v.21).

A lame man healed   3.1-11

        This is one of the 'wonders and signs' of 2.43.
1   Peter and John are leaders of the Christians but still join in
        the regular Jewish prayers at three in the afternoon, the
        time of the evening sacrifice.
2   The exact site of the 'Beautiful' gate is not known: it is
        probably one of the nine gates leading from the Court of
        Gentiles to the Court of Women.
6   The lame man expects money: he gets far more in the power
        of Jesus.
7   As in many of Jesus' miracles there is the healing touch.

his feet and ankles were made strong. [8] And leaping up he stood and walked and entered the temple with them, walking and leaping and praising God. [9] And all the people saw him walking and praising God, [10] and recognized him as the one who sat for alms at the Beautiful Gate of the temple; and they were filled with wonder and amazement at what had happened to him.

[11] While he clung to Peter and John, all the people ran together to them in the portico called Solomon's, astounded. [12] And when Peter saw it he addressed the people, "Men of Israel, why do you wonder at this, or why do you stare at us, as though by our own power or piety we had made him walk? [13] The God of Abraham and of Isaac and of Jacob, the God of our fathers, glorified his servant[c] Jesus, whom you delivered up and denied in the presence of Pilate, when he had decided to release him. [14] But you denied the Holy and Righteous One, and asked for a murderer to be granted to you, [15] and killed the Author of life, whom God raised from the dead. To this we are witnesses. [16] And his name, by faith in his name, has made this man strong whom you see and know; and the faith which is through Jesus[d] has given the man this perfect health in the presence of you all.

[17] "And now, brethren, I know that you acted in ignorance, as did also your rulers. [18] But what God foretold by the mouth of all the prophets, that his Christ should suffer, he thus fulfilled. [19] Repent therefore, and turn again, that your sins may be blotted out, that times of refreshing may come from the presence of the Lord, [20] and that he may send the Christ appointed for you, Jesus, [21] whom heaven must receive until the time for establishing all that God spoke by the mouth of his holy prophets from of old. [22] Moses said, 'The Lord God will raise up for you a prophet from your brethren as he raised me up. You shall listen to him in whatever he tells you. [23] And it shall be that every soul that does not listen to that prophet shall be destroyed from the people.' [24] And all the prophets who have spoken, from Samuel and those who came afterward, also proclaimed these days. [25] You are the sons of the prophets and of the covenant which God gave to your fathers, saying to Abraham, 'And in your posterity shall all the families of the earth be blessed.' [26] God, having raised up his servant,[c] sent him to you first, to bless you in turning every one of you from your wickedness."

c Or 'child'
d Greek 'him'

12

| 8 | 'Walking and leaping' — a complete healing. |
| 11 | 'The portico called Solomon's' is probably a covered area by the Court of Gentiles, on the eastside of the Temple. |

Peter's speech   3.12-26   (cf. the speech in 2.14-36)

12	Peter takes the chance to speak to the crowd and tell them it is not the Apostles' power but the power of Jesus that has done this miracle (cf. v.16).
13	'The God of Abraham. . . ' — the God of the Old Covenant (cf. Exodus 3.6). 'His servant Jesus' (see R.S.V. note and Acts 3.26; 4.25, 27, 30). God's 'servant' probably refers to the servant of God in Isaiah chapters 40 to 55 and in the Psalms, where the servant's suffering is God's will. For the Jews these prophecies are not Messianic, but for the Christians they fit the sufferings of Jesus: His sufferings (v.18) open the door to forgiveness (v.26).
14	'The Holy and Righteous One' — Messianic titles. 'Asked for a murderer' (cf. Matthew 27.16-21; Mark 15.6-11; Luke 23.18-19).
15	'The Author of life' leads people into the real life. The Apostles are witnesses to the guilt of the Jewish religious leaders in rejecting and killing Jesus, and also to His Resurrection — 'whom God raised from the dead'.
16	In the Gospels, faith in Jesus plays an important part in miracles of healing: now it is 'faith in his name'.
17-18	'Ignorance' can be understood, but God's will is done: Luke sees Jesus' sufferings as part of God's will (cf. 17.3; 26.23 and Luke 24.26, 44ff). All the prophets foretell the suffering of the Messiah.
19	Peter makes his appeal: 'turn again' back to God. 'Times of refreshing' — the Parousia (Second Coming).
20-21	Jesus will come again, from Heaven, when God chooses.
22	Jesus is the prophet like Moses (Deuteronomy 18.15-16).
23	He must be obeyed.
24	All the prophets support Peter's words (cf. v.18).
25-26	God's covenant and promise are for those who hear, through God's 'servant' Jesus. 'Sent him to you first' — i.e. to the Jews: the story of Acts is one of rejection of Jesus by the Jews and the preaching of the Gospel to the Gentiles.

4 And as they were speaking to the people, the priests and the captain of the temple and the Sad'ducees came upon them, ² annoyed because they were teaching the people and proclaiming in Jesus the resurrection from the dead. ³ And they arrested them and put them in custody until the morrow, for it was already evening. ⁴ But many of those who heard the word believed; and the number of the men came to about five thousand.

⁵ On the morrow their rulers and elders and scribes were gathered together in Jerusalem, ⁶ with Annas the high priest and Ca'iaphas and John and Alexander, and all who were of the high-priestly family. ⁷ And when they had set them in the midst, they inquired, "By what power or by what name did you do this?" ⁸ Then Peter, filled with the Holy Spirit, said to them, "Rulers of the people and elders, ⁹ if we are being examined today concerning a good deed done to a cripple, by what means this man has been healed, ¹⁰ be it known to you all, and to all the people of Israel, that by the name of Jesus Christ of Nazareth, whom you crucified, whom God raised from the

14

The arrest of Peter and John   4.1-7

1   'The priests' have regular duties in the Temple. 'The captain of the temple' is probably in charge of the Temple police who keep order there. 'The Sadducees' are aristocratic priests who include the high priestly families and are the chief Temple administrators: they do not hold with the oral traditions (see note on v.5), only the written Law contained in the Pentateuch (first five Books of the Bible). They reject the idea of resurrection.

2   The Sadducees are angry: they do not believe in resurrection.

4   The religious leaders reject the Apostles' words: many ordinary folk believe. Five thousand is a round number.

5   Jewish religious leaders meet in council, the Sanhedrin: by law it may not meet at night. It consists of the 'rulers', mainly priests; 'elders', heads of important families; 'scribes' or lawyers, mainly Pharisees. The Pharisees' main interest is in synagogues and synagogue worship. They follow the written Law of the Old Testament and also the laws laid down by Rabbis through the years, known as 'the Tradition of the Elders'. They believe in resurrection, angels and spirits. The difference in ideas between Sadducees and Pharisees often leads to disputes, even in the Council. Nevertheless, the Sanhedrin, with seventy members under the High Priest, is a very powerful body. 'In Jerusalem' — the headquarters of Jewish authority. Annas, High Priest from A.D. 6 to 14 and then deposed by the Romans. His son-in-law, Caiaphas, follows him (A.D. 18-36), but Annas has still great power (cf. John 18.13). A son of Annas, Jonathan, high priest in A.D. 36, may be the 'John' mentioned: Alexander is not known.

7   The vital question is about the name of Jesus.

Peter addresses the Sanhedrin   4.8-12

8   The promise of Jesus (Mark 13.11; Luke 12.11-12) comes true for Peter.

9   The irony is in their arrest for doing good.

10   Peter is able to proclaim the Resurrection of Jesus, whom the Sanhedrin has put to death.

dead, by him this man is standing before you well. [11] This is the stone which was rejected by you builders, but which has become the head of the corner. [12] And there is salvation in no one else, for there is no other name under heaven given among men by which we must be saved."

[13] Now when they saw the boldness of Peter and John, and perceived that they were uneducated, common men, they wondered; and they recognized that they had been with Jesus. [14] But seeing the man that had been healed standing beside them, they had nothing to say in opposition. [15] But when they had commanded them to go aside out of the council, they conferred with one another, [16] saying, "What shall we do with these men? For that a notable sign has been performed through them is manifest to all the inhabitants of Jerusalem, and we cannot deny it. [17] But in order that it may spread no further among the people, let us warn them to speak no more to any one in this name." [18] So they called them and charged them not to speak or teach at all in the name of Jesus. [19] But Peter and John answered them, "Whether it is right in the sight of God to listen to you rather than to God, you must judge; [20] for we cannot but speak of what we have seen and heard." [21] And when they had further threatened them, they let them go, finding no way to punish them, because of the people; for all men praised God for what had happened. [22] For the man on whom this sign of healing was performed was more than forty years old.

[23] When they were released they went to their friends and reported what the chief priests and the elders had said to them. [24] And when they heard it, they lifted their voices together to God and said, "Sovereign Lord, who didst make the heaven and the earth and the sea and everything in them, [25] who by the mouth of our father David, thy servant,[c] didst say by the Holy Spirit,

'Why did the Gentiles rage,
and the peoples imagine vain things?
[26] The kings of the earth set themselves in array,
and the rulers were gathered together,
against the Lord and against his Anointed'—[e]
[27] for truly in this city there were gathered together against thy holy servant[c] Jesus, whom thou didst anoint, both Herod and Pontius Pilate, with the Gentiles and the peoples of Israel, [28] to do whatever

c Or 'child'
e Or 'christ'

11   The Early Church applies these words (Psalm 118.22) to Jesus, 'rejected' by the Jewish leaders yet glorified by God (cf. Luke 20.17). In the Psalm the reference is to Israel, derided by other nations, important in the eyes of God. The picture is that of a stone, cast out by the builders as useless, but later found to be the exact stone for a place of great importance.

12   Jesus is the only way to salvation.

The Sanhedrin decide   4.13-22

13   The Apostles' 'boldness' is the work of the Holy Spirit. 'Uneducated, common men' — Jews are mostly well-educated, but these men have no high professional learning. 'With Jesus' — as His disciples during His lifetime: this is the answer to their question (v.7).

14   It seems that the lame man has also been arrested: this proof of healing makes the authorities careful.

15-18   The Sanhedrin cannot ignore the 'notable sign' and all they can do is caution the Apostles. 'In this name' (cf. v.7).

19-20   Peter and John do not accept the decision: they must obey God rather than men (cf. 5.29).

21-22   The miracle has aroused such interest the Sanhedrin can do no more.

Christian prayers   4.23-31

23   Peter and John go back to the other Christians — not all, for they now number thousands — perhaps to Mary's house (cf. 12.12).

24-30   A Christian prayer for help in persecution, probably typical of prayers in the Early Church, beginning with God as Creator.

25-26   These words (Psalm 2.1-2) concern the threat to Israel by her enemies.

27   They are now related to Jesus and His persecution: the Gentiles, peoples, kings and rulers (25-26) now become Herod, Herod, Pilate, Gentiles and peoples of Israel.

28   Messiah's sufferings are part of God's plan (cf. 2.22-24; 3.18).

thy hand and thy plan had predestined to take place. ²⁹ And now, Lord, look upon their threats, and grant to thy servants*f* to speak thy word with all boldness, ³⁰ while thou stretchest out thy hand to heal, and signs and wonders are performed through the name of thy holy servant*c* Jesus." ³¹ And when they had prayed, the place in which they were gathered together was shaken; and they were all filled with the Holy Spirit and spoke the word of God with boldness.

THE LIFE OF THE EARLY CHURCH   4.32-37

³² Now the company of those who believed were of one heart and soul, and no one said that any of the things which he possessed was his own, but they had everything in common. ³³ And with great power the apostles gave their testimony to the resurrection of the Lord Jesus, and great grace was upon them all. ³⁴ There was not a needy person among them, for as many as were possessors of lands or houses sold them, and brought the proceeds of what was sold ³⁵ and laid it at the apostles' feet; and distribution was made to each as any had need. ³⁶ Thus Joseph who was surnamed by the apostles Barnabas (which means, Son of encouragement), a Levite, a native of Cyprus, ³⁷ sold a field which belonged to him, and brought the money and laid it at the apostles'feet.

f Or 'slaves'   *c Or 'child'*

ANANIAS AND SAPPHIRA   5.1-11

5 But a man named Anani'as with his wife Sapphi'ra sold a piece of property, ² and with his wife's knowledge he kept back some of the proceeds, and brought only a part and laid it at the apostles' feet. ³ But Peter said, "Anani'as, why has Satan filled your heart to lie to the Holy Spirit and to keep back part of the proceeds of the land? ⁴ While it remained unsold, did it not remain your own? And after it was sold, was it not at your disposal? How is it that you have contrived this deed in your heart? You have not lied to men but to God." ⁵ When Anani'as heard these words, he fell down and died. And great fear came upon all who heard of it. ⁶ The young men rose and wrapped him up and carried him out and buried him.

⁷ After an interval of about three hours his wife came in, not knowing what had happened. ⁸ And Peter said to her, "Tell me whether you sold the land for so much." And she said, "Yes, for so much." ⁹ But Peter said to her, "How is it that you have agreed together to tempt the Spirit of the Lord? Hark, the feet of those that have buried your husband are at the door, and they will carry you out." ¹⁰ Immediately she fell down at his feet and died. When

29-30   A prayer for continued 'boldness' and God's presence, shown in healing and 'signs and wonders'.

31   The Holy Spirit is with them, as at Pentecost (cf. 2.1-4). 'Shaken' — a sign of God's presence (cf. Exodus 19.18; Isaiah 6.4).

The life of the Early Church   4.32-37   (cf. 2.42-47)

32   The importance of unity, shown in sharing 'everything in common'.

33   'Great power' and 'great grace' are the answer to prayer (cf. 29-30).

34-35   More detail about sharing (v.32) and the Apostles' work of distributing.

36-37   An example of sharing: Barnabas is a Jew, born in Cyprus where his family lives. 'A Levite' — Levites are families who hold a hereditary right to perform certain duties in the Temple.

Ananias and Sapphira   5.1-11

1-2   Ananias and Sapphira belong to the Christian group who hold 'everything in common' (4.32), but they keep back what, in fact, belongs to God.

3-4   They can do what they like with their own property but, in pretending, they lie, not only to the Apostles but also to the Holy Spirit and God. Note the different behaviour of Barnabas (4.36-37).

5-6   The death of Ananias, perhaps at the shock of being found out, is seen as punishment by God, and has a great effect on those present.

7-8   Sapphira continues the lie.

9-10   She suffers the same fate as her husband.

the young men came in they found her dead, and they carried her out and buried her beside her husband. [11] And great fear came upon the whole church, and upon all who heard of these things.

SIGNS AND WONDERS 5.12-16

[12] Now many signs and wonders were done among the people by the hands of the apostles. And they were all together in Solomon's Portico. [13] None of the rest dared join them, but the people held them in high honor. [14] And more than ever believers were added to the Lord, multitudes both of men and women, [15] so that they even carried out the sick into the streets, and laid them on beds and pallets, that as Peter came by at least his shadow might fall on some of them. [16] The people also gathered from the towns around Jerusalem, bringing the sick and those afflicted with unclean spirits, and they were all healed.

THE ARREST OF THE APOSTLES 5.17-42

[17] But the high priest rose up and all who were with him, that is, the party of the Sad'ducees, and filled with jealousy [18] they arrested the apostles and put them in the common prison. [19] But at night an angel of the Lord opened the prison doors and brought them out and said, [20] "Go and stand in the temple and speak to the people all the words of this Life." [21] And when they heard this, they entered the temple at daybreak and taught.

Now the high priest came and those who were with him and called together the council and all the senate of Israel, and sent to the prison to have them brought. [22] But when the officers came, they did not find them in the prison, and they returned and reported, [23] "We found the prison securely locked and the sentries standing at the doors, but when we opened it we found no one inside." [24] Now when the captain of the temple and the chief priests heard these words, they were much perplexed about them, wondering what this would come to. [25] And some one came and told them, "The men whom you put in prison are standing in the temple and teaching the people." [26] Then the captain with the officers went and brought them, but without violence, for they were afraid of being stoned by the people.

[27] And when they had brought them, they set them before the council. And the high priest questioned them, [28] saying, "We strictly charged you not to teach in this name, yet here you have filled Jerusalem with your teaching and you intend to bring this man's blood upon us." [29] But Peter and the apostles answered, "We must obey God rather than men. [30] The God of our fathers raised Jesus

11   'Great fear' is added to 'great power' and 'great grace' (4.33).
       For the first time in Acts the word 'church', ecclesia (meaning
       assembly) is used to describe the Christian community.

Signs and wonders   5.12-16   (cf. 2.43-47)
12   'Solomon's Portico' (cf. 3.11) — the Apostles still meet in the
       Temple Court to preach to the people.
13   'None of the rest' is not clear: it suggests that many admire
       the Apostles but dare not join.
14   Even so, many do join the Christians.
15-16   (cf. Mark 6.55-56). Peter is leader: his shadow represents the
       presence and power of God (cf. Luke 1.35; 9.34). A similar
       belief is found in the story of Paul (19.11-12).

The arrest of the Apostles   5.17-21
17   The authorities are 'filled with jealousy' because of the
       success of the Apostles' preaching.
18   They are arrested because they fail to obey the order of
       4.18.
19   'An angel' appears often in Luke's writings (cf. Luke 1.11,
       26; 2.9; 22.43). A similar escape story is found in Acts
       12.1-11.
20   'The words of this Life' — the Gospel of new life in Christ.
21   Probably in Solomon's Portico again (cf. 5.12). 'The Council
       and all the senate of Israel' — the Sanhedrin (see note on
       4.5).
22   'The officers' — the Temple police.
24   'The captain of the temple' (cf. 4.1).
26   The second arrest is made 'without violence' because they are
       afraid of the people who view the Apostles with favour
       (cf. v.13).

Trial by the Sanhedrin   5.27-42
28   'We strictly charged you not to teach in this name' — the
       religious leaders know that the Apostles blame them for
       Jesus' death. 'You intend to bring this man's blood upon us'
       — perhaps the leaders are afraid that the Christians plan
       revenge.
29   Cf. 4.19. Peter's speech is like 3.13-15.
30   'Hanging him on a tree' — the Crucifixion of Jesus: refers to
       Deuteronomy 21.22 (cf. 10.39; 13.29).

whom you killed by hanging him on a tree. ³¹ God exalted him at his right hand as Leader and Savior, to give repentance to Israel and forgiveness of sins. ³² And we are witnesses to these things, and so is the Holy Spirit whom God has given to those who obey him."

³³ When they heard this they were enraged and wanted to kill them. ³⁴ But a Pharisee in the council named Gama'li-el, a teacher of the law, held in honor by all the people, stood up and ordered the men to be put outside for a while. ³⁵ And he said to them, "Men of Israel, take care what you do with these men. ³⁶ For before these days Theu'das arose, giving himself out to be somebody, and a number of men, about four hundred, joined him; but he was slain and all who followed him were dispersed and came to nothing. ³⁷ After him Judas the Galilean arose in the days of the census and drew away some of the people after him; he also perished, and all who followed him were scattered. ³⁸ So in the present case I tell you, keep away from these men and let them alone; for if this plan or this undertaking is of men, it will fail; ³⁹ but if it is of God, you will not be able to overthrow them. You might even be found opposing God!"

⁴⁰ So they took his advice, and when they had called in the apostles, they beat them and charged them not to speak in the name of Jesus, and let them go. ⁴¹ Then they left the presence of the council, rejoicing that they were counted worthy to suffer dishonor for the name. ⁴² And every day in the temple and at home they did not cease teaching and preaching Jesus as the Christ.

THE CHOICE OF THE SEVEN   6.1-7

6 Now in these days when the disciples were increasing in number, the Hellenists murmured against the Hebrews because their widows were neglected in the daily distribution. ² And the twelve summoned the body of the disciples and said, "It is not right that we should give up preaching the word of God to serve tables. ³ Therefore, brethren, pick out from among you seven men of good repute, full of the Spirit and of wisdom, whom we may appoint to this duty. ⁴ But we will devote ourselves to prayer and to the ministry of the

31	The word 'Saviour' is not found often in the New Testament but is used by Luke in his Gospel and Acts. 'Repentance' and 'forgiveness' are important in Luke's writings.
32	This is their message and the Holy Spirit works through them.
33-34	'Enraged' (cf. 7.54) but the wise Gamaliel stops any rash action. He is a well-known rabbi, teacher of Paul (22.3), a Pharisee, and not so much against the Apostles as the Sadducees. Gamaliel advises caution: man-made projects tend to die out; if this is God-inspired it cannot be defeated.
36-37	Luke cannot have a direct record of a speech made in the Sanhedrin. He makes an error: Theudas and Judas are rebels against the Romans, Judas over a census in Palestine in A.D. 6, while the revolt of Theudas is in A.D. 44 (the speech by Gamaliel is at least ten years before this).
38	The death and failure of these two may be repeated in the present case: Jesus is already dead.
39	But if God is behind it take care, lest you oppose God.
40	The verdict as before, 'not to speak in the name of Jesus' (cf. 4.18), but this time the Apostles are beaten as well.
41	They find joy in persecution (cf. Matthew 5.11-12).
42	The authorities make no further move against them: the next persecution follows the death of Stephen (8.1ff.) 'Teaching' the Christians: 'preaching' to would-be converts.

The choice of the Seven 6.1-7

1	The presence of the 'Hellenists' (Greek-speaking Jews) and a group of 'widows' suggests that 'these days' are probably quite a time after the previous events. The 'Hebrews' are Aramaic-speaking Jews, including the Apostles. 'Disciples' — used for the first time in Acts as a title for Christians. 'The daily distribution' is some kind of help based on Christian sharing (cf. 2.44-45; 4.32-35).
2	'The twelve' — only here in Acts are they so called.
3-4	'Seven men' (often called Deacons) to help the Apostles and leave them to their work of preaching, although Stephen and Philip preach as well (8.5-40; 21.8): their story is told in chapters 7 and 8.

word." **5** And what they said pleased the whole multitude, and they chose Stephen, a man full of faith and of the Holy Spirit, and Philip, and Proch'orus, and Nica'nor, and Timon, and Par'menas, and Nicola'us, a proselyte of Antioch. **6** These they set before the apostles, and they prayed and laid their hand upon them.

7 And the word of God increased; and the number of the disciples multiplied greatly in Jerusalem, and a great many of the priests were obedient to the faith.

STEPHEN'S PREACHING 6.8-15

8 And Stephen, full of grace and power, did great wonders and signs among the people. **9** Then some of those who belonged to the synagogue of the Freedmen (as it was called), and of the Cyre'nians, and of the Alexandrians, and of those from Cili'cia and Asia, arose and disputed with Stephen. **10** But they could not withstand the wisdom and the Spirit with which he spoke. **11** Then they secretly instigated men, who said, "We have heard him speak blasphemous words against Moses and God." **12** And they stirred up the people and the elders and the scribes, and they came upon him and seized him and brought him before the council, **13** and set up false witnesses who said, "This man never ceases to speak words against this holy place and the law; **14** for we have heard him say that this Jesus of Nazareth will destroy this place, and will change the customs which Moses delivered to us." **15** And gazing at him, all who sat in the council saw that his face was like the face of an angel.

5   The whole assembly chooses seven, probably Hellenists since
     they have Greek names: one is a 'proselyte', a convert to
     Judaism and so not a Jew — this suggests that the rest are all
     Jews.
6   The Apostles pray and lay their hands on the seven to fulfil
     verse 3, 'whom we may appoint'. Rabbis lay on hands when
     ordaining other rabbis.
7   A further increase in the number of 'disciples' (cf. 2.41; 4.4;
     5.14; 6.1). There is no other mention of priests' joining.

Stephen's preaching   6.8-10
     The story of Stephen's speech to the Sanhedrin and his death
     is told in 6.15 to 8.3.
8   'The grace and power' (cf. 4.33) granted to the Apostles are
     found also in Stephen.
9   'The synagogue of the Freedmen' — perhaps more than one
     synagogue, used by Jews from Asia Minor and North Africa.
     The 'Freedmen' may be Greek-speaking descendants of
     Jewish captives taken to Rome by Pompey in 63 B.C.
     Stephen's preaching causes argument.
10   'The wisdom and the Spirit' are too much for these men.

Stephen before the Sanhedrin   6.11-15
11   The accusations of blasphemy against 'Moses' (the Law) and
     God are like those made in the trial of Jesus (cf. Mark
     14.56-59).
12   Stephen is brought before the Sanhedrin (see note on 4.5).
13   They add blasphemy against 'this holy place', the Temple
     (cf. 21.28).
14   This is the charge brought against Jesus, not mentioned in
     Luke's Gospel but found in the others (Matthew 26.61;
     27.40; Mark 14.58; 15.29; John 2.19). 'The customs' are
     probably the Pharisees' oral traditions (see note on 4.5),
     handed down over the years, made by men to govern everyday
     life and ritual.
15   The Holy Spirit inspires Stephen and his face reflects God's
     glory (cf. Moses in Exodus 34.29-30).

7 And the high priest said, "Is this so?" ² And Stephen said: "Brethren and fathers, hear me. The God of glory appeared to our father Abraham, when he was in Mesopota'mia, before he lived in Haran, ³ and said to him, 'Depart from your land and from your kindred and go into the land which I will show you.' ⁴ Then he departed from the land of the Chalde'ans, and lived in Haran. And after his father died, God removed him from there into this land in which you are now living; ⁵ yet he gave him no inheritance in it, not even a foot's length, but promised to give it to him in possession and to his posterity after him, though he had no child. ⁶ And God spoke to this effect, that his posterity would be aliens in a land belonging to others, who would enslave them and ill-treat them four hundred years. ⁷ 'But I will judge the nation which they serve,' said God, 'and after that they shall come out and worship me in this place.' ⁸ And he gave him the covenant of circumcision. And so Abraham became the father of Isaac, and circumcised him on the eighth day; and Isaac became the father of Jacob, and Jacob of the twelve patriarchs.

⁹ "And the patriarchs, jealous of Joseph, sold him into Egypt; but God was with him, ¹⁰ and rescued him out of all his afflictions, and gave him favor and wisdom before Pharaoh, king of Egypt, who made him governor over Egypt and over all his household. ¹¹ Now there came a famine throughout all Egypt and Canaan, and great affliction, and our fathers could find no food. ¹² But when Jacob heard that there was grain in Egypt, he sent forth our fathers the first time. ¹³ And at the second visit Joseph made himself known to his brothers, and Joseph's family became known to Pharaoh. ¹⁴ And Joseph sent and called to him Jacob his father and all his kindred, seventy-five souls; ¹⁵ and Jacob went down into Egypt. And he died, himself and our fathers, ¹⁶ and they were carried back to Shechem and laid in the tomb that Abraham had bought for a sum of silver from the sons of Hamor in Shechem.

¹⁷ "But as the time of the promise drew near, which God had granted to Abraham, the people grew and multiplied in Egypt ¹⁸ till there arose over Egypt another king who had not known Joseph. ¹⁹ He dealt craftily with our race and forced our fathers to expose their infants, that they might not be kept alive. ²⁰ At this time Moses was born, and was beautiful before God. And he was

Stephen's speech to the Sanhedrin   7.1-53

Stephen does not defend himself against the charges
(6.11-13). He reminds his hearers that their rejection of the
Messiah is like Israel's constant rejection of God and of the
teaching of the prophets all through their history. He shows
that God is with His people wherever they go.

The story of Abraham   7.1-8

2-4   'The God of glory' (cf. Psalm 29.3) = Glorious God. Some of
Stephen's facts do not agree with the Genesis story, e.g.
'Depart from your land': the command comes in Haran
(Genesis 12.1) where Abraham's family have moved from Ur
in 'the land of the Chaldeans' (Genesis 11.31).

5   Abraham is given no permanent home in Canaan: he lives as
a nomad, often outside the Promised Land.

6-7   Israel in Egypt and the Exodus (Genesis 15.13-14 and Acts
7.17-45).

8   'Circumcision' — a sign of the covenant between God and
Abraham (Genesis 17.1-14) and of great religious significance
to all Jews.

The story of Joseph   7.9-16

9   God is with Joseph, even in a strange land. 'Jealous of
Joseph' recalls the priests' jealousy of the Apostles (5.17).
(cf. Genesis 37).

10   Genesis 39-41. Joseph is freed from prison and made
'governor over Egypt': Jesus is freed from death and exalted
as Lord.

11-16   Genesis 41-50.

The story of Moses   7.17-43

Stephen draws a likeness between Moses and Jesus: their
authority (verses 25,35), their miracles (36), their rejection
(27,39).

17-29   Exodus 1.7 to 2.15.

17   'The promise' (cf. v.5).

20   'Beautiful before God' — recalls Jesus (Luke 2.52).

brought up for three months in his father's house; ²¹ and when he was exposed, Pharaoh's daughter adopted him and brought him up as her own son. ²² And Moses was instructed in all the wisdom of the Egyptians, and he was mighty in his words and deeds.

²³ "When he was forty years old, it came into his heart to visit his brethren, the sons of Israel. ²⁴ And seeing one of them being wronged, he defended the oppressed man and avenged him by striking the Egyptian. ²⁵ He supposed that his brethren understood that God was giving them deliverance by his hand, but they did not understand. ²⁶ And on the following day he appeared to them as they were quarrelling and would have reconciled them, saying, "Men, you are brethren, why do you wrong each other?' ²⁷ But the man who was wronging his neighbor thrust him aside, saying, 'Who made you a ruler and a judge over us? ²⁸ Do you want to kill me as you killed the Egyptian yesterday?' ²⁹ At this retort Moses fled, and became an exile in the land of Mid'ian, where he became the father of two sons.

³⁰ "Now when forty years had passed, an angel appeared to him in the wilderness of Mount Sinai, in a flame of fire in a bush. ³¹ When Moses saw it he wondered at the sight; and as he drew near to look, the voice of the Lord came, ³² 'I am the God of your fathers, the God of Abraham and of Isaac and of Jacob.' And Moses trembled and did not dare to look. ³³ And the Lord said to him, 'Take off the shoes from your feet, for the place where you are standing is holy ground. ³⁴ I have surely seen the ill-treatment of my people that are in Egypt and heard their groaning, and I have come down to deliver them. And now come, I will send you to Egypt.'

³⁵ "This Moses whom they refused, saying, 'Who made you a ruler and a judge?' God sent as both ruler and deliverer by the hand of the angel that appeared to him in the bush. ³⁶ He led them out, having performed wonders and signs in Egypt and at the Red Sea, and in the wilderness for forty years. ³⁷ This is the Moses who said to the Israelites, 'God will raise up for you a prophet from your brethren as he raised me up.' ³⁸ This is he who was in the congregation in the wilderness with the angel who spoke to him at Mount Sinai, and with our fathers; and he received living oracles to give to us. ³⁹ Our fathers refused to obey him, but thrust him aside, and in their hearts they turned to Egypt, ⁴⁰ saying to Aaron, 'Make for us gods to go before us; as for this Moses who led us out from the land of Egypt, we do not know what has become of him.' ⁴¹ And they made a calf in those days, and offered a sacrifice to the idol and rejoiced in the works of their hands. ⁴² But God turned and gave them over to worship the

22	Moses is brought up in Egypt but God is with him even there (again Luke 2.52). 'Mighty in his words and deeds' like Jesus (Luke 24.19).
23	'To visit his brethren, the sons of Israel' as Jesus comes to His people.
25	Moses is rejected.
26	Moses shows the spirit of Jesus.
27-28	He is rejected again.
29	He flees to a strange land, like Abraham and the patriarchs and Israel in their wanderings.
30-34	See Exodus 3.1-10.
32	Like the voice of God at Jesus' Baptism (Matthew 3.17; Mark 1.11; Luke 3.22).
33-35	'Holy ground' — God does not live in temples: He is here in a foreign land. 'I will send you' — as God sends Jesus — 'as both ruler and deliverer.' 'The hand of the angel' is the hand of God.
36	'Wonders and signs' — God is present 'in Egypt' (Exodus 7-12), 'at the Red Sea' (Exodus 14), 'and in the wilderness' (Exodus 15-17).
37	'A prophet' — Jesus Himself (cf. Deuteronomy 18.15,18; Luke 24.19; Acts 3.22).
38	See Exodus 19-20. Moses, the mediator between God and man, to whom the 'living oracles' (the Law, the Commandments) were given. Stephen does not disparage the Law (cf. 6.11; 7.53).
39	Rejection of Moses. 'Turned to Egypt' (Numbers 14.3-4).
40-41	Rebellion against God (Exodus 32).
42	'God turned' — gave the people the idolatry they wanted: 'the host of heaven' (Jeremiah 19.13) are pagan gods.
42-43	The words from Amos (5.25-27), where Israel is accused of worshipping foreign gods, probably Assyrian: the names vary slightly in Amos. 'Beyond Babylon' (Amos says 'Exile beyond Damascus') — the actual Exile of the Jews is the Captivity in Babylon in the sixth century B.C.

host of heaven, as it is written in the book of the prophets:
'Did you offer to me slain beasts and sacrifices,
forty years in the wilderness, O house of Israel?
⁴³ And you took up the tent of Moloch,
and the star of the god Rephan,
the figures which you made to worship;
and I will remove you beyond Babylon.'
⁴⁴ "Our fathers had the tent of witness in the wilderness, even as
he who spoke to Moses directed him to make it, according to the
pattern that he had seen. ⁴⁵ Our fathers in turn brought it in with
Joshua when they dispossessed the nations which God thrust out
before our fathers. So it was until the days of David, ⁴⁶ who found
favor in the sight of God and asked leave to find a habitation for
the God of Jacob. ⁴⁷ But it was Solomon who built a house for him.
⁴⁸ Yet the Most High does not dwell in houses made with hands; as
the prophet says,
⁴⁹ 'Heaven is my throne,
and earth my footstool.
What house will you build for me, says the Lord,
or what is the place of my rest?
⁵⁰ Did not my hand make all these things?'
⁵¹ "You stiff-necked people, uncircumcised in heart and ears, you
always resist the Holy Spirit. As your fathers did, so do you. ⁵² Which
of the prophets did not your fathers persecute? And they killed
those who announced beforehand the coming of the Righteous One,
whom you have now betrayed and murdered, ⁵³ you who received the
law as delivered by angels and did not keep it."

THE DEATH OF STEPHEN   7.54-8.1

⁵⁴ Now when they heard these things they were enraged, and they
ground their teeth against him. ⁵⁵ But he, full of the Holy Spirit,
gazed into heaven and saw the glory of God, and Jesus standing at
the right hand of God; ⁵⁶ and he said, "Behold, I see the heavens
opened, and the Son of man standing at the right hand of God."
⁵⁷ But they cried out with a loud voice and stopped their ears

The House of God   7.44-53

44   'The tent of witness' — the movable Tabernacle and Ark, made to God's orders, symbolic of God's presence (Exodus 35-40).

45   It is brought into the Promised Land by Joshua (Joshua 3-4).

46-47 David wants to build a house for God (Psalm 132.1-5; 2 Samuel 7.8-16), but it is his son, Solomon, who builds the Temple (I Kings 6).

48   God is not in one building or in one land.

49-50 The prophet says that the Temple cannot hold God, Maker of all (Isaiah 66.1-2). Stephen shows that Christianity needs no sacrifices or idols, or even a temple: Christ Himself is the Temple. This will anger the priests, guardians of the Temple and of the Law, but more is to come.

The death of Stephen   7.54-8.1

51   Stephen's account of Israel's rejection of God and His messengers now turns into an attack on the religious leaders for their rejection of Jesus and the Holy Spirit. 'Stiff-necked' as in the story of the Golden Calf (Exodus 32.9; 33.3,5). 'Uncircumcised in heart and ears' (cf. Jeremiah 9.26; 6.10).

52   Just as their ancestors have persecuted God's messengers, so they have rejected and killed 'the Righteous One' (cf. 3.14).

53   There is a tradition of 'angels' (cf. v.38) who act as mediators between God and man.

54   This is too much for the Sanhedrin: they are 'enraged' (cf. 5.33).

55   Stephen is inspired and has a vision of the glory of God and of Jesus at God's right hand (cf. Luke 22.69, Mark 14.62).

56   'I see the heavens opened' (cf. Matthew 3.16; Mark 1.10; Luke 3.21). 'The Son of man' — used in Daniel 7.13-14 for a heavenly figure, probably symbolic of Israel: this title is often used by Jesus in the Gospels, only here in Acts.

57   The Sanhedrin will hear no more.

and rushed together upon him. [58] Then they cast him out of the city and stoned him; and the witnesses laid down their garments at the feet of a young man named Saul. [59] And as they were stoning Stephen, he prayed, "Lord Jesus, receive my spirit." [60] And he knelt down and cried with a loud voice, "Lord, do not hold this sin against them." And when he had said this, he fell asleep.

PERSECUTION AND PREACHING: PHILIP IN SAMARIA   8.1-8

8 [1] And Saul was consenting to his death.

And on that day a great persecution arose against the church in Jerusalem; and they were all scattered throughout the region of Judea and Samar'ia, except the apostles. [2] Devout men buried Stephen, and made great lamentation over him. [3] But Saul laid waste the church, and entering house after house, he dragged off men and women and committed them to prison.

[4] Now those who were scattered went about preaching the word. [5] Philip went down to a city of Samar'ia, and proclaimed to them the Christ. [6] And the multitudes with one accord gave heed to what was said by Philip, when they heard him and saw the signs which he did. [7] For unclean spirits came out of many who were possessed, crying with a loud voice; and many who were paralyzed or lame were healed. [8] So there was much joy in that city.

58	'They cast him out of the city and stoned him' (cf. Numbers 15.35; Leviticus 24.10-16). 'Witnesses' — those who accuse (6.11-14) must, by law, cast stones. Saul is present (cf. 22.20).
	N.B. Stoning is the Jewish punishment for blasphemy, but we cannot be sure if this stoning is legal or not, or if the Sanhedrin has the power of life and death. In the case of Jesus, condemned for blasphemy (Matthew 26.65-66; Mark 14.63-64), He is taken to Pilate to make the proceedings legal. Here, it seems, the Jews take matters into their own hands. In an official stoning the victim's clothes are removed, he is thrown over a cliff, and stones are rolled on him. If it is a lynching, as it may seem in this case (cf. Jesus in John 8.59 and 10.31-33 and Paul in Acts 14.19) then the throwers will remove their clothes.
59-60	Like the prayers of Jesus (Luke 23.34,46) — Stephen shares His spirit and forgiveness.
8.1	'Saul was consenting' — it is possible that he is a member of the Sanhedrin.

Persecution and Preaching: Philip in Samaria   8.1-8

1	The death of Stephen begins persecution in Jerusalem, but this only spreads the Gospel into 'Judea and Samaria.' 'Except the apostles' — they remain in Jerusalem. This suggests that the persecution may have been against the Greek-speaking Jews (the Hellenists of 6.1), the friends of Stephen. The Apostles, Palestinian Jews, are left alone for the time.
2	'Devout men' recalls the burial of Jesus by Joseph of Arimathea (Luke 23.50-53).
3	Luke makes Saul an ardent persecutor.
4	Persecution just spreads 'the word'.
5	Jews in general hate Samaritans: Jesus has no room for such hatred (Luke 10.25-35; 17.11-19) and His followers must be the same. Philip is one of the Seven (6.5).
6-7	Preaching is followed by 'signs', as with Jesus Himself and the Apostles. Luke, a doctor, has great interest in healings.
8	'Much joy' comes with the Holy Spirit (cf. 8.39; 13.52; 16.34).

SIMON THE MAGICIAN   8.9-25

⁹ But there was a man named Simon who had previously practised magic in the city and amazed the nation of Samar'ia, saying that he himself was somebody great. ¹⁰ They all gave heed to him, from the least to the greatest, saying, "This man is that power of God which is called Great." ¹¹ And they gave heed to him, because for a long time he had amazed them with his magic. ¹² But when they believed Philip as he preached good news about the kingdom of God and the name of Jesus Christ, they were baptized, both men and women. ¹³ Even Simon himself believed, and after being baptized he continued with Philip, And seeing signs and great miracles performed, he was amazed.

¹⁴ Now when the apostles at Jerusalem heard that Samar'ia had received the word of God, they sent to them Peter and John, ¹⁵ who came down and prayed for them that they might receive the Holy Spirit; ¹⁶ for it had not yet fallen on any of them, but they had only been baptized in the name of the Lord Jesus. ¹⁷ Then they laid their hands on them and they received the Holy Spirit. ¹⁸ Now when Simon saw that the Spirit was given through the laying on of the apostles' hands, he offered them money, ¹⁹ saying, "Give me also this power, that any one on whom I lay my hands may receive the Holy Spirit." ²⁰ But Peter said to him, "Your silver perish with you, because you thought you could obtain the gift of God with money! ²¹ You have neither part nor lot in this matter, for your heart is not right before God. ²² Repent therefore of this wickedness of yours, and pray to the Lord that, if possible, the intent of your heart may be forgiven you. ²³ For I see that you are in the gall of bitterness and in the bond of iniquity." ²⁴ And Simon answered, "Pray for me to the Lord, that nothing of what you have said may come upon me."

²⁵ Now when they had testified and spoken the word of the Lord, they returned to Jerusalem, preaching the gospel to many villages of the Samaritans.

PHILIP AND THE ETHIOPIAN   8.26-40

²⁶ But an angel of the Lord said to Philip, "Rise and go toward the south[g] to the road that goes down from Jerusalem to Gaza." This is a desert road. ²⁷ And he rose and went. And behold, an Ethiopian, a eunuch, a minister of the Canda'ce, queen of the Ethiopians, in charge of all her treasure, had come to Jerusalem to worship ²⁸ and was returning; seated in his chariot, he was reading the prophet Isaiah.

g   Or 'at noon'

34

Simon the magician   8.9-25

9   Simon, known as Simon Magus, is well known in the
        traditions of the Early Church, and often appears as a rival
        to Peter and the Apostles. 'Magus' is a Persian word for a
        member of the priestly class of Persia, or a magician. The
        wise men from the East who visited the infant Jesus
        (Matthew 2.1-12) are known as the Magi.

10   Some think he has the 'power of God'.

11   His magic has great effect on the people of Samaria.

12-13   Philip's message is more effective still, resulting in baptisms,
        even Simon's, and in 'signs and great miracles'.

14   The leading Apostles, Peter and John, come to confirm and
        approve Philip's mission to the Samaritans: John is not
        mentioned again in Acts.

15-16   It is believed that baptism and the gift of the Holy Spirit go
        together (cf. 2.38). 'The Holy Spirit' here suggests some
        outward signs, as at Pentecost (cf. 2.1-4).

17   This has been called 'a Samaritan Pentecost'. A Gentile
        Pentecost comes later (10.44).

18-19   Simon wants not the gift but the authority to give the
        Spirit.

20-21   Peter condemns his attitude, but

22   there is still hope for forgiveness.

23   A vague reference to Deuteronomy 29.18 and Isaiah 58.6,
        suggests the bitter and sinful position of Simon.

24   Simon needs help.

25   The journey back to Jerusalem gives an opportunity to take
        the Gospel to other parts of Samaria.

Philip and the Ethiopian   8.26-40

26   Again Philip of the Seven (8.5), not the Apostle (1.13). 'An
        angel' (cf. 7.38,53) gives divine direction. See R.S.V. note
        'at noon' — this is no time to travel and it is not usual to see
        anyone on a desert road at such a time because of the heat.
        Gaza is the last town before the desert on the road to Egypt:
        Gaza of the Old Testament destroyed by Alexander the
        Great: the new Gaza destroyed by the Romans in A.D. 66.

27-28   Ethiopia, rather to the south of the present country, the
        Sudan. 'Candace' is a title for the Queen Mother. The eunuch
        may be a Jew, but more probably a Gentile worshipping the
        Jewish God: a God-fearer (see note on 2.10).

²⁹ And the Spirit said to Philip, "Go up and join this chariot." ³⁰ So Philip ran to him, and heard him reading Isaiah the prophet, and asked, "Do you understand what you are reading?" ³¹ And he said, "How can I, unless some one guides me?" And he invited Philip to come up and sit with him. ³² Now the passage of the scripture which he was reading was this:

"As a sheep led to the slaughter
or a lamb before its shearer is dumb,
so he opens not his mouth.
³³ In his humiliation justice was denied him.
Who can describe his generation?
For his life is taken up from the earth."

³⁴ And the eunuch said to Philip, "About whom, pray, does the prophet say this, about himself or about some one else?" ³⁵ Then Philip opened his mouth, and beginning with this scripture he told him the good news of Jesus. ³⁶ And as they went along the road they came to some water, and the eunuch said, "See, here is water! What is to prevent my being baptized?"^b ³⁸ And he commanded the chariot to stop, and they both went down into the water, Philip and the eunuch, and he baptized him. ³⁹ And when they came up out of the water, the Spirit of the Lord caught up Philip; and the eunuch saw him no more, and went on his way rejoicing. ⁴⁰ But Philip was found at Azo′tus, and passing on he preached the gospel to all the towns till he came to Caesare′a.

b *Other ancient authorities add all or most of verse 37, 'And Philip said, "If*
   you believe with all your heart, you may." And he replied, "I believe that
   Jesus Christ is the Son of God." '

29   'The Spirit' (cf. the 'angel' of v.26).

30   'Heard him reading' — the normal practice to read aloud.

32-33   One of the prophet's 'servant' poems (Isaiah 53.7-8) foretelling the death of the Messiah. The early Christians speak of Jesus as the 'servant' of God (cf. 3.13,26;4.27,30).

34-35   The question gives Philip a starting point to preach 'the good news of Jesus.'

✳ 36   The eunuch also seizes his opportunity.

✳ 37   See R.S.V. note — this suggests some kind of early creed, to be said at baptism.

39   Philip goes on his way, led by the Spirit. The eunuch goes 'on his way rejoicing' — the joy of the Holy Spirit (cf. 13.52; 16.34).

40   Azotus — the ancient Philistine city of Ashdod. Philip preaches in this area: the next time we hear of him he is living at Caesarea (21.8).

Acts 1.15-26 The Choice of Matthias

After the Ascension which took place on the Mount of Olives, the remaining eleven disciples returned to Jerusalem and went to the Upper Room -- probably the home of John Mark's mother (**Luke 22.12; Acts 12.12**) where Jesus took His Last Supper with His disciples. Peter soon assumed the position of leadership among the disciples. (After all, when Jesus was still physically present, Peter had always taken the initiative as the disciples' spokesman; he was almost always the first to answer questions asked of the disciples, for instance during the confession at Caesarea Philippi (**Luke 9.20**), and he was the disciple bold enough to challenge Jesus' prediction of His death (**Mark 8.32**). Because of his leadership qualities, which were recognized by Jesus, he had been given the mantle of leadership by Jesus Himself (**Luke 22.31-32**)).

Peter addressed the brethren, numbering about one hundred and twenty, on the need to restore the number of Apostles to twelve, as it had been before Judas betrayed Jesus and Judas's subsequent death by hanging. He referred to the Old Testament (**Psalms 69.25; 109.8**) to prove that what Judas had done was according to God's plan, and that he would squarely bear the consequences of his betrayal of our Lord.

Having said this, Peter set out the qualifications which this substitute Apostle must have, namely, he must have been with Jesus from His Baptism by John, right through to His Resurrection. Two of the brethren passed the initial test and were therefore put forward. After prayers they cast lots, and the lot fell on Matthias. He was then enrolled with the eleven Apostles.

Casting of lots: it is significant to note that until this time the Apostles still adopted the traditional method of discerning the will of God by means of casting lots. But after the gift of the Holy Spirit on the Day of Pentecost, the disciples began to decide such issues by prayer, fasting and reasoning. For example, this method of casting lots was no longer used when the seven deacons were chosen (**Acts 6.5-6**).

Lots were cast, either by writing names on stones which were placed in a pot and then shaken: the stone which fell out first gave the name of the winner, or by throwing two pieces of flat stone or wood, sometimes called 'urim' and 'thummim':

the face in view when the stones or wood landed on the ground revealed the winner.

Matthias: nothing else is known about Matthias after his election. This does not suggest, however, that he was a failure. Luke's interest was mainly in the course of the Gospel of Christ and the work of the Holy Spirit in the Christian Church, not in the men themselves. Thus, even in the case of Peter and Paul, two of the most prominent among the Apostles, about whom Luke wrote extensively, we are not told what happened to them in the end.

Acts 2.14-36 Peter's Defence: the First 'Christian' Sermon
In **Acts 2.1-13** we have the account of the gift of the Holy Spirit on the Day of Pentecost, fifty days after the feast of the Passover, when Jesus had been crucified. There were three great Jewish feasts: Passover, Pentecost and Tabernacles. During these feasts Jerusalem was packed with pilgrims from local Jewish towns and villages and from abroad. The latter were either Jews living abroad (called Jews of the Dispersion or Diaspora, especially after 70 A.D. when, following the destruction of Jerusalem by the Roman military commander Titus, later an Emperor, the Jews were dispersed by force throughout the Roman Empire), or proselytes, that is, non-Jews who had accepted the Jewish religion and had undergone Mosaic and Jewish rites of circumcision etc. Luke here gives us a long list of the pilgrims' home countries.

What happened to the disciples on this day? They felt a sudden impulse, 'a sound came from heaven like the rush of a mighty wind, and it filled all the house . . . And there appeared to them tongues as of fire, distributed and resting on each one of them. And they were all filled with the Holy Spirit and began to speak in other tongues.' (**Acts 2.2-4**).

The disciples felt the power of God coming upon them in an unusual way. Their fears were washed away and they began to speak excitedly 'in other tongues.' This experience is met with again in **Acts 10.46** at the conversion of Cornelius. Although in some ways it may be similar to what we find today among the so-called spiritualist churches, the Pentecost experience had ingredients which marked it out as different. We are told that, while the disciples spoke in tongues, the congregation understood what they were saying in their diverse and individual languages: there was no need for interpreters. In latter-day spiritualist churches there is always an interpreter who professes the ability to understand the inspired utterances of the 'visioner'.

What did Peter say? He refuted the charge of drunkenness levelled against the disciples. (It was, after all, only the third hour of the day, i.e. 9.00 a.m., too early even for a habitual drunkard to have taken enough to make himself drunk.) The Jews, who had for many years lost their independence, were expecting the Day of the Lord, the Age to come when God would restore to them their lost glory. Earlier prophets, like Joel, had painted pictures of this day. Peter then quoted from the Old Testament (**Joel 2.28-32**) to prove that what the people were witnessing was the fulfilment of their age-old expectations. Then followed Peter's proclamation: the announcement of the Good News of Jesus. Jesus was the Messiah, as proved by the mighty works and wonders which God did through Him; in Him the promises had been fulfilled and the Age to come had been ushered in (**v.22**); He came from David's line, but in spite of His mighty works wicked men had conspired against Him and had Him killed (**v.23**); but God had raised Him from the dead and made Him Lord and Christ (**vv.24, 36**). (**vv.24, 36**).

Effect of the Address: the congregation were impressed by Peter's address and asked what they were to do.

Peter asked them to repent and to be baptized in the Name of Jesus Christ for the forgiveness of their sins, and they would receive the gift of the Holy Spirit.

Those who received the word were baptized; they numbered three thousand. Immediately they began to show signs of their new fellowship by being attentive to the teaching and maintaining a new bond by joining in the daily breaking of bread and prayers. Later, the believers also sold their belongings and offered the proceeds into a common fund which was distributed amongst all members of the Church.

This first sermon of Peter became typical, in many ways, of the first sermons of the Early Church. Such early sermons endeavoured to prove, with quotations from the Old Testament, that Jesus was the fulfilment of the Scriptures; that He did many mighty works, but that He was crucified, and ascended into glory. All should repent, be baptized, for the gift of the Holy Spirit which was to ensure their salvation.

Acts 3.12-26 Peter's Second Speech

The strange and new teaching which began on the Day of Pentecost was accompanied by miracles of healing, more often referred to as 'wonders and signs'. One of these was to attract the attention, not only of the common people who flocked to the Temple during the usual hours of prayer, but also of the Jewish leaders. At the Gate called 'Beautiful', Peter and John had healed a lame man (**Acts 3.1-10**). The congregation who had assembled for the ninth hour of prayer (i.e. 3.00 p.m.) were amazed when they saw the cripple 'walking, leaping and praising God'. Peter addressed them.

Peter spoke to his fellow Jews ('Men of Israel') and asked them why they wondered at the miracle. They had performed the miracle, he added, not by their own power, but by the power of Jesus Christ. Then followed a short sermon typical of early Christian teaching and preaching. Jesus was the 'servant' of God, the God of the patriarchs (Abraham, Isaac and Jacob), and He had been killed after a trial which was a total travesty of justice. Pilate had actually decided to release Him (seeing that He was innocent), but the Jews had in His stead preferred a murderer, and had called vehemently for the murder of the innocent. However, God had raised Him from the dead. The lame man had been healed through their faith in Jesus.

Peter conceded that the Jews, especially the commoners, had acted in mob ignorance. He therefore called on them to repent and to have faith in the Risen Jesus as God's Messiah. Since Peter was talking to fellow Jews who were conversant with the Old Testament Scriptures, he again supported his argument with quotations from the Scriptures. The coming of Jesus had been foretold by Moses (**v.22**) and by Samuel and later prophets (**v.24**): see **Deuteronomy 18.15-16; Leviticus 23.29**.

If the Jews had killed Jesus in ignorance, the days of ignorance were now over: having recognized their mistake, they would no longer have any excuse for failing to repent. Repentance would bring about forgiveness — 'that times of refreshing may come from the presence of the Lord' (**v.19**). For 'every soul that does not listen . . . shall be destroyed from the people' (**v.23**): see **Deuteronomy 18.19**. Peter called on them to turn away from their wickedness since they were sons of Abraham with whom God had made a covenant with the promise that in his 'posterity shall all the families of the earth be blessed' (**v.25**). They would be forfeiting their right should they fail to appreciate the great responsibility that went with their higher privilege.

Acts 4.1-12 Trouble with the Authorities: Peter's Third Speech
The healing of the lame man was soon to attract the attention of the Jewish leaders. They had to so something, before it was too late, to halt the spread of this new teaching, or else their position would be in jeopardy. The sensational healing led to the arrest of Peter and John by the Temple police. The Temple was controlled by the Sadducees, who had collaborated with Pilate to crucify Jesus. They were not prepared to weaken their position by allowing Jesus' followers the freedom to foment trouble. The leaders were incensed firstly, because the Apostles were preaching the resurrection of the dead and secondly, many people had come to believe the Gospel (v.2).

After Peter and John had spent a night in custody, the Council of the Jews (the Sanhedrin) convened to try the two Apostles. They asked them 'By what power or by what name did you do this?' In response to this, Peter made his third recorded speech (vv.8-12).

Peter answered with great courage: he was 'filled with the Holy Spirit'. They had acted, he asserted, 'by the name of Jesus of Nazareth whom you crucified, whom God raised from the dead': this was both an affront and a direct challenge, and Peter supported his words with a quotation from **Psalm 118.22**: 'The stone which the builders rejected has become the head of the corner.' He assured them that there was salvation in no one other than Jesus. After all, the Jews and their leaders were a very religious people who looked forward earnestly to salvation: it was therefore proper that they should be duly warned not to continue to reject Jesus.

The members of the Sanhedrin were surprised at the boldness of these 'uneducated, common men'. Although they were incensed by this bold assertion from the accused, they could not find sufficient reason to do them harm, since the lame man who had been healed, a man of forty, was there in the court, and the people had seen that he was genuinely cured. They therefore decided to merely threaten them, and gave them a serious warning to desist from preaching further in Jesus' name (v.18).

Peter was not intimidated. Since they had not committed any offence, Peter reasserted their uncompromising stand — 'whether it is right in the sight of God to listen to you rather than to God, you must judge; for we cannot but speak of what we have seen and heard.' (vv.19-20).

Result of the First Trial 4.23-31: when Peter and John were released, they reported to the other believers and all joined in a hymn of praise and thanksgiving. Then follows another Old Testament quotation, **Psalm 2.1-2**, which they applied to the situation in which they found themselves in their discipleship of Christ.

They concluded with a prayer for strength to preach and power to heal and perform 'signs and wonders' in the name of Jesus (vv.29-30).

After this prayer, the Apostles experienced a second outpouring of the Holy Spirit (as at Pentecost) and they spoke the word of God with even greater boldness than before.

Acts 5.17-42 The Second Trial and Peter's Fourth Speech

In Acts chapter 4 we found that no amount of intimidation by the Jewish leaders would deter the Apostles from their mission. The Holy Spirit was guiding them and leading them on to fresh victories. More and more signs and wonders were being performed by them, and people came from far and near, bringing all their sick and those possessed, all of whom were healed. More and more believers were being added daily to the Church and the fame of the Apostles spread like wildfire.

In chapter 5 the Sanhedrin (or Council) were aroused to jealousy by the growing power of the Gospel. The Apostles, instead of heeding their warning, ignored the consequences and energetically went about their evangelism. The Sanhedrin, therefore, for the second time, ordered the arrest of the Apostles, who were then miraculously rescued from prison and went back to the Temple to continue their preaching as if nothing had happened.

This was a grave affront to the Council who, although in no mood to tolerate it, nevertheless treated the Apostles with some respect (v.26). They asked the Apostles why, in spite of earlier warnings, they had continued to fill Jerusalem with their teaching, thereby intending to 'bring this man's blood upon us'.

Peter once again reminded them of their message: 'The God of our fathers raised Jesus whom you killed . . . God exalted him . . . to give repentance to Israel and forgiveness of sins. And we are witnesses to these things, and so is the Holy Spirit whom God has given to those who obey Him.'

In this speech Peter did not go into as much detail as before; he did not support his argument with words from the Scriptures. However, under the guidance of the Holy Spirit — who had been controlling and directing the course of the Gospel — a Jewish leader and respected Pharisaic member of the Sanhedrin called Gamaliel, intervened on the Apostles' behalf.

Gamaliel made references to 'past' Jewish history and cautioned the Sanhedrin to adopt a 'wait and see' policy in their attitude towards the Apostles and their new teaching. 'Men of Israel,' he said, 'take care what you do with these men. For before these days Theudas arose, giving out to be somebody . . . but he was slain and all who followed him were dispersed and came to nothing. After him Judas the Galilean arose in the days of the census and drew away some of the people after him; he also perished, and all who followed him were scattered.' (5.35-37).

If these two uprisings failed, it was because they had no divine direction; by the same token, if the Apostles' Gospel preaching was man-initiated, it would also fail. 'But if it is of God,' the Sanhedrin 'will not be able to overthrow them.' In fact the action of the Council would be in opposition to God, whose agents they were claiming to be; this would be a terrible irony.

The Sanhedrin took Gamaliel's advice. After beating the Apostles they again charged them not to speak in the Name of Jesus, and dismissed them. As in the previous case, the Apostles went out rejoicing that they were counted worthy to suffer dishonour for Jesus' Name. They continued daily in the Temple and elsewhere, teaching and preaching Jesus as the Christ.

The References to Theudas and Judas: In his preamble to his Gospel, Luke claims that he was writing 'an orderly account for most excellent Theophilus'. In the Acts of the Apostles Luke no doubt intended to continue his self-imposed task and tell the second part of the story of Jesus, beginning with His Ascension and showing how His Gospel was spread from Jerusalem to the uttermost parts of the world.

In spite of Luke's claim to orderliness and accuracy, Gamaliel's references to history, as reported by Luke, raise serious doubts as to their historical exactitude. Gamaliel's address is dated about A.D. 36, that is, during the first few years of apostolic preaching. The rebellion of Theudas took place in A.D. 44, so Gamaliel could not have mentioned an event that was yet to happen. Again, the rebellion of Judas came much earlier than that of Theudas, in A.D. 6, and therefore, could not rightly be referred to by Gamaliel as coming after the rebellion of Theudas.

In defence of Luke, it has been suggested that there might have been an earlier, but otherwise unknown, rebellion led by another Theudas, a namesake of the Theudas of A.D. 44, this being a common abbreviation for a number of contemporary Jewish names.

Acts 7.1-53 Stephen's Defence
In Acts chapter 6 we read about the phenomenal growth of the Church, in spite of the considerable opposition spearheaded by the Jewish leaders. The believers included Greek-speaking Jews (Hellenists) who had now returned 'home' to Jerusalem and Judea, as well as proselytes, that is, non-Jews who had accepted the Jewish religion and now turned 'Christian'. With this infusion of 'tribal' groups into the Church, there was bound to be internal dissension sooner or later. The simple, communal mode of life introduced right at the beginning of the evangelical period was to create problems of administration. Hellenist widows had a right to full support from the common funds but realized that they were not getting a fair deal and complained bitterly.

It was soon appreciated that this state of affairs, if left unresolved, would lead the Church to schism. The twelve Apostles saw that they would be distracted from their work of prayer and preaching unless the problem were dealt with once and for all, and so they asked the Hellenists to choose 'seven men of good repute, full of the Spirit and of wisdom' to take charge of all distribution. Seven men, called deacons, were thus selected.

Stephen, Philip, Prochorus, Nicanor, Timon, Parmenas and Nicolaus, a proselyte of Antioch (a converted Gentile) were chosen. Note that unlike the selection of Matthias to replace Judas Iscariot, in Acts 1.21-26, there was no casting of lots; this method was no longer in use in the Church after the Day of

Pentecost and the descent of the Holy Spirit on the Apostles. Such decisions were now made through prayers and reasoning. The Apostles prayed and commissioned the seven deacons to their important task by 'laying hands upon them'.

One of the seven deacons, Stephen, very soon proved to be much more than a mere 'server of tables'; he involved himself in preaching and in disputing with opponents of the Church, putting them completely on the defensive by his wisdom and power of argument. In the synagogue of the Freedmen (probably Jews who had been enslaved by the Romans but later freed and allowed to return home), Stephen disputed with non-believing Hellenists and soon fell foul of them; they accused him of the deadly Jewish sin of blasphemy 'against Moses and God'. He was arraigned before the Sanhedrin, the first apart from the Twelve to face the wrath of the Jewish leaders.

The High Priest, as President of the Council, asked him, 'Is it so?': in other words he asked Stephen whether he was guilty or not of the charge of blasphemy preferred against him. There is no doubt that Stephen understood the seriousness of the charge which, if proved, would earn him death by stoning. But rather than defend himself, Stephen began a lengthy speech which was not a defence in the true sense of the word but rather an attack against his accusers (**7.2-53**).

(**vv.2-16**) Stephen reviewed the early history of the people, beginning with Abraham in Mesopotamia, on to Isaac and Jacob and his sojourn with his family in Egypt.

(**vv.17-34**) After many years of prosperity and later of enslavement in Egypt, God heard their groaning and raised Moses, charging him with the task of delivering the people from bondage.

(**vv.35-53**) Although the people had rejected Moses when he first appeared to them, he remained undaunted and eventually led them out, giving them God's promises in the wilderness. Yet they rejected Yahweh and worshipped other gods. Hence Amos had, much later, condemned them (**Amos 5.25-27**). In the wilderness Moses had made the tent of witness for the worship of Yahweh and handed it over to his successor, Joshua, who finally led them into Canaan. All worship, even in their settled life in Palestine, continued in the tent until David's time. It was Solomon who eventually built the Temple as a permanent place of worship. Thus there was no logic in the claim that the Temple was indispensable in the worship of God, since for many years, in the wilderness and afterwards, there was no Temple, and even after Solomon had built it he still said that the Most High did not dwell in houses made with hands. Stephen then quoted again from Scripture, Isaiah 66.1-2, to support his stand.

From verse 51-53 Stephen declared that the history of the Jews had been one long rebellion against God. They had rejected all the prophets of God and failed to appreciate the true place of the Temple, only as a vessel, not as the essence, of worship. As if to compound their sins, they had rejected and murdered the Righteous One, Jesus Christ, who was the true Temple of God.

(vv.55-56.) In a moment of ecstasy and vision, Stephen cried out that he had seen Jesus standing at the right hand of God.

Effect of Stephen's Defence: Before Stephen announced his vision, the Sanhedrin had already become so infuriated by Stephen's condemnation of their hypocrisy that 'they ground their teeth against him' (v.54). His statement concerning the vision was the last straw; the charge of blasphemy had been proved beyond any doubt. Stephen had disgraced the name of God by claiming that a crucified criminal was the 'Righteous One' and sitting at the right hand of God. Punishment for blasphemy was death by stoning (Leviticus 24.16f). They threw Stephen out of the city and stoned him. As they were stoning him, he recalled what Our Lord had done on a similar occasion: prayed for His enemies. So Stephen prayed, 'Lord, do not hold this sin against them', and died.

In this way, Stephen became the first Christian martyr. His death marked a new phase in the history of the Early Church. The irony of this new wave of opposition to the Church, in which the first blood was shed, was that the man who, at this stage, appeared to be the most active persecutor, Saul of Tarsus, who 'was consenting to his (Stephen's) death' (Acts 8.1), was soon to take up where Stephen had left off, advancing the work of God as far afield as no one so far had ever imagined possible.

Acts 8.1-24 Stephen's Death leads to Progress

The death of Stephen led to an upsurge in the persecution of the Church in and around Jerusalem, headed by Saul, who ravaged the Church, entering house after house, dragging off men and women and committing them to prison. The believers took flight and found refuge in remote parts of Judea and in Samaria; only the Twelve still had sufficient courage and reason to remain in Jerusalem, determined to continue, against all odds, to direct operations from their headquarters. Fortunately for the Church, wherever the believers went they took with them the Good News and planted the seed of the Gospel on fresh ground.

Among the believers who fled from Jerusalem was Philip, one of the first seven deacons. He was perhaps, after Stephen, the most learned of the seven. Philip went down to Samaria and proclaimed the Christ there. Considering the mutual hatred existing between the Jews and the Samaritans, it was a remarkable success on the part of Philip, who was himself a Jew, that the Samaritans 'with one accord gave heed to what was said by Philip, when they heard him and saw the signs which he did'.

In Samaria Philip converted, among others, a man called Simon, a magician very well known in Samaria. People referred to him as 'that power of God which is called Great', because he had amazed them with his magical arts. However, Simon was convinced that Philip was preaching about a greater name than his: he accepted baptism , and kept close to Philip.

News soon reached the mother Church in Jerusalem that Samaria had accepted the Gospel. The Church sent Peter and John to Samaria to confirm the new converts so that they might receive the Holy Spirit. On reaching Samaria they were impressed by what they saw: the Apostles laid their hands on the converts and they received the Holy Spirit.

It was at this stage that Simon revealed his unworthiness. His baptism had been a sham, because he had not changed spiritually. He pleaded with the Apostles to sell the Holy Spirit to him so that he might, in turn, be able to sell it to the highest bidder and thereby usurp the power of God. Peter's rebuke was sharp: Simon had no part in the work of the Holy Spirit, for his heart was not right before God' (**v.21**). **vv.26-40.** Philip continued on his preaching mission, winning more souls for Christ. An angel of the Lord ordered him to rise and go south, along the road that leads from Jerusalem to Gaza. On that road Philip met an Ethiopian eunuch who was returning home in his chariot after a pilgrimage to Jerusalem. He was reading a passage from **Isaiah 53.7-8.** He invited Philip into his chariot to expound to him the real meaning of the passage that he was reading. Philip explained to him that the suffering servant of the Lord, who was like a sheep led to the slaughter, referred to none other than Jesus Christ. He then told the eunuch the Good News of Jesus. The eunuch accepted the Good News and was baptized. He continued on his homeward way, rejoicing.

Nothing more is heard about this Ethiopian, but the ancient Church in Ethiopia claims that he was the founder of the Christian Church in that country.

Philip, on the other hand, was 'caught up' by the Spirit of the Lord and went to Azotus from where he continued the work of preaching until he reached Caesarea, where he made his permanent home with his daughters (**Acts 21.8**).

QUESTIONS

1 Who were Joseph, called Barsabbas, and Matthias? **Acts 1.23**
Describe what part they played in the early story of Acts.

2 They were all filled with the Holy Spirit. **Acts 2.4**
What were the signs of the Spirit's presence with the Apostles? What was the effect on a) the Apostles, and b) the people?

3 Peter and John were going up to the temple at the hour of prayer. **Acts 3.1**
Describe carefully what happened there.

4 They arrested them (Peter and John) and put them in custody. **Acts 4.3**
What were the exact reasons for their arrest? What happened when they were brought before the authorities?

5 They had everything in common. **Acts 4.32**
What is meant by this description of the Early Christians?
Describe the part played by Barnabas in this connection.

6 When they had called in the apostles, they beat them and charged them not to speak in the name of Jesus, and let them go. **Acts 5.40**
Describe what had been happening just before this.

7 They chose Stephen, a man full of faith and of the Holy Spirit. **Acts 6.5**
Who was Stephen and for what job was he chosen?
Describe briefly what happened to him.

8 An angel of the Lord said to Philip, 'Rise and go toward the south to the road that goes down from Jerusalem to Gaza.' **Acts 8.26**
Describe carefully what happened next.

SAUL GOES TO DAMASCUS 9.1-24

9 But Saul, still breathing threats and murder against the disciples of the Lord, went to the high priest ² and asked him for letters to the synagogues at Damascus, so that if he found any belonging to the Way, men or women, he might bring them bound to Jerusalem. ³ Now as he journeyed he approached Damascus, and suddenly a light from heaven flashed about him. ⁴ And he fell to the ground and heard a voice saying to him, "Saul, Saul, why do you persecute me?" ⁵ And he said, "Who are you, Lord?" And he said, "I am Jesus, whom you are persecuting; ⁶ but rise and enter the city, and you will be told what you are to do." ⁷ The men who were travelling with him stood speechless, hearing the voice but seeing no one. ⁸ Saul arose from the ground; and when his eyes were opened, he could see nothing; so they led him by the hand and brought him into Damascus. ⁹ And for three days he was without sight, and neither ate nor drank.

Saul goes to Damàscus 9.1-9

1   Saul is still keen to destroy the Christians (cf. 8.3).

2   Damascus is outside Jewish territory, but has many Jews and several synagogues. 'Letters' from the Sanhedrin to the leaders of the synagogues would help Saul to kidnap rather than arrest 'any belonging to the Way'. The early Christians describe themselves as 'the Way' (cf. 24.14), Christianity being the 'Way' of life: many Christians have fled to Damascus from the persecution in Jerusalem.

3   Saul is full of his eagerness to support the Jewish Law, Gamaliel's words (5.34-39) are probably in his mind — he is a pupil of Gamaliel (cf. 22.3) — and Stephen's death is fresh in his memory. This must be his own story of what happened on the way to Damascus (cf. 22.4-16; 26.9-20). He describes 'a light from heaven' at about noon (cf. 22.6; 26.13) a time when travellers rest to avoid the heat of the sun (cf. note on 8.26).

4-6   In persecuting the Christians, Saul is persecuting Christ Himself (cf. Matthew 25.34-45). The sudden shock and the voice bring Saul to recognize Jesus as 'Lord'.

7   Saul's friends also hear the voice.

8   So far Saul has been blind to the truth: now the blindness is physical and he has to be led into Damascus.

9   Fasting may be the result of shock or Saul's way of thinking things out.

¹⁰ Now there was a disciple at Damascus named Anani'as. The Lord said to him in a vision, "Anani'as." And he said, "Here I am, Lord." ¹¹ And the Lord said to him, "Rise and go to the street called Straight, and inquire in the house of Judas for a man of Tarsus named Saul; for behold, he is praying, ¹² and he has seen a man named Anani'as come in and lay his hands on him so that he might regain his sight." ¹³ But Anani'as answered, "Lord, I have heard from many about this man, how much evil he has done to thy saints at Jerusalem; ¹⁴ and here he has authority from the chief priests to bind all who call upon thy name." ¹⁵ But the Lord said to him, "Go, for he is a chosen instrument of mine to carry my name before the Gentiles and kings and the sons of Israel; ¹⁶ for I will show him how much he must suffer for the sake of my name." ¹⁷ So Anani'as departed and entered the house. And laying his hands on him he said, "Brother Saul, the Lord Jesus, who appeared to you on the road by which you came, has sent me that you may regain your sight and be filled with the Holy Spirit." ¹⁸ And immediately something like scales fell from his eyes and he regained his sight. Then he rose and was baptized, ¹⁹ and took food and was strengthened.

For several days he was with the disciples at Damascus. ²⁰ And in the synagogues immediately he proclaimed Jesus saying, "He is the Son of God." ²¹ And all who heard him were amazed, and said, "Is not this the man who made havoc in Jerusalem of those who called on this name? And he has come here for this purpose, to bring them bound before the chief priests." ²² But Saul increased all the more in strength, and confounded the Jews who lived in Damascus by proving that Jesus was the Christ.

²³ When many days had passed, the Jews plotted to kill him, ²⁴ but their plot became known to Saul. They were watching the gates day and night, to kill him; ²⁵ but his disciples took him by night and let him down over the wall, lowering him in a basket.

Saul and Ananias   9.10-19

10   Ananias is a well-known Jewish Christian.

11   'He is praying' — Luke often makes a point of the importance
        of prayer (cf. 1.24-25). 'A man of Tarsus' — Saul's home
        town.

12   The two visions (v.10,12) prepare both men for what is to
        come.

13   'Saints' — Christians.

14-15   Ananias has heard of Saul and is not keen to go to him: he
        goes because Saul is God's 'chosen instrument'. 'Gentiles and
        kings and the sons of Israel' — in Acts we read of Saul's
        mission to the Gentiles, his stand before Governors Felix and
        Festus (chapters 24-25) and King Agrippa (chapters 25-26),
        his journey to Caesar in Rome, as well as his preaching to
        Israel.

16   'He must suffer' as Jesus Himself has suffered.

17-18   Ananias greets Saul as a Christian 'brother' — through him
        Saul receives healing, baptism and the Holy Spirit.

19   Food renews his strength: recovery is complete.

Saul's work in Damascus   9.19-25

20-22   Saul is a changed man. His preaching is 'the Son of God' and
        'the Christ': Jesus is Messiah.
        N.B. In Paul's letter to the Galatians (1.16-17) he speaks of
        going to Arabia after his conversion, then returning to
        Damascus. Arabia may mean an area near Damascus where
        many Arabs live (cf. note on v.23).

23-24   'The Jews' — in 2 Corinthians 11.32-33 Paul speaks of these
        events and says the plot is by 'the governor under King
        Aretas' — and his preaching may have angered the King of the
        Arabs.

25   'His disciples' — the Christians in Damascus (cf. 2 Corinthians
        11.33).

SAUL RETURNS TO JERUSALEM   9.26-31

²⁶ And when he had come to Jerusalem he attempted to join the disciples; and they were all afraid of him, for they did not believe that he was a disciple. ²⁷ But Barnabas took him, and brought him to the apostles, and declared to them how on the road he had seen the Lord, who spoke to him, and how at Damascus he had preached boldly in the name of Jesus. ²⁸ So he went in and out among them at Jerusalem, ²⁹ preaching boldly in the name of the Lord. And he spoke and disputed against the Hellenists; but they were seeking to kill him. ³⁰ And when the brethren knew it, they brought him down to Caesare'a, and sent him off to Tarsus.

³¹ So the church throughout all Judea and Galilee and Samar'ia had peace and was built up; and walking in the fear of the Lord and in the comfort of the Holy Spirit it was multiplied.

PETER IN LYDDA AND JOPPA   9.32-43

³² Now as Peter went here and there among them all, he came down also to the saints that lived at Lydda. ³³ There he found a man named Aene'as, who had been bedridden for eight years and was paralyzed. ³⁴ And Peter said to him, Aene'as, Jesus Christ heals you; rise and make your bed." And immediately he rose. ³⁵ And all the residents of Lydda and Sharon saw him, and they turned to the Lord.

³⁶ Now there was at Joppa a disciple named Tabitha, which means Dorcas or Gazelle. She was full of good works and acts of charity. ³⁷ In those days she fell sick and died; and when they had washed her, they laid her in an upper room. ³⁸ Since Lydda was near Joppa, the disciples, hearing that Peter was there, sent two men to him entreating him, "Please come to us without delay." ³⁹ So Peter rose and went with them. And when he had come, they took him to the upper room. All the widows stood beside him weeping, and showing coats and garments which Dorcas made while she was with them. ⁴⁰ But Peter put them all outside and knelt down and prayed; then turning to the body he said, "Tabitha, rise." And she opened her eyes, and when she saw Peter she sat up. ⁴¹ And he gave her his hand and lifted her up. Then calling the saints and widows he presented her alive. ⁴² And it became known throughout all Joppa, and many believed in the Lord. ⁴³ And he stayed in Joppa for many days with one Simon, a tanner.

Saul returns to Jerusalem 9.26-31

26   According to Galatians 1.18 it is three years before Saul goes to Jerusalem: he stays fifteen days with Peter. The disciples are naturally 'afraid' and suspicious of him.

27-28   As usual Barnabas is helpful (cf. 4.36-37). 'The apostles' (the Twelve) accept his conversion.

29   Saul works among Hellenists as Stephen has done (cf. 6.8-10) and they try to do with him what they have done with Stephen.

30   Saul goes to Tarsus for safety ('regions of Syria and Cilicia' in Galatians 1.21) — Tarsus is in Cilicia.

31   This verse prepares us for Peter's work, leading to the mission to the Gentiles.

Peter in Lydda and Joppa 9.32-43

32   Peter sets off to visit Christians. Lydda is on the road from Jerusalem to Joppa.

33-34   Jesus Christ is still the power that heals, as in His own ministry. 'Make your bed' can mean 'get a meal ready'.

35   Sharon is the coastal plain between Joppa and Mount Carmel.

36   Joppa is the modern port of Jaffa. Tabitha (Aramaic) and Dorcas (Greek) both mean 'gazelle'.

39   'All the widows' would receive Christian help (cf. 2.45; 4.35; 6.1). Dorcas has given much help.

40-41   The miracle is the answer to prayer — it recalls the story of the daughter of Jairus (Matthew 9.23-25; Mark 5.40-42; Luke 8.51-55).

42   'Many' become Christians (cf. 2.41,47; 4.4; 6.1; 8.12).

43   'Simon, a tanner' is distinguished from 'Simon who is called Peter' (10.5).

10 At Caesare'a there was a man named Cornelius, a centurion of what was known as the Italian Cohort, ²a devout man who feared God with all his household, gave alms liberally to the people, and prayed constantly to God. ³About the ninth hour of the day he saw clearly in a vision an angel of God coming in and saying to him, "Cornelius." ⁴And he stared at him in terror, and said, "What is it, Lord?" And he said to him, "Your prayers and your alms have ascended as a memorial before God. ⁵And now send men to Joppa, and bring one Simon who is called Peter; ⁶he is lodging with Simon, a tanner, whose house is by the seaside." ⁷When the angel who spoke to him had departed, he called two of his servants and a devout soldier from among those that waited on him, ⁸and having related everything to them, he sent them to Joppa.

⁹The next day, as they were on their journey and coming near the city, Peter went up on the housetop to pray, about the sixth hour. ¹⁰And he became hungry and desired something to eat; but while they were preparing it, he fell into a trance ¹¹and saw the heaven opened, and something descending, like a great sheet, let down by four corners upon the earth. ¹²In it were all kinds of animals and reptiles and birds of the air. ¹³And there came a voice to him, "Rise, Peter; kill and eat." ¹⁴But Peter said, "No, Lord; for I have never eaten anything that is common or unclean." ¹⁵And the voice came to him again a second time, "What God has cleansed, you must not call common." ¹⁶This happened three times, and the thing was taken up at once to heaven.

¹⁷Now while Peter was inwardly perplexed as to what the vision which he had seen might mean, behold, the men that were sent by Cornelius, having made inquiry for Simon's house, stood before the gate ¹⁸and called out to ask whether Simon who was called Peter was lodging there. ¹⁹And while Peter was pondering the vision, the Spirit said to him. "Behold, three men are looking for you. ²⁰Rise and go down, and accompany them without hesitation; for I have sent them." ²¹And Peter went down to the men and said, "I am the one you are looking for; what is the reason for your coming?" ²²And they said, "Cornelius, a centurion, an upright and God-fearing man, who is well spoken of by the whole Jewish nation, was directed by a holy angel to send for you to come to his house, and to hear what you have to say." ²³So he called them in to be his guests.

The next day he rose and went off with them, and some of the

Peter and Cornelius: Cornelius's vision   10.1-8

1   Caesarea — a seaport north of Joppa and headquarters of the Roman government in Judea.

2   Cornelius is a God-fearer (see note on 2.10), not a proselyte and not circumcised. 'The people' are the Jews (cf. the story of the centurion in Luke 7.4-5).

3   'The ninth hour' — 3 p.m., the hour of prayer (cf. 3.1); this is a daylight vision, not a dream.

4   'As a memorial' — like a sacrifice.

5-8   Cornelius hears and obeys God's order.

Peter's vision   10.9-23

9   Once again, prayer is important (cf. 9.11,40). 'The housetop' is a quiet place for prayer: 'the sixth hour' is noon.

10   Peter is hungry, and his mind is probably full of ideas about the mission to the Gentiles: as a Jew, he has doubts about this.

11   The 'sheet' may be an awning on the roof, to keep off the sun, or a sail in the harbour that can be seen from the roof.

12-15   The vision and the voice take away any distinction between clean and unclean foods (cf. Jesus in Mark 7.19): the food laws are found in Leviticus 11.

16   'Three times' to emphasize the importance of the lesson.

17   'What the vision . . . might mean' — the removal of any distinction between Jew and Gentile.

19-20   The Spirit urges Peter to go with the messengers at once.

brethren from Joppa accompanied him. ²⁴And on the following day they entered Caesare'a. Cornelius was expecting them and had called together his kinsmen and close friends. ²⁵When Peter entered, Cornelius met him and fell down at his feet and worshipped him. ²⁶But Peter lifted him up, saying, "Stand up; I too am a man." ²⁷And as he talked with him, he went in and found many persons gathered; ²⁸and he said to them, "You yourselves know how unlawful it is for a Jew to associate with or to visit any one of another nation; but God has shown me that I should not call any man common or unclean. ²⁹So when I was sent for, I came without objection. I ask then why you sent for me."

³⁰And Cornelius said, "Four days ago, about this hour, I was keeping the ninth hour of prayer in my house; and behold, a man stood before me in bright apparel, ³¹saying, 'Cornelius, your prayer has been heard and your alms have been remembered before God. ³²Send therefore to Joppa and ask for Simon who is called Peter; he is lodging in the house of Simon, a tanner, by the seaside.' ³³So I sent to you at once, and you have been kind enough to come. Now therefore we are all here present in the sight of God, to hear all that you have been commanded by the Lord."

³⁴And Peter opened his mouth and said; "Truly I perceive that God shows no partiality, ³⁵but in every nation any one who fears him and does what is right is acceptable to him. ³⁶You know the word which he sent to Israel, preaching good news of peace by Jesus Christ (he is Lord of all), ³⁷the word which was proclaimed throughout all Judea, beginning from Galilee after the baptism which John preached: ³⁸how God anointed Jesus of Nazareth with the Holy Spirit and with power; how he went about doing good and healing all that were oppressed by the devil, for God was with him. ³⁹And we are witnesses to all that he did both in the country of the Jews and in Jerusalem. They put him to death by hanging him on a tree; ⁴⁰but God raised him on the third day and made him manifest; ⁴¹not to all the people but to us who were chosen by God as witnesses, who ate and drank with him after he rose from the dead. ⁴²And he commanded us to preach to the people, and to testify that he is the one ordained by God to be judge of the living and the dead. ⁴³To him all the prophets bear witness that every one who believes in him receives forgiveness of sins through his name."

⁴⁴While Peter was still saying this, the Holy Spirit fell on all who heard the word. ⁴⁵And the believers from among the circumcised who came with Peter were amazed, because the gift of the Holy Spirit

Peter goes to Cornelius   10.24-33

24   Cornelius is ready: he gathers friends and relatives.

25   'Worshipped him' — Peter is a messenger of God.

26   'I too am a man' (cf. 14.11-15).

27-28   It is 'unlawful' for a Jew to go into the house of a
         Gentile ('anyone of another nation'): Peter explains why he
         does so — he has learnt from his vision.

30-33   Cornelius answers Peter's question (v.29).

Peter's speech to Cornelius and his friends   10.34-43
         Cf. his speech in Jerusalem (2.22-24).

34-36   God has no favourites: 'the word' (the Gospel) is for all and
         Jesus 'is Lord of all' (cf. 4.12).

38   'God anointed Jesus' (cf. 4.27).

39   The Apostles are witnesses to the Gospel. 'Hanging him on a
         tree' (cf. 5.30).

40-41   They are witnesses also to the Resurrection. 'Who ate and
         drank with him' (cf. 1.4 R.S.V. note; Luke 24.30, 42-43).

42   'He commanded us' (cf. 1.8; Luke 24.47-48) — this is what
         Cornelius wants to hear (v.33). Jesus is 'judge' (cf. Paul at
         Athens (17.31).

43   The Gospel means forgiveness of sins to 'every one who
         believes' through faith in Jesus.

Gentile converts   10.44-48

44   The Holy Spirit comes to them, even before baptism.

45   'The circumcised' — the Jewish Christians who have come
         with Peter.

had been poured out even on the Gentiles. **46** For they heard them speaking in tongues and extolling God. Then Peter declared, **47** "Can any one forbid water for baptizing these people who have received the Holy Spirit just as we have?" **48** And he commanded them to be baptized in the name of Jesus Christ. Then they asked him to remain for some days.

PETER RETURNS TO JERUSALEM   11.1-18

11 Now the apostles and the brethren who were in Judea heard that the Gentiles also had received the word of God. **2** So when Peter went up to Jerusalem, the circumcision party criticized him, **3** saying, "Why did you go to uncircumcised men and eat with them?" **4** But Peter began and explained to them in order: **5** "I was in the city of Joppa praying; and in a trance I saw a vision, something descending, like a great sheet, let down from heaven by four corners; and it came down to me. **6** Looking at it closely I observed animals and beasts of prey and reptiles and birds of the air. **7** And I heard a voice saying to me, 'Rise, Peter; kill and eat.' **8** But I said, 'No, Lord; for nothing common or unclean has ever entered my mouth.' **9** But the voice answered a second time from heaven, 'What God has cleansed you must not call common.' **10** This happened three times, and all was drawn up again into heaven. **11** At that very moment three men arrived at the house in which we were, sent to me from Caesare′a. **12** And the Spirit told me to go with them without hesitation. These six brethren also accompanied me, and we entered the man's house. **13** And he told us how he had seen the angel standing in his house and saying, 'Send to Joppa and bring Simon called Peter; **14** he will declare to you a message by which you will be saved, you and all your household.' **15** As I began to speak, the Holy Spirit fell on them just as on us at the beginning. **16** And I remembered the word of the Lord, how he said, 'John baptized with water, but you shall be baptized with the Holy Spirit.' **17** If then God gave the same gift to them as he gave to us when we believed in the Lord Jesus Christ, who was I that I could withstand God?" **18** When they heard this they were silenced. And they glorified God, saying, "Then to the Gentiles also God has granted repentance unto life."

THE CHURCH AT ANTIOCH   11.19-30

19 Now those who were scattered because of the persecution that

46 The Gentiles are 'speaking in tongues' (cf. 2.1-4), a sign of the Spirit.

47 'Can anyone forbid water for baptizing' (cf. 8.36 'What is to prevent my being baptized?'). 'Just as we have' — i.e. the original disciples at Pentecost.

48 ✳ Baptism receives them into the fellowship of Christ and the Christian Church.

Peter returns to Jerusalem 11.1-18

1 The Church in Jerusalem keeps in touch with what goes on elsewhere, as in the mission to Samaria (8.14) and the mixed Jewish and Gentile Church at Antioch (11.22).

2-3 'The circumcision party' — all the early Christians are Jews, except the Ethiopian (8.26-39) and Cornelius and his family and friends (chapter 10): they do not agree with mixing with Gentiles at meals. These difficulties are still to be found later on (15.1-35).

4-16 Peter tells the whole story.

14 'All your household' — it is common for whole families rather than individuals to adopt a new religion (cf. 16.15; 31-34; 18.8).

16 Peter ends with the words of Jesus (1.5).

17 He cannot hinder God by refusing baptism.

18 Gentiles can have 'repentance unto life' without first becoming Jews.

The Church at Antioch 11.19-30

19 This verse picks up the story from 8.4. Phoenicia lies along the coast north of Mount Carmel. Cyprus, an island in the eastern Mediterranean, plays a part in the mission of Paul and Barnabas (13.4ff.). Antioch, a great city, capital of Syria: it has many Jews and proselytes among the Gentile population. The Gospel is preached first to the Jews.

arose over Stephen travelled as far as Phoeni′cià and Cyprus and Antioch, speaking the word to none except Jews. ²⁰ But there were some of them, men of Cyprus and Cyre′nė, who on coming to Antioch spoke to the Greeksⁱ also, preaching the Lord Jesus. ²¹ And the hand of the Lord was with them, and a great number that believed turned to the Lord. ²² News of this came to the ears of the church in Jerusalem, and they sent Barnabas to Antioch. ²³ When he came and saw the grace of God, he was glad; and he exhorted them all to remain faithful to the Lord with steadfast purpose; ²⁴ for he was a good man, full of the Holy Spirit and of faith. And a large company was added to the Lord. ²⁵ So Barnabas went to Tarsus to look for Saul; ²⁶ and when he had found him, he brought him to Antioch. For a whole year they met with^j the church, and taught a large company of people; and in Antioch the disciples were for the first time called Christians.

²⁷ Now in these days prophets came down from Jerusalem to Antioch. ²⁸ And one of them named Ag′abus stood up and foretold by the Spirit that there would be a great famine over all the world; and this took place in the days of Claudius. ²⁹ And the disciples determined, every one according to his ability, to send relief to the brethren who lived in Judea; ³⁰ and they did so, sending it to the elders by the hand of Barnabas and Saul.

i Other ancient authorities read 'Hellenists' j Or 'were guests of'

HEROD AND THE CHURCH 12.1-19

12 About that time Herod the king laid violent hands upon some who belonged to the church. ² He killed James the brother of John with the sword; ³ and when he saw that it pleased the Jews, he proceeded to arrest Peter also. This was during the days of Unleavened

20-21   Before long the Gospel is brought to the Greeks (Hellenists) also. 'Men of Cyprus and Cyrene' — cf. Barnabas (4.36) and Lucius (13.1). For the first time the Gospel comes to Gentiles in large numbers (v.21,24. cf. 2.41,47).

22-23   The Church in Jerusalem is concerned (cf. 11.1) and sends Barnabas (cf. the check on Philip's mission to Samaria (8.14)).

24   Barnabas is just the man for the job (cf. 4.36-37; 9.27).

25   He asks Saul, a Greek-speaking Jew, to help him. Tarsus, capital of the province of Cilicia (cf. 9.30).

26   'Christians' — a nickname given by non-Christians (cf. 26.28). The Christians often called themselves 'Followers of the Way' i.e. the Way of Life (cf. 9.2).

27   'Prophets' — men inspired by the Holy Spirit (cf. 13.1; 15.32; 21.10).

28   Historians record severe local famines, but none empire-wide, in the time of Claudius, A. D. 46-48.

29-30   The Church at Antioch helps the Mother Church in Jerusalem. 'Elders' — similar to men in the synagogues who look after synagogue affairs and worship. The Church in Jerusalem follows this idea: James, the Lord's brother, is their leader (cf. 12.17; 15.13).

Herod and the Church   12.1-19

1   Herod is Herod Agrippa I, grandson of Herod the Great and nephew of Herod Antipas ruler of Galilee in the time of Jesus (cf. Luke 23.7-12). Between A.D. 37 and 41 he is given Trachonitis, territory of his uncle Philip, by the Emperor Gaius (and probably Abilene as well): then he receives Galilee and Perea, territory of Herod Antipas, and Judea. He is given the title 'King'. His death in A.D. 44 is seen by Luke (and by the historian Josephus) as divine punishment (12.20-23).

2   Jesus' prophecy (Mark 10.39) is fulfilled. James is the first of the Apostles to be killed. There is a tradition, with little evidence, that John shares his fate: a far stronger tradition has John living to a great age in Ephesus. If John has died, surely Luke would mention it.

3   'The Jews' are presumably those who oppose the Christians. 'The days of Unleavened Bread' — the week following the Passover.

Bread. ⁴ And when he had seized him, he put him in prison, and delivered him to four squads of soldiers to guard him, intending after the Passover to bring him out to the people. ⁵ So Peter was kept in prison; but earnest prayer for him was made to God by the church.

⁶ The very night when Herod was about to bring him out, Peter was sleeping between two soldiers, bound with two chains, and sentries before the door were guarding the prison; ⁷ and behold, an angel of the Lord appeared, and a light shone in the cell; and he struck Peter on the side and woke him, saying. "Get up quickly." And the chains fell off his hands. ⁸ And the angel said to him, "Dress yourself and put on your sandals." And he did so. And he said to him, "Wrap your mantle around you and follow me." ⁹ And he went out and followed him; he did not know that what was done by the angel was real, but thought he was seeing a vision. ¹⁰ When they had passed the first and the second guard, they came to the iron gate leading into the city. It opened to them of its own accord, and they went out and passed on through one street; and immediately the angel left him. ¹¹ And Peter came to himself, and said, "Now I am sure that the Lord has sent his angel and rescued me from the hand of Herod and from all that the Jewish people were expecting."

¹² When he realized this, he went to the house of Mary, the mother of John whose other name was Mark, where many were gathered together and were praying. ¹³ And when he knocked at the door of the gateway, a maid named Rhoda came to answer. ¹⁴ Recognizing Peter's voice, in her joy she did not open the gate but ran in and told that Peter was standing at the gate. ¹⁵ They said to her, "You are mad." But she insisted that it was so. They said, "It is his angel!" ¹⁶ But Peter continued knocking; and when they opened, they saw him and were amazed. ¹⁷ But motioning to them with his hand to be silent, he described to them how the Lord had brought him out of the prison. And he said, "Tell this to James and to the brethren." Then he departed and went to another place.

¹⁸ Now when day came, there was no small stir among the soldiers over what had become of Peter. ¹⁹ And when Herod had sought for him and could not find him, he examined the sentries and ordered that they should be put to death. Then he went down from Judea to Caesare'a, and remained there.

THE DEATH OF HEROD 12.20-25

²⁰ Now Herod was angry with the people of Tyre and Sidon; and

4	'Four squads of soldiers' suggests one squad for each of the four night watches: but all may be on duty together to prevent a repeat of 5.19. Herod wants no trouble during the Passover time.
5	Prayer is important (cf. 9.11,40; 10.9) and is followed by events which, to Luke, are quite miraculous.
6	There seems little chance of escape.
7-9	All that happens seems unreal to Peter: the angel gives orders: he does what he is told.
10-11	In the cool night air Peter realises the truth. 'The Jewish people' suggests that there is considerable opposition to the Christians.
12	'The house of Mary' — a meeting place for Early Christians, such as the disciples before Pentecost: probably the scene of the Last Supper. John Mark is probably the author of the Gospel of that name (cf. 12.25; 13.5, 13; 15.37-39), and nephew (cousin) of Barnabas (Colossians 4.10). 'Praying' (cf. v.5).
17	James, the brother of Jesus (Mark 6.3) already holds an important position in the Church (cf. 21.17-18), particularly when Peter is not in Jerusalem. 'Went to another place' — perhaps Antioch: he is back again in chapter 15.
19	Caesarea — the seat of the Roman government (see note on 10.1).

The death of Herod   12.20-25

20	Tyre and Sidon — chief ports of Phoenicia, north-west of Palestine. The quarrel may be over economic matters.

they came to him in a body, and having persuaded Blastus, the king's chamberlain, they asked for peace, because their country depended on the king's country for food. ²¹ On an appointed day Herod put on his royal robes, took his seat upon the throne, and made an oration to them. ²² And the people shouted, "The voice of a god, and not of man!" ²³ Immediately an angel of the Lord smote him, because he did not give God the glory; and he was eaten by worms and died.

²⁴ But the word of God grew and multiplied.

²⁵ And Barnabas and Saul returned from^k Jerusalem when they had fulfilled their mission, bringing with them John whose other name was Mark.

PAUL'S FIRST MISSIONARY JOURNEY   13.1-14.28
IN CYPRUS   13.1-12

13 Now in the church at Antioch there were prophets and teachers, Barnabas, Symeon who was called Niger, Lucius of Cyre′ne, Man′a-en a member of the court of Herod the tetrarch, and Saul. ² While they were worshipping the Lord and fasting, the Holy Spirit said, "Set apart for me Barnabas and Saul for the work to which I have called them." ³ Then after fasting and praying they laid their hands on them and sent them off.

⁴ So, being sent out by the Holy Spirit, they went down to Seleu′cia; and from there they sailed to Cyprus. ⁵ When they arrived at Sal′amis, they proclaimed the word of God in the synagogues of the Jews. And they had John to assist them. ⁶ When they had gone through the whole island as far as Paphos, they came upon a certain magician, a Jewish false prophet, named Bar-Jesus. ⁷ He was with the proconsul, Sergius Paulus, a man of intelligence, who summoned Barnabas and Saul and sought to hear the word of God. ⁸ But El′ymas the magician (for that is the meaning of his name) withstood them, seeking to turn away the proconsul from the faith. ⁹ But Saul, who is also called Paul, filled with the Holy Spirit, looked intently

---

k   Other ancient authorities read 'to'.

21-22	Flattery of 'the people', probably Phoenicians who admire the glory of Herod's clothes and speech, leads to a dreadful end.
23	Herod's death, in A.D. 44 is put down to punishment by God. His son, Herod Agrippa II, takes his place.
24	In spite of persecution, the Gospel spreads.
25	The mission of Barnabas and Saul (cf. 11.29-30) is completed and they come back to Antioch. John Mark (cf. v.12).

Paul's first missionary journey 13.1-14.28
In Cyprus 13.1-12

1	Antioch, where the Gospel is first preached to large numbers of Gentiles (cf. 11.20). Only Barnabas and Saul are known: 'Symeon who was called Niger' (black) could be Simon of Cyrene (Luke 23.26) but there is no evidence. Herod the terarch is Herod Antipas, ruler of Galilee in the time of Jesus and deposed by the Romans in A.D. 30.
2	Again a time of prayer (cf. 9.11,40; 10.9; 12.5) and fasting. The Holy Spirit's call comes to Barnabas and Saul perhaps through one of the prophets (v.1).
3	'They laid their hands on them' — an act of blessing on those who are to represent the Church at Antioch. After this Luke calls Barnabas and Saul 'apostles' (14.4,14).
4	Seleucia is the port of Antioch. Cyprus, home of Barnabas (4.36) has a large Jewish population.
5	Salamis is the main harbour. Their mission is to the Jews. John Mark (cf. 12.12,25; 13.5,13; 15.37-39). 'To assist' — perhaps to organize and to teach converts.
6-7	Paphos — Roman capital of Cyprus: the Roman proconsul (governor) is friendly. 'Magician' (Greek 'magus'), probably an astronomer, foretelling the future.
8	'The Jewish false prophet' interferes: perhaps Elymas is his Greek name and Bar-Jesus (son of Jesus) is Aramaic. It is common for a Jew to have two names, one Aramaic and one Greek or Latin, e.g. Cephas — Petros, John — Marcus.
9	Saul (Jewish name) becomes Paul (Roman 'Paulus'): the Gentiles, and Paul himself, would call him Paul. There may be a hint here that Luke is writing for the Church in Rome and that Paul's mission is to the Gentiles.

at him [10] and said, "You son of the devil, you enemy of all righteous-ness, full of all deceit and villainy, will you not stop making crooked the straight paths of the Lord? [11] And now, behold, the hand of the Lord is upon you, and you shall be blind and unable to see the sun for a time." Immediately mist and darkness fell upon him and he went about seeking people to lead him by the hand. [12] Then the proconsul believed, when he saw what had occurred, for he was astonished at the teaching of the Lord.

IN ASIA MINOR   13.13-52

[13] Now Paul and his company set sail from Paphos, and came to Perga in Pamphyl'ia. And John left them and returned to Jerusalem; [14] but they passed on from Perga and came to Antioch of Pisid'ia. And on the sabbath day they went into the synagogue and sat down. [15] After the reading of the law and the prophets, the rulers of the synagogue sent to them, saying, "Brethren, if you have any word of exhortation for the people say it." [16] So Paul stood up, and motioning with his hand said:

"Men of Israel, and you that fear God, listen. [17] The God of this people Israel chose our fathers and made the people great during their stay in the land of Egypt, and with uplifted arm he led them out of it. [18] And for about forty years he bore with[m] them in the wilderness. [19] And when he had destroyed seven nations in the land of Caanan, he gave them their land as an inheritance, for about four hundred and fifty years. [20] And after that he gave them judges until Samuel the prophet. [21] Then they asked for a king; and God gave them Saul the son of Kish, a man of the tribe of Benjamin, for forty years. [22] And when he had removed him, he raised up David to be their king; of whom he testified and said, 'I have found in David the son of Jesse a man after my heart, who will do all my will.' [23] Of this man's posterity God has brought to Israel a Savior, Jesus, as he promised. [24] Before his coming John had preached a baptism of repentance to all the people of Israel. [25] And as John was finishing his course, he said, 'What do you suppose that I am? I am not he. No, but after me one is coming, the sandals of whose feet I am not worthy to untie.'

[26] "Brethren, sons of the family of Abraham, and those among you that fear God, to us has been sent the message of this salvation. [27] For those who live in Jerusalem and their rulers, because they did not

m Other ancient authorities read 'cared for' (Deuteronomy 1.31)

10-11 Paul, in the power of the Spirit, defeats Elymas (cf. Peter in
8.18ff.) The effect on Elymas is similar to that on Paul on
the Damascus road, but in reverse — here it is punishment
by God.

12 We do not know if Paulus is converted to Christianity but
Luke seems to suggest this.

In Asia Minor   13.13-52
13 Perga is in the unhealthy coastal area and they press on.
'John left them' — no reason is given, but perhaps it is his
fear and inexperience.

14 'Antioch of Pisidia' — the chief town of southern Galatia, a
Roman colony with a number of Jews.

15 'The rulers of the synagogue' look after the services, etc. A
visitor may be invited to read and speak.

16 Paul speaks to the Jews and God-fearers (cf. v.26 and note on
2.10 and 10.2). His speech is like those of Peter (chapters 2
and 3) and Stephen (chapter 7).

17-22 Paul's short history of events is well known to the Jews: it
will help the Gentiles to understand what follows.

23-25 He speaks of the coming of Jesus as Messiah, heralded by
John the Baptist.

27-28 The blame for Jesus' death is laid on the Jews, not on Pilate:
the Jews have not understood their prophets.

recognize him nor understand the utterances of the prophets which are read every sabbath, fulfilled these by condemning him. [28] Though they could charge him with nothing deserving death, yet they asked Pilate to have him killed. [29] And when they had fulfilled all that was written of him, they took him down from the tree, and laid him in a tomb. [30] But God raised him from the dead; [31] and for many days he appeared to those who came up with him from Galilee to Jerusalem, who are now his witnesses to the people. [32] And we bring you the good news that what God promised to the fathers, [33] this he has fulfilled to us their children by raising Jesus; as also it is written in the second psalm,

'Thou art my Son,

today I have begotten thee.'

[34] And as for the fact that he raised him from the dead, no more to return to corruption, he spoke in this way,

'I will give you the holy and sure blessings of David.'

[35] Therefore he says also in another psalm,

'Thou wilt not let thy Holy One see corruption.'

[36] For David, after he had served the counsel of God in his own generation, fell asleep, and was laid with his fathers, and saw corruption; [37] but he whom God raised up saw no corruption. [38] Let it be known to you therefore, brethren, that through this man forgiveness of sins is proclaimed to you, [39] and by him every one that believes is freed from everything from which you could not be freed by the law of Moses. [40] Beware, therefore, lest there come upon you what is said in the prophets:

[41] 'Behold, you scoffers, and wonder, and perish;

for I do a deed in your days,

a deed you will never believe, if one declares it to you.' "

[42] As they went out, the people begged that these things might be told them the next sabbath. [43] And when the meeting of the synagogue broke up, many Jews and devout converts to Judaism followed Paul and Barnabas, who spoke to them and urged them to continue in the grace of God.

[44] The next sabbath almost the whole city gathered together to hear the word of God. [45] But when the Jews saw the multitudes, they were filled with jealousy, and contradicted what was spoken by Paul, and reviled him. [46] And Paul and Barnabas spoke out boldly, saying, "It was necessary that the word of God should be spoken first to you. Since you thrust it from you, and judge yourselves unworthy of eternal life, behold, we turn to the Gentiles. [47] For so the Lord has

29   God's will has been fulfilled (cf. 3.18).

30-31 The Resurrection cancels what they have done: Jesus is Messiah, as the Apostles witness (cf. 1.21-22).

32-37 It is the habit of rabbis to explain one section of the Scriptures by referring to others, here Psalm 2.7 (v.33), Isaiah 55.3 (34) and Psalm 16.10 (35). 'The Holy One' (35) is not David, but Messiah (37).

38-41 The speech reaches its climax, 'forgiveness of sins' for believers in Jesus Christ, and a warning from Habakkuk 1.5 (cf. 3.23). The words in vv. 40-41 foretell rejection by the Jews and the taking of the Gospel to the Gentiles (46).

42-43 Some Jews and proselytes are keen to hear more, and follow Paul and Barnabas to listen to them elsewhere.

44   'The whole city' is an exaggeration, but includes a mixed audience of Jews. God-fearers and others.

45   'The Jews' are probably the synagogue leaders, 'filled with jealousy' (cf. 5.17) and afraid of a Gospel that does not distinguish between Jew and Gentile.

46   Paul and Barnabas warn the Jews of Asia Minor: later their warning comes to those who live in Greece (18.6) and in Rome (28.23-28).

47   See Isaiah 49.6 — the 'servant of God' is sent to Jews and Gentiles.

commanded us, saying,

'I have set you to be a light for the Gentiles,
that you may bring salvation to the uttermost parts of the
earth.' "

⁴⁸ And when the Gentiles heard this, they were glad and glorified the word of God; and as many as were ordained to eternal life believed. ⁴⁹ And the word of the Lord spread throughout all the region. ⁵⁰ But the Jews incited the devout women of high standing and the leading men of the city, and stirred up persecution against Paul and Barnabas, and drove them out of their district. ⁵¹ But they shook off the dust from their feet against them, and went to Ico'nium. ⁵² And the disciples were filled with joy and with the Holy Spirit.

AT ICONIUM   14.1-7

14 Now at Ico'nium they entered together into the Jewish synagogue, and so spoke that a great company believed, both of Jews and Greeks. ² But the unbelieving Jews stirred up the Gentiles and poisoned their minds against the brethren. ³ So they remained for a long time, speaking boldly for the Lord, who bore witness to the word of his grace, granting signs and wonders to be done by their hands. ⁴ But the people of the city were divided; some sided with the Jews, and some with the apostles. ⁵ When an attempt was made by both Gentiles and Jews, with their rulers, to molest them and to stone them, ⁶ they learned of it and fled to Lystra and Derbe, cities of Lycao'nia, and to the surrounding country; ⁷ and there they preached the gospel.

⁸ Now at Lystra there was a man sitting, who could not use his feet; he was a cripple from birth, who had never walked. ⁹ He listened to Paul speaking; and Paul, looking intently at him and seeing that he had faith to be made well, ¹⁰ said in a loud voice, "Stand upright on your feet." And he sprang up and walked. ¹¹ And when the crowds saw what Paul had done, they lifted up their voices, saying in Lycao'nian, "The gods have come down to us in the likeness of

48	The Jews reject the Gospel: the Gentiles are ready to believe (cf. 28.28). 'They were glad' (cf. 8.8,39).
49	'The word of the Lord spread' not only through the Apostles but also through the converts.
50	'The devout women' influence 'the leading men'.
51	'They shook off the dust' (cf. Luke 9.5; 10.11) — a symbolic act for rejection. Iconium, south-east of Antioch (the modern Konja), a Roman colony and trade centre. Paul and Barnabas go to the towns: the people will spread the word elsewhere (cf. v.49).
52	'The disciples' — the new Church at Antioch.

At Iconium   14.1-7

1	As Jews, Paul and Barnabas preach in the synagogues and are made welcome. The 'Greeks' are probably God-fearing Gentiles.
2	But their enemies are busy (cf. v.5).
3	Paul and Barnabas speak 'boldly' (cf. 9.27; 18.26; 19.8). 'Signs and wonders' (cf. 2.43; 5.12; 6.8; 8.6).
4	'The apostles' — so called only here and v.14 in Acts: the title may mean that they are representatives, sent out by the Church at Antioch (13.3).
5	The 'rulers' may be the synagogue leaders, but more probably the town authorities who fear riots caused by the two sides. The threat of v.2 becomes real.
6	Paul and Barnabas flee. Lystra (modern Zoldera), a Roman colony to the south of Iconium. Derbe, believed to be the modern Kerti Huyuk, south-east of Lystra.
7	We do not know how long they stay (cf. v.20).

At Lystra   14.8-20

	A story like that of Peter and John and the lame man at the Temple (cf. 3.1-12).
8	Luke lays threefold stress on the man's condition.
9	'Faith' is present in healing miracles (cf. Luke 5.20; Acts 3.16).
10	'He sprang up and walked' (cf. 3.8).
11	In excitement over the miracle the crowd talk in their own language: Paul has been speaking in Greek and does not understand.

men!" [12] Barnabas they called Zeus, and Paul, because he was the chief speaker, they called Hermes. [13] And the priest of Zeus, whose temple was in front of the city, brought oxen and garlands to the gates and wanted to offer sacrifice with the people. [14] But when the apostles Barnabas and Paul heard of it, they tore their garments and rushed out among the multitude, crying, [15] "Men, why are you doing this? We also are men, of like nature with you, and bring you good news, that you should turn from these vain things to a living God who made the heaven and the earth and the sea and all that is in them. [16] In past generations he allowed all the nations to walk in their own ways; [17] yet he did not leave himself without witness, for he did good and gave you from heaven rains and fruitful seasons, satisfying your hearts with food and gladness." [18] With these words they scarcely restrained the people from offering sacrifice to them.

AT LYSTRA AND DERBE   14.21-28

[19] But Jews came there from Antioch and Ico'nium; and having persuaded the people, they stoned Paul and dragged him out of the city, supposing that he was dead. [20] But when the disciples gathered about him, he rose up and entered the city; and on the next day he went on with Barnabas to Derbe. [21] When they had preached the gospel to that city and had made many disciples, they returned to Lystra and to Ico'nium and to Antioch, [22] strengthening the souls of the disciples, exhorting them to continue in the faith, and saying that through many tribulations we must enter the kingdom of God. [23] And when they had appointed elders for them in every church, with prayer and fasting, they committed them to the Lord in whom they believed.

[24] Then they passed through Pisid'ia, and came to Pamphyl'ia. [25] And when they had spoken the word in Perga, they went down to Attali'a; [26] and from there they sailed to Antioch, where they had been commended to the grace of God for the work which they had fulfilled. [27] And when they arrived, they gathered the church together and declared all that God had done with them, and how he had opened a door of faith to the Gentiles. [28] And they remained no little time with the disciples.

12	Zeus (Roman Jupiter), chief of the gods, and Hermes (Roman Mercury), messenger of the gods: there is a legend of their visit to earth as beggars. 'The gates' are perhaps those of the city, where the lame man has been begging. 'To offer sacrifice' — to the supposed gods: the 'garlands' adorn the oxen before sacrifice.
14	Paul and Barnabas may not understand the language (cf. v.11), but they do understand what is happening. 'They tore their garments' as a sign of their displeasure with an act of blasphemy (cf. Mark 14.63).
15	This speech and the speech at Athens (17.22-31) differ from others in that they are made to pagans. The 'good news' is the Gospel. 'Turn from these vain things', i.e. idols, to the true God who is revealed in His Creation.
16	God has overlooked their ignorance and idolatry in the past,
17	but He has revealed Himself in Nature.
19	Enemies from Antioch (cf. 13.45-50) and Iconium (cf. 14.2-5) come to stir up trouble. 'They stoned Paul' — throwing stones rather than a real attempt at execution.
20	'The disciples' — there are already believers: perhaps Paul and Barnabas have been there for some time (cf. note on v.7).

To Derbe and back to Antioch in Syria   14.21-28

21-22	The mission is a success. Instead of going back to Antioch in Syria by the short route overland, the Apostles retrace their steps (a bold and dangerous move) to encourage the new Christian Churches in the new faith.
23	'Elders' as in the synagogues, to look after the young Churches (cf. 11.30; 15.6; 20.17). 'With prayer and fasting' as at the beginning of their journey (cf. 13.2-3).
24-26	They preach in Perga this time (cf. 13.13-14) then, from Attalia, go direct to Antioch in Syria.
27	They report to the whole Church. 'A door of faith' is open for Gentiles into the Christian Church.
28	They remain in Antioch a long time.

15 But some men came down from Judea and were teaching the brethren, "Unless you are circumcised according to the custom of Moses, you cannot be saved." ² And when Paul and Barnabas had no small dissension and debate with them, Paul and Barnabas and some of the others were appointed to go up to Jerusalem to the apostles and the elders about this question. ³ So, being sent on their way by the church, they passed through both Phoeni'cia and Samar'ia, reporting the conversion of the Gentiles, and they gave great joy to all the brethren. ⁴ When they came to Jerusalem, they were welcomed by the church and the apostles and the elders, and they declared all that God had done with them. ⁵ But some believers who belonged to the party of the Pharisees rose up, and said, "It is necessary to circumcise them, and to charge them to keep the law of Moses."

⁶ The apostles and the elders were gathered together to consider this matter. ⁷ And after there had been much debate, Peter rose and said to them, "Brethren, you know that in the early days God made choice among you, that by my mouth the Gentiles should hear the word of the gospel and believe. ⁸ And God who knows the heart bore witness to them, giving them the Holy Spirit just as he did to us; ⁹ and he made no distinction between us and them, but cleansed their hearts by faith. ¹⁰ Now therefore why do you make trial of God by putting a yoke upon the neck of the disciples which neither our fathers nor we have been able to bear? ¹¹ But we believe that we shall be saved through the grace of the Lord Jesus, just as they will."

¹² And all the assembly kept silence; and they listened to Barnabas and Paul as they related what signs and wonders God had done through them among the Gentiles. ¹³ After they finished speaking, James replied, "Brethren, listen to me. ¹⁴ Symeon has related how God first visited the Gentiles, to take out of them a people for his name. ¹⁵ And with this the words of the prophets agree, as it is written,

¹⁶ 'After this I will return,
and I will rebuild the dwelling of David, which has fallen;
I will rebuild its ruins,
and I will set it up,
¹⁷ that the rest of men may seek the Lord,
and all the Gentiles who are called by my name,
¹⁸ says the Lord, who has made these things known from of old.'

The Council of Jerusalem: A problem about Gentiles   15.1-21

N.B. The Jerusalem Church is more conservative than that at Antioch, centre of the Gentile mission (cf. 11.1ff). It is not certain if these verses are about one or two meetings: Luke may have combined the two (cf. 15.2-5 and 15.6ff).

1   'From Judea' — from Jerusalem, from James the brother of Jesus (cf. 12.17) and the elders.

2   'no small dissension' — the problem is acute (cf. 11.2).

3   The attitude of Phoenicia and Samaria is favourable to Paul and Barnabas.

4   They receive a welcome in Jerusalem and show how God has worked through them.

5   Their main critics are some ex-Pharisees.

6   After the story of this Council the 'apostles' do not appear again in Acts.

7   'In the early days' — Peter refers to the conversion of Cornelius (chapter 10) when God originates the mission to the Gentiles.

8   'God who knows the heart' (cf. 1.24). 'Giving them the Holy Spirit' (cf. 10.44) and so accepting them equally with Jews.

9   'Cleansed' (cf. 10.15; 11.9) suggests there is no need for circumcision.

10   The Law is a 'yoke', both duty and privilege: it is often too heavy for Jews and impossible for Gentiles.

11   Salvation is by faith, not by Law.

12   'Signs and wonders' are proof of God's presence in the Gentile mission.

13   James, head of the Jerusalem Church, sums up.

14   'Symeon' — Aramaic form of Simon — is the last mention of Peter in Acts. 'God first visited the Gentiles' (cf. v.7). 'A people for his name' — a covenant people, like Israel in the Old Testament.

15-18   God has acted as Old Testament prophets foretell (cf. Amos 9.11-12; Jeremiah 12.15; Isaiah 45.21).

¹⁹ Therefore my judgment is that we should not trouble those of the Gentiles who turn to God, ²⁰ but should write to them to abstain from the pollutions of idols and from unchastity and from what is strangled" and from blood. ²¹ For from early generations Moses has had in every city those who preach him, for he is read every sabbath in the synagogues."

²² Then it seemed good to the apostles and the elders, with the whole church, to choose men from among them and send them to Antioch with Paul and Barnabas. They sent Judas called Barsabbas, and Silas, leading men among the brethren, ²³ with the following letter: "The brethren, both the apostles and the elders, to the brethren who are of the Gentiles in Antioch and Syria and Cili'cia, greeting. ²⁴ Since we have heard that some persons from us have troubled you with words, unsettling your minds, although we gave them no instructions, ²⁵ it has seemed good to us in assembly to choose men and send them to you with our beloved Barnabas and Paul, ²⁶ men who have risked their lives for the sake of our Lord Jesus Christ. ²⁷ We have therefore sent Judas and Silas, who themselves will tell you the same things by word of mouth. ²⁸ For it has seemed good to the Holy Spirit and to us to lay upon you no greater burden than these necessary things: ²⁹ that you abstain from what has been sacrificed to idols and from blood and from what is strangled" and from unchastity. If you keep yourselves from these, you will do well. Farewell."

³⁰ So when they were sent off, they went down to Antioch; and having gathered the congregation together, they delivered the letter. ³¹ And when they read it, they rejoiced at the exhortation. ³² And Judas and Silas, who were themselves prophets, exhorted the brethren with many words and strengthened them. ³³ And after they had spent some time, they were sent off in peace by the brethren to those who had sent them.º ³⁵ But Paul and Barnabas remained in Antioch, teaching and preaching the word of the Lord, with many others also.

n *Other early authorities omit 'and from what is strangled'*
o *Other ancient authorities insert verse 34, 'But it seemed good to Silas to remain there'*

19	James agrees with Peter — they should not 'trouble' the Gentiles by forcing the Law upon them, i.e. circumcision.
20	James puts forward four requirements: these were orders, in the first place, for Jews and 'strangers' alike:

a) to refrain from meat that has been offered to 'idols' in heathen temples (Leviticus 17.8-9);

b) to refrain from 'unchastity', e.g. prohibited marriages (Leviticus 18.6-23);

c) to refrain from 'what is strangled';

d) to refrain from 'blood' (Leviticus 17.10-14) i.e. not to eat meat with blood in it.

c and d refer to meat not killed in the Jewish (kosher) way.

21	Jews and their synagogues are widely spread and the Law is taught 'every sabbath' — Gentiles should know what the Law says.

A letter from the Council   15.22-35

22	To 'the apostles and the elders' (15.2,6) is now added 'the whole church' to choose men to go with Paul and Barnabas to Antioch with the Council's message. 'Judas called Barsabbas' may be a brother of Joseph (1.23). Silas is almost certainly the one who goes with Paul on later missions (15.40ff).
23	The usual beginning for letters of the time, with the writer and addressee.
24	The 'men' referred to in v.1 are disowned.
26	'Risked their lives' — given their lives to Jesus.
28	'The Holy Spirit' is present (cf. 13.2; 20.23).
29	cf. v.20.
30	'They delivered the letter' probably first by 'word of mouth' (v.27).
32	Judas and Silas, previously called 'leading men' (v.22), are now called 'prophets' (cf. 11.27; 13.1) probably meaning preachers in the Early Church.
34	See R.S.V. note — this leads naturally to v.40.

Acts 9.1-31 The Conversion of Saul

After the martyrdom of Stephen, Saul, who had been a student under Gamaliel and who had, in his testimony in **Philippians 3.5**, called himself 'a Hebrew born of Hebrews, as to the law a Pharisee', ravaged 'the church and, entering house after house, dragged off men and women and committed them to prison' (**Acts 8.3**).

The believers fled from Jerusalem to Judea and Samaria and preached the word of God wherever they went. The Twelve, as was said earlier, remained in Jerusalem. The opposition, which had gained a new impetus with the death of Stephen, failed to achieve its purpose: instead of the desired result, the Gospel was scattered abroad, where it germinated and bore much fruit.

Saul was violently opposed to the Gospel, and was particularly angered by Stephen's blasphemous claims. He therefore obtained letters of authority from the High Priest to go to Damascus and to arrest all the believers there. Although, at this stage, Saul was convinced that 'the Way' (as Christianity was then called), was a threat to his orthodox Judaism, the death of Stephen and the way he had prayed for his murderers must have given him food for thought. On his journey from Jerusalem to Damascus, a distance of 140 miles (225 km.), Saul must have began to examine his role so far as the defender of Judaism.

As he approached the city, Luke tells us that he was struck down by a light from heaven and that a voice spoke to him in Hebrew, 'Saul, Saul, why do you persecute me? . . . I am Jesus, whom you are persecuting; but rise and enter the city, and you will be told what you are to do.' When Saul arose he could see nothing: he was blind.

In this wonderful revelation, Jesus told Saul that the persecution of His followers meant the persecution of Christ Himself. Saul could not easily divorce himself from this experience and for three days he could not bring himself either to eat or to drink.

There was in Damascus, we are told, a disciple (not one of the Twelve) called Ananias. In a vision the Lord had directed him to go to the street called Straight, to the house of Judas, to meet Saul and lay his hands on him so that he might receive his sight. Naturally Ananias was afraid of Saul, because the news of his staunch opposition to the Church had travelled faster than Saul himself and had reached Damascus. But the Lord convinced him to go to meet Saul, because Saul was a chosen instrument 'to carry my name before the Gentiles and kings and the sons of Israel'.

Saul's experience on the road to Damascus can be compared with the Apostles' experience on the Day of Pentecost. Saul always recalled it with a sense of his unworthiness for his call, since he had been an outspoken and uncompromising enemy of the Church. In his Letters he returns to this theme again and again, thus leaving no doubt as to the reality, to him, of the experience (see **Galatians 1.15-16; I Corinthians 15.8-9).** The gift of the Holy Spirit to the Apostles on the Day of Pentecost was, they knew, the source of their energy and conviction for preaching the Gospel; for Saul, his experience on the road to Damascus was his equivalent of Pentecost, and he was eternally proud of this personal call by Jesus.

After Ananias had laid his hands on Saul and had spoken to him, something like scales fell from his eyes and he regained his sight. After this he was baptized and, having taken food, he became strengthened for the work ahead.

Saul remained in Damascus for several days and in the synagogues he soon started to preach Christ Crucified. The Jews were not prepared to allow him to continue like this: they plotted to kill him, but the disciples in the city were able to let him down over the wall in a basket and he escaped to Jerusalem.

In Jerusalem, things were not any easier for Saul until Barnabas (who was later to accompany him on his first missionary journey) intervened and introduced him to the Church. They were convinced and admitted him into their congregation. Later, however, some outsiders, Hellenists, plotted against him in Jerusalem and he escaped to Caesarea: from there he returned to Tarsus, his home city.

Luke then adds, on a rather optimistic note which was not borne out by later events, that 'the Church throughout all Judea and Galilee and Samaria had peace and was built up' **(Acts 9.31).** The position following the conversion of Saul was that, for the moment, the opponents of the Church, were soundly defeated. It was to take them some time to recover from the rude shock and to reorganize themselves for a confrontation which was to decide whether the Church was to be swallowed up or to mature and grow as an independent body.

Acts 10.34-48 The Conversion of Cornelius

So far we have seen the Gospel preached in Judea and Samaria. The persecution of the Church had scattered its believers, who preached the Good News wherever they went. We have seen how Samaria was converted and how the Samaritans received the Holy Spirit after Peter and John had prayed and laid their hands on them. Philip had gone on to convert the Ethiopian eunuch and from Gaza travelled to Azotus and Caesarea.

The conversion of non-Jews did not at first create many problems for the Church; any doubts that were raised must have been muted. As long as the field of conversion was limited, the strict Jews kept calm. However, as more and more non-Jews were converted, there was a clash of interests: it would appear that none of the non-Jewish converts had been compelled to first become proselytes (by undergoing the Jewish rites of circumcision, etc.) before being baptized and admitted to the Church.

This was the difficult state of affairs when an important Roman military officer was converted by none other than Peter himself. This man was Cornelius, a centurion of the Italian Cohort, described as 'a devout man who feared God with all his household', and who gave alms liberally and prayed constantly to God (**Acts 10.1-2**). Cornelius must have been impressed by Jewish religion and adopted it (he was probably a God-fearer), but we are not told that he accepted circumcision (this would have made him a proselyte). He practised almsgiving and prayer, two very important Jewish religious practices.

While Peter was in Joppa, where he had raised Dorcas from the dead, he and Cornelius, who was stationed at Caesarea, had experiences which eventually brought them face to face. Peter had a vision of animals and birds, clean and unclean, which were let down to him from heaven in a sheet: it taught him not to call unclean aything which God had cleansed.

Cornelius also had a vision, in which he was directed to send for Peter at Joppa to come down to Caesarea and preach the Good News to him. He sent two servants and a soldier to Joppa to fetch Peter.

While Peter was contemplating the meaning of his vision, the three men sent by Cornelius arrived and related their mission to him. The following day Peter left for Caesarea and when he met

Cornelius, a Gentile, he was no longer left in any doubt as to the meaning of his vision. He addressed Cornelius (**v.28**) and confessed that God had taught him that he should not regard any man as common or unclean. He then asked Cornelius to tell him why he had sent for him.

Cornelius narrated his own vision and formally invited Peter to address the large audience gathered in his house. Peter began with the affirmation that God was an impartial judge who accepted all men from all nations who walked in his ways. God had sent Jesus Christ who preached the Good News in Galilee and Judea and worked miracles. In spite of all these things, the Jews put Him to death. He rose on the third day and appeared to His disciples and then commanded them to preach to the people that He, Jesus, was ordained by God as Judge of the living and the dead, and that all who believed in Him would gain forgiveness of sins.

We should note, in this sermon of Peter (**10.34-43**), the absence of Old Testament references: Peter was talking to non-Jews who were not familiar with the Scriptures. There would have been no sense, therefore, in quoting the Scriptures in support of the claim that Jesus was the Messiah (Christ) fore-ordained to bring salvation to those who believed in Him.

A remarkable thing happened during the preaching of Peter: the Holy Spirit descended on all who heard him. Hitherto, apart from on the Day of Pentecost, the Holy Spirit had fallen upon believers after their baptism, and usually after the laying-on of hands by the Apostles. This inversion of the order surprised Peter's companions. To the further consternation of Peter's friends the new converts even spoke in tongues. Peter had no choice but to baptize Cornelius and the others, and he remained in Caesarea for some days, engaged in further teaching.

When Peter returned to Jerusalem (**chapter 11**) he was questioned by the strict Jewish believers (here called 'the circumcision party') who challenged his decision to go to uncircumcised men and to eat with them. In **vv.4-17** Peter related the experiences which had led him to Cornelius and was able, at least temporarily, to contain the opposition to his action. However, the question of whether or not Gentiles were to be admitted was still a live issue and one requiring urgent attention, if the Church was to survive.

External opposition resumes: It has been said that Luke's optimism in **chapter 9.31** to the effect that 'the church throughout all Judea and Galilee and Samaria had peace and was built up' was tenuous and short-lived. While the Church was dealing with the internal issue of admission of Gentiles into the Church following Peter's conversion of Cornelius, a more invidious attack was launched against the believers. Before now, all external opposition had come from the strong Sadducean party, the chief priests and the Sanhedrin. In **chapter 12**, Herod Agrippa I (c. 10 B.C. — A.D. 44) who had been granted the title of King by the Emperor Claudius in 41 A.D., renewed the hostility against the Church. He was the grandson of Herod the Great who had tried, but failed, to kill the infant Jesus during the notorius slaughter of the children (reported in **Matthew 2.16ff.**). Herod Agrippa knew that his family had never been liked by the Jews because they were not strictly speaking, Jews, but Idumaeans who had, through cunning and intrigue, obtained for themselves the official title of kings or tetrarchs of the regions beginning with Herod the Great. Therefore, in order to ingratiate himself with the Jews, he decided to lend his support to their opposition and hostility towards the Church. Some time between A.D. 41 and A.D. 44 (when he died) he began to persecute the Church. He killed James, the brother of John, who thus became the first martyr among the Twelve. When Agrippa I saw that this pleased the Jews he arrested Peter also and fixed a date, after the Passover, for his execution (**12.4-5**).

The Church was in dire peril and made earnest prayer for Peter. The angel of the Lord again intervened, and Peter was miraculously rescued from prison. After reporting his escape to the anxious brethren, Peter went into hiding. Learning of the escape of Peter the following morning, Herod Agrippa I vented his anger on the unlucky soldiers who kept guard at the prison. But the threat from that quarter soon disappeared, when the King died of bubonic plague.

With Peter driven underground, the opportunity presented itself to Saul, now probably called Paul, to assume greater responsibility in the task of spreading the Gospel further into Gentile territory than Peter himself, in spite of his Cornelius experience, could have been prepared to go. Again, according to St. Luke, in the Acts of the Apostles, Antioch in Syria began to play a significant role in the progress of the Gospel: Jerusalem had been the scene of deadly persecution, and for the Church to survive, other centres of operation had to spring up to serve as refuge to the missionaries. Antioch took the initiative and attracted many believers, teachers and prophets: among them Barnabas, whom we met earlier during the introduction of Saul to the Jerusalem Church (9.26-27). The Church grew rapidly in Antioch, and during a time of famine in Jerusalem we are told in Acts 11.28ff that Antioch sent relief to the Jerusalem Church as a practical sign of the comradeship and fellow-feeling which the Church represented. It was in the realization of the activity of the Church in Antioch that the believers there were first called 'Christians' (11.26).

Acts 13.1-52 Paul's First Missionary Journey

We read in Acts 11.19 that many believers who were scattered after the martyrdom of Stephen went to Antioch, among other places. Many people in Antioch were converted following the preaching of these new arrivals. When news of the wide acceptance of the Word by Antioch reached Jerusalem, the Church sent Barnabas to Antioch. Barnabas was glad at what he saw and, after exhorting the young Church to remain faithful to the Lord, he decided to send for Paul (who was still at Tarsus) to come down to Antioch and to join with him in reaping the large harvest to Christendom, and to help him in strengthening the faith of the new converts. For a whole year the two of them taught there.

The Church in Antioch, very strong in constant prayers, with fasting and other Christian rites, was one day during prayers directed by the Holy Spirit to 'set apart . . . Barnabas and Paul' for the work to which God had called them (13.2). After due fasting and prayers, the Church laid their hands on them and sent them off on what has become St. Paul's first missionary tour. This journey was epoch-making: for the first time the Church was fulfilling, in a very practical way, one of the last charges given by the Master to be His 'witnesses in Jerusalem and in all Judea and Samaria and to the end of the earth' (Acts 1.8). The Church was now formally launching itself on a missionary journey to unspecified destinations: it was left to the Holy Spirit to direct their steps.

Paul and Barnabas went down to Seleucia and from there set sail for Cyprus. They preached in the synagogue at Salamis and moved across country to Paphos. Here they were confronted by a false Jewish magician called Bar-Jesus or Elymas (Peter had met a similar fellow, in the person of Simon Magus in Samaria). Bar-Jesus did everything he could to distract the attention of the Roman proconsul, Sergius Paulus, from the good news for which he had specifically invited the Apostles to his residence. Paul, filled with the Holy Spirit and with righteous indignation, would not tolerate this confrontation against the work of God. He cursed Bar-Jesus: 'You son of the devil, you enemy of all righteousness, full of all deceit and villainy, will you not stop making crooked the straight paths of the Lord? . . . Behold, the hand of the Lord is upon you, and you shall be blind . . . for a time' (vv.10-11).

We read that Bar-Jesus was immediately struck blind and the punishment had an immediate result: 'The proconsul believed . . . for he was astonished at the teaching of the Lord' (v.12).

Leaving Paphos, Paul and Barnabas set sail for the mainland of Asia Minor and disembarked at Perga, where John Mark left the two Apostles and returned to Jerusalem. When they arrived in Antioch in Pisidia they preached in the synagogue of the Jews (13.16-41). This was St. Paul's first recorded sermon in the Acts. It was addressed to 'Men of Israel' i.e. the Jews, and 'you that fear God' i.e. religious Gentiles or proselytes. As in earlier Church sermons, especially those by Peter, Paul raised a number of points in the hope of convincing his audience that Jesus was the Son of God:

- **13.16.25:** A summary of Jewish history from their sojourn in Egypt, through the wilderness days, to their settlement in Canaan after God had destroyed seven Canaanite nations. He reminded them that God had always led them to many victories, that God had given them judges, then King David from whose family was born the Saviour, Jesus Christ, whose forerunner was John the Baptist.
- **13.26-32:** Paul then gave a short account of Jesus' life, pointing out how unbelieving Jewish leaders in Jerusalem had condemned Him to death and had induced Pilate to crucify Him. But He rose from the dead and appeared to His disciples who were then His witnesses. Hence the Good News was now being brought to them.
- **13.33-37:** Paul cited Old Testament passages to prove the truth of the Resurrection (Psalms 2.7; 16.10 and Isaiah 55.3); Jesus, unlike David, did not see corruption in the grave.
- **13.38-39:** Through the Risen Jesus Christ men could gain forgiveness of sins; it was only through Jesus that man could gain salvation, which not even the Law of Moses could give.
- **13.40-41:** Paul then concluded with a warning. Should

the Jews reject the message, they would lose the only chance offered to them; the Good News would be taken to others, as the Old Testament clearly says in **Habakkuk 1.5.**

The reaction of the hearers seemed at first to be positive; they asked Paul kindly to speak to them on the next sabbath. Many of them clung to Paul and Barnabas and were exhorted to continue in the grace of God.

The following sabbath, however, the crowd which gathered to hear Paul included non-Jews **(vv.44-52)**. The Jews became jealous and reacted with unexpected hostility. They contradicted Paul and reviled him. In an expression of utter hopelessness and frustration **(v.46)**, Paul announced that since they had rejected the word of God which should be preached to the Jews first, he and Barnabas would address themselves to the Gentiles. In support of his decision Paul again quoted from the Old Testament **(Isaiah 49.6)**. The Jews were not moved by Paul's denunciation. The wealthy women among them and the leading men of the city were urged to drive Paul and Barnabas out of Antioch. The two Apostles moved on to Iconium, some ninety miles (145 km.) further east, after shaking the dust from their feet.

The rejection of the Good News by the Jews, which prompted Paul to turn to the Gentiles, made a deep impression in the mind of Luke, himself a Gentile, when he was writing the Acts of the Apostles. What was a loss to the Jews became an eternal gain for the Gentiles. The Jews had never thought that the Gentiles would partake of eternal life on the Day of the Lord; to them it was therefore unthinkable that fellow Jews like Paul and Barnabas would openly announce that they were turning to the Gentiles. Naturally, Paul was filled with deep sorrow at this turn of events and said so in his Letter to the Romans (see **Romans 9.1-5; 10.1-4**). But in spite of his feelings the work of God had to go on, and be taken to the 'uttermost parts of the earth', whether the Jews like it or not.

It is significant to observe at this point that, although Paul left Antioch and went further and further away into pagan territory, Jewish opposition was so intense that it dogged his footsteps. In the next city, Iconium, the audience who listened to his preaching was divided: one side believed the Gospel but the other side believed the Jews. Very soon a riotous situation developed; a plot was hatched to stone Paul and Barnabas and they fled to Lystra, thus escaping the fate that had befallen Stephen **(14.1-6)**.

Lystra (14.8-20): At Lystra, Paul and Barnabas healed a man who had been a cripple from birth. Most of the natives, who spoke the native language of Lycaonia and not Greek, and who worshipped ancient gods, thought that two of these gods had come to them in human form. The priest of Zeus collected oxen and garlands to sacrifice to Barnabas, whom they called Zeus. It was with great difficulty that the Apostles dissuaded them.

Paul preached to the people that the purpose of the visit was to make them desist from their worship of the gods of the earth, sky, trees, etc., and turn to worship only the true God, the Creator of the Universe. He warned them that, since God had now sent witnesses to assert His goodness, the days of ignorance were over: God would no longer be pleased should they continue to worship as of old. Since God satisfied all human needs they should worship Him alone.

The Outcome: The Jews from Antioch would not be outdone. Joined by other hostile Jews from Iconium, they trooped down to Lystra and persuaded the people to stone Paul. The people dragged him out of the city, supposing him to be dead. But when the believers gathered about him he rose up, and they left on the following day for Derbe, where they also preached and made converts.

Later they left Derbe and traced their journey home, making short stops in all the towns they have visited earlier and where they had established young churches. Their task was to exhort the new converts to remain steadfast in their faith and to warn them that the Kingdom of God meant that they must bear whatever persecutions came their way. They appointed elders in every church and encouraged them to remain constant in prayer and fasting.

On finally returning to Antioch in Syria, their base, they recounted their successes, especially among the Gentiles, and remained in Antioch for some time in order to deal with a crisis within the Church itself.

Acts 15.1-35 The First Christian Council in Jerusalem
As long as the Gospel was limited to the Jews with a slight infusion of proselytes or civilized 'God-fearers', that is, those Gentiles who had had long contact with Jews in cities with large Jewish settlements, all was well with the Church. The question of the unfair treatment of Hellenist widows had been amicably

settled by the appointment of the seven deacons. Before Paul decided to take the Gospel far into pagan territories, it had still been possible to tolerate a few non-Jewish converts — the Samaritans, the Ethiopian eunuch, Cornelius, the Church at Antioch, and a few others. Any opposition to the admission of these people into the Church was at this stage either half-spirited or mute. For example, Peter had been able to convince the strict Jews in the Church that he had had to baptize Cornelius and his friends in spite of himself, because God had impelled him to do so and had given them the Holy Spirit just as they, the Apostles, had been given the Holy Spirit at Pentecost.

But the situation was soon to change, and there was, for the Jewish Christians, the fear that unless drastic action were taken they would soon be swamped by the Gentiles and become a minority in the Church, which was, as far as they were concerned, a Jewish Church. To some of these Jewish Christians the Church was rightfully part of the Jewish heritage, not a separate body. Paul and Barnabas, in their missionary journey into the interior of Asia Minor, had gone beyond the limits of what was acceptable; a halt now had to be called to their favouring of Gentiles. Those Jews who were stongly opposed to Paul came to Antioch, seat of the new missionary effort, in order to tackle the problem and get Paul to conform.

The Judaizers' point was that, for non-Jews to be fully admitted into the Christian Church, they must first of all undergo the Jewish rite of circumcision and be prepared to accept the Law of Moses and the Traditions of the Jews. In other words, they must first become proselytes before communion with the Jews. It was inconceivable to these strict Jews that they should have anything to do with pagans and their uncivilised practices in food, morals and social intercourse. For instance, pagans ate food sacrificed to idols, ate strangled animals and blood, and often had unnatural and promiscuous sexual dealings even of an incestuous nature. How could Jews sit down at the same table as these uncouth Gentiles?

When Paul and Barnabas returned to Antioch the battle line was already drawn. Their opponents had prepared their case very well and their arguments were irrefutable. The Church at Antioch was unable to resolve the issue and wisely referred the matter to the Mother Church at Jerusalem. Paul and Barnabas, among others, were delegated to Jerusalem.

The two Apostles were warmly received in Jerusalem (a few

years back they had led a relief mission from Antioch to Jerusalem). Now they declared to the Church all that God had done through them among the Gentiles and how many Gentiles had been converted into the Church.

Their opponents, the Judaizers, together with converted Pharisees, maintained that it was 'necessary to circumcise the Gentiles, and to charge them to keep the law of Moses' (**15.5**).

Peter was the first to address the Council. He reminded them how he had been first chosen to preach the Gospel to the Gentiles. This was clear reference to his conversion of Cornelius and his household in **Acts chapter 10**. He pointed out how Cornelius and the others had received the Holy Spirit, just as they, the Apostles, had received the Holy Spirit at Pentecost: God did not make any distinction between Jews and Gentiles in this most important gift. It would therefore be mocking God if they imposed on the Gentiles' neck a yoke (meaning the Law and the Traditions) which neither their fathers nor they themselves were able to bear. In effect, Peter was saying that the Jews as a race had not succeeded in keeping the laws of God: it would therefore be futile to impose such laws on others. Salvation came through faith in Jesus and not by struggling to keep the Law (**15.7-11**).

Then Paul and Barnabas were given the opportunity to address the Council (**15.12**). They recounted all the signs and wonders which God had performed through them among the Gentiles. Their report dealt with their first missionary journey into Galatia in Asia Minor.

James, the brother of Jesus, who was now the leader of the Church in Jerusalem, did the summing-up for the Council (**15.13-21**). (We are told by Paul in his First Letter to the Corinthians (**15.7**) that, after His Resurrection, Jesus appeared to James, among others. This appearance must have shaken James who, like the other brothers of Jesus, was not a believer during the earthly life of Our Lord: later, when he joined the Church, he very soon rose to a position of leadership.)

James delivered a speech which, for its power and insight, dealt a fatal blow to the hopes of the Judaizing Christians, 'the circumcision party'. He made the following points:

● Peter had related to them how Gentiles had been admitted into the Kingdom of God: nobody now doubted the veracity of this (**v.14**).

● The admission of Gentiles agreed with Old Testament

prophecy which, as in **Amos 9.11-12**, declares that Gentiles would seek the Lord (**vv.15-18**).

● Therefore converted Gentiles should not be forced to accept circumcision or to keep the entire Jewish Law which had been preached every sabbath in the synagogues for many generations since first proclaimed by Moses (**vv.19, 21**).

● Therefore they should urge the Gentiles to keep only (4) Therefore they should urge the Gentiles to keep only those rules of social contact which offended the Jewish Christians, namely: they should avoid 'the pollutions of idols, unchastity, what is strangled, and blood' (**v.20**).

The Council then decided (**vv.22-29**) to convey their proposals in a letter to the Church at Antioch. The letter was to be carried by Paul and Barnabas as official delegates from Antioch and its contents confirmed by Judas Barsabbas and Silas.

It might be helpful to explain what the clauses of the decision meant. Gentile Christians were being urged to abstain from certain practices offensive to their Jewish brethren and which might prejudice the Jews against Gentiles full communion as Christian brethren:

● 'What has been sacrificed to idols' — in the ancient pagan world most meat offered for sale in markets, and therefore meant for domestic consumption, came from animals which were first offered to pagan gods. Gentiles saw no harm in eating such meat, but some Jewish Christians would be horrified if such meat were offered to them.

● 'Blood' — this meant either meat with its blood not drained off (in **Leviticus 17.10** the Law forbids eating of blood), or 'shedding of human blood or murder', a practice which was not uncommon among pagan Gentiles who were still very primitive.

● 'What is strangled' — this meant meat from animals that had not been killed as was laid down by Mosaic law: the neck had to be cut open to drain off the blood (that is the 'life') of the animal.

● 'Unchastity' — this meant sexual immorality, for which a number of Greek (or Gentile) cities were notorious. It might also include marriage between close relatives, which was contrary to Jewish Law: some Gentile nations had no such inhibitions.

When the Church at Antioch received the letter and the oral report, they rejoiced at the exhortation (**v.31**). The decision

had been a compromise solution and ushered in the peace which had been seriously threatened. Jewish and Gentile Christians now had some basis for coexistence and, despite occasional minor disagreements the Church was launched on a fresh voyage of evangelization, again led by Paul and Barnabas, but this time as two, and no longer one, separate missions.
missions.

Paul's First Missionary Journey: a Summary   (13.4-14.28)

Country	Town	Bible Reference	Incidents
Cyprus	Salamis	Acts 13.4-5	Paul and Barnabas preached in the synagogues.
	Paphos	13.6-12	Paul confronted a Jewish magician, Bar-Jesus or Elymas, who withstood their teaching and distracted the proconsul, Sergius Paulus, from the Gospel. Paul cursed Elymas with blindness. Sergius Paulus believed.
Pamphylia	Perga	13.13	John Mark deserted Paul and Barnabas and returned to Jerusalem.
Pisidia	Antioch	13.14-51	Paul preached in the synagogue: many believed. They were invited to preach on the following sabbath, but the Jews became jealous because many non-Jews also assembled. The Jews instigated a mob and Paul and Barnabas were expelled.
Galatia	Iconium	14.1-6	Paul preached in the synagogue. The audience were divided: one side believed, the other supported the Jewish opposition. A plot was hatched to stone the Apostles: they fled to Lystra.

Country	Town	Bible Reference	Incidents
	Lystra	14.7-20	They preached the Gospel and healed a cripple from birth. The natives called them Zeus and Hermes. The priest of Zeus brought oxen for sacrifice: Paul and Barnabas had difficulty in stopping him. Paul preached the need to worship only the true God, the Creator, not vain gods. Jews came from Antioch and Iconium, stirred up the people, and Paul was stoned. He later arose and they fled to Derbe.
	Derbe	14.21-26	They preached and made many converts. From Derbe they returned home, passing through the cities they had visited, strengthening the young Churches by appointing leaders among them.

See map on
page 95

QUESTIONS

1 Now as he journeyed he approached Damascus. **Acts 9.3**
Why was Saul going to Damascus? What happened to him that day?
Describe briefly the events of the next few days.

2 Who were Aeneas **Acts 9.33** and Tabitha **9.36**?
What part did Peter play in their lives?

3 Describe carefully the visions of Cornelius **Acts 10.1-16** and Peter
Acts 10.11-16.

4 Herod the king laid violent hands upon some who belonged to the
church. **Acts 12.1**
Two of the apostles were involved. What happened to them?

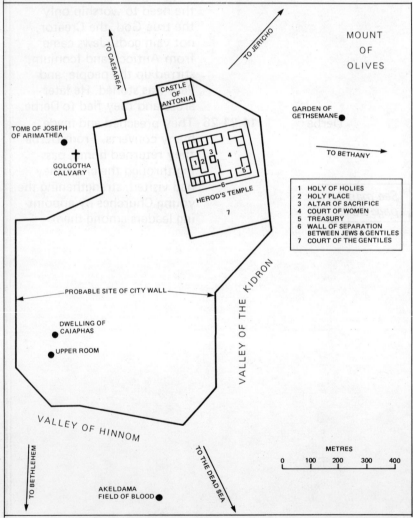

Diagram of Jerusalem and the Temple in the time of Jesus Christ.

5 Set apart for me Barnabas and Saul. **Acts 13.2**
Who said this and why were they to be 'set apart'?
Describe their work in Cyprus.

6 Behold we turn to the Gentiles. **Acts 13.46**
Where did Paul speak these words, and why?

7 The gods have come down to us in the likeness of men. **Acts 14.11**
Where was this said and by whom? Describe carefully what had just
taken place and what happened later.

8 What discussions took place in Jerusalem between Paul and Barnabas
and the Apostles and the elders? **Acts 15.2**
What message was to be sent to the Gentiles?

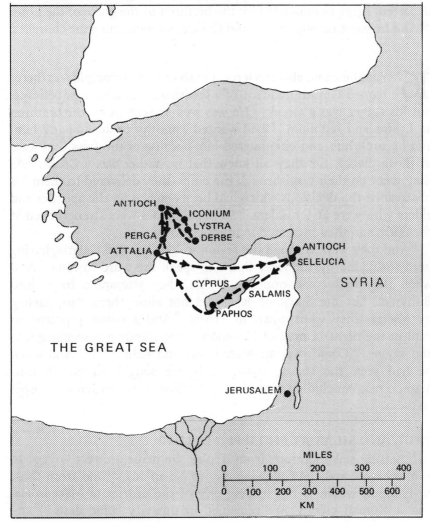

Paul's first missionary journey.

PAUL'S SECOND MISSIONARY JOURNEY   15.36-18.22
IN ASIA MINOR   15.36-41

36 And after some days Paul said to Barnabas, "Come, let us return and visit the brethren in every city where we proclaimed the word of the Lord, and see how they are." **37** And Barnabas wanted to take with them John called Mark. **38** But Paul thought best not to take with them one who had withdrawn from them in Pamphyl'ia, and had not gone with them to the work. **39** And there arose a sharp contention, so that they separated from each other; Barnabas took Mark with him and sailed away to Cyprus, **40** but Paul chose Silas and departed, being commended by the brethren to the grace of the Lord. **41** And he went through Syria and Cili'cia, strengthening the churches.

16 And he came also to Derbe and to Lystra. A disciple was there, named Timothy, the son of a Jewish woman who was a believer; but his father was a Greek. **2** He was well spoken of by the brethren at Lystra and Ico'nium. **3** Paul wanted Timothy to accompany him; and he took him and circumcised him because of the Jews that were in those places, for they all knew that his father was a Greek. **4** As they went on their way through the cities, they delivered to them for observance the decisions which had been reached by the apostles and elders who were at Jerusalem. **5** So the churches were strengthened in the faith, and they increased in numbers daily.

6 And they went through the region of Phry'gia and Galatia, having been forbidden by the Holy Spirit to speak the word in Asia. **7** And when they had come opposite My'sia, they attempted to go into Bithyn'ia, but the Spirit of Jesus did not allow them; **8** so, passing by My'sia, they went down to Tro'as. **9** And a vision appeared to Paul in the night: a man of Macedo'nia was standing beseeching him and saying, "Come over to Macedo'nia and help us." **10** And when he had seen the vision, immediately we sought to go on into Macedo'nia, concluding that God had called us to preach the gospel to them.

PAUL AND SILAS AT PHILIPPI   16.11-40

11 Setting sail therefore from Tro'as, we made a direct voyage to Sam'othrace, and the following day to Ne-ap'olis, **12** and from there to Philippi, which is the leading city of the district of Macedo'nia, and a Roman colony. We remained in this city some days; **13** and on the sabbath day we went outside the gate to the riverside, where

Paul's second missionary journey   15.36-18.22
In Asia Minor   15.36-16.10
36   Paul intends to visit the converts of his first journey.
37-38   There is a difference of opinion about John Mark, who had
         left them on their first journey (13.13).
39   There is a definite quarrel: Barnabas goes to his own home
         island (4.36) with Mark. He is not mentioned again in Acts.
40   Paul takes Silas (cf. 15.22, 32-34): perhaps they carry the
         letter from the Council (15.23. See also 16.4).
         N.B. Paul and Barnabas and Mark are reconciled later (cf.
         1 Corinthians 9.6; Philemon 24; Colossians 4.10; 2 Timothy
         4.11).
16.1   Paul starts from the east, overland. Timothy is the son of a
         mixed marriage, against Jewish Law: the Law regards him as
         a Jew because he has a Jewish mother.
2   He may already be a preacher.
3   Paul wants him, perhaps in Mark's place. Circumcision
         suggests that Paul sees him as a Jew, not as a Gentile convert:
         to circumcise him will please Jewish Christians.
4   The Council's letter goes to places beyond those to which it
         is addressed.
5   A typical description of early Christianity (cf. 14.22; 15.41).
6-8   Hard to follow because of lack of detail by Luke, but he
         points clearly to the guidance of the Holy Spirit. They arrive
         at Troas, seaport and Roman colony on the site of ancient
         Troy. Paul must be wondering about the next move.
9   Paul dreams 'of a man of Macedonia' — some think this may
         by Luke himself, because the 'we passage'begins here
         (vv.9-17) hinting at Luke's presence with Paul on parts of his
         journey: there is no definite proof. Other 'we passages' are
         found in 20.5-16; 21.1-18; 27.1-28.16.
10   They obey what they believe to be God's call.

Paul and Silas at Philippi 16.11-40
11   Samothrace, a mountainous island half-way to Neapolis: a
         place to stop the night. From Neapolis a road leads to Rome.
12   Philippi, a Roman colony and important city of Macedonia,
         named after Philip, father of Alexander the Great.
13   'A place of prayer' by the river may be a synagogue or
         simply a place where Jews, mainly women, meet for worship.

we supposed there was a place of prayer; and we sat down and spoke to the women who had come together. ¹⁴ One who heard us was a woman named Lydia, from the city of Thyati′ra, a seller of purple goods, who was a worshipper of God. The Lord opened her heart to give heed to what was said by Paul. ¹⁵ And when she was baptized, with her household, she besought us, saying, "If you have judged me to be faithful to the Lord, come to my house and stay." And she prevailed upon us.

¹⁶ As we were going to the place of prayer, we were met by a slave girl who had a spirit of divination and brought her owners much gain by soothsaying. ¹⁷ She followed Paul and us, crying, "These men are servants of the Most High God, who proclaim to you the way of salvation." ¹⁸ And this she did for many days. But Paul was annoyed, and turned and said to the spirit, "I charge you in the name of Jesus Christ to come out of her." And it came out that very hour.

¹⁹ But when her owners saw that their hope of gain was gone, they seized Paul and Silas and dragged them into the market place before the rulers; ²⁰ and when they had brought them to the magistrates they said, "These men are Jews and they are disturbing our city. ²¹ They advocate customs which it is not lawful for us Romans to accept or practise." ²² The crowd joined in attacking them; and the magistrates tore the garments off them and gave orders to beat them with rods. ²³ And when they had inflicted many blows upon them, they threw them into prison, charging the jailer to keep them safely. ²⁴ Having received this charge, he put them into the inner prison and fastened their feet in the stocks.

²⁵ But about midnight Paul and Silas were praying and singing hymns to God, and the prisoners were listening to them, ²⁶ and suddenly there was a great earthquake, so that the foundations of the prison were shaken; and immediately all the doors were opened and every one's fetters were unfastened. ²⁷ When the jailer woke and saw that the prison doors were open, he drew his sword and was about to kill himself, supposing that the prisoners had escaped. ²⁸ But Paul cried with a loud voice, "Do not harm yourself, for we are all here." ²⁹ And he called for lights and rushed in, and trembling with fear he fell down before Paul and Silas, ³⁰ and brought them out and said, "Men, what must I do to be saved?" ³¹ And they said, "Believe in the Lord Jesus, and you will be saved, you and your household." ³² And they spoke the word of the Lord to him and to all that were in his house. ³³ And he took them the same hour of the night, and washed their wounds, and he was baptized at once, with all his family.

14	Thyatira, famous for the manufacture and dyeing of purple cloth. 'A worshipper of God' — not a Jew but a God-fearer. 'Opened her heart' (cf. Luke 24.45).
15	Baptism follows faith (cf. the Ethiopian, 8.36-38 and the jailer, 16.30-33). 'With her household' (cf. note on 11.14; 16.31-34; 18.8).
16	'A spirit of divination' (or 'a spirit python') — the snake-god giving oracles to the priestess at Delphi. This girl gives such oracles (tells fortunes) in a pretended trance, probably using ventriloquism.
17	'The Most High God' — a Gentile way of referring to the Jewish God (cf. Luke 8.28). 'The way of salvation' (cf. 4.12). *N.B.* The 'we passage' ends here, until the journey to Troas (20.5) — see note on v.9.
18	Healing in the Name of Jesus (cf. 3.6; 9.34).
19	Her owners receive money she earns by fortune telling. 'The market place' — the forum: the court and prison are here. 'The rulers' — the magistrates.
20-21	'These men are Jews' — the Jews are allowed to practise their religion, but not to convert people. Anti-Jewish feeling may start a riot.
22	'Beat them with rods' — a common Roman punishment for non-Romans: they do not know that the Apostles are Roman citizens (cf. v.37).
23-24	The jailer is keen to carry out his strict orders: 'the inner prison' may be a dungeon, and their feet are fastened in wooden 'stocks'.
25	Again the importance of prayer (cf. 1.24-25; 9.10-11). Note the faith and confidence of Paul and Silas.
26	The answer to prayer — 'the foundations of the prison were shaken' (cf. 4.31).
27-28	The jailer, afraid of failing in his duty (23) is going to kill himself (cf. 12.19): he is saved by Paul.
29	The jailer realizes the presence of a great power associated with Paul and Silas.
30	'To be saved' (cf. v.17 'the way of salvation').
31-32	Paul and Silas tell him the answer is Jesus, and preach 'the word of the Lord' to him and his family.
33-34	His conversion is followed by caring for the prisoners and the baptism of himself and family (see note on v.15). Once more joy comes with salvation (cf. 8.8,39; 13.48,52).

³⁴ Then he brought them up into his house, and set food before them; and he rejoiced with all his household that he had believed in God.

³⁵ But when it was day, the magistrates sent the police, saying, "Let those men go." ³⁶ And the jailer reported the words to Paul, saying, "The magistrates have sent to let you go; now therefore come out and go in peace." ³⁷ But Paul said to them, "They have beaten us publicly, uncondemned, men who are Roman citizens, and have thrown us into prison; and do they now cast us out secretly? No! let them come themselves and take us out." ³⁸ The police reported these words to the magistrates, and they were afraid when they heard that they were Roman citizens; ³⁹ so they came and apologized to them. And they took them out and asked them to leave the city. ⁴⁰ So they went out of the prison, and visited Lydia; and when they had seen the brethren, they exhorted them and departed.

PAUL AT THESSALONICA   17.1-9

17 Now when they had passed through Amphip′olis and Apollo′nia, they came to Thessaloni′ca, where there was a synagogue of the Jews. ² And Paul went in, as was his custom, and for three weeks*ᵖ* he argued with them from the scriptures, ³ explaining and proving that it was necessary for the Christ to suffer and to rise from the dead, and saying, "This Jesus, whom I proclaim to you, is the Christ." ⁴ And some of them were persuaded, and joined Paul and Silas; as did a great many of the devout Greeks and not a few of the leading women. ⁵ But the Jews were jealous, and taking some wicked fellows of the rabble, they gathered a crowd, set the city in an uproar, and attacked the house of Jason, seeking to bring them out to the people. ⁶ And when they could not find them, they dragged Jason and some of the brethren before the city authorities, crying, "These men who have turned the world upside down have come here also, ⁷ and Jason has received them; and they are all acting against the decrees of Caesar, saying that there is another king, Jesus." ⁸ And the people and the city authorities were disturbed when they heard this. ⁹ And when they had taken security from Jason and the rest, they let them go.

p Or 'sabbaths'

35-37   The magistrates send to release the prisoners and learn of
        their error — Roman citizens are immune from flogging and
        imprisonment without trial: apparently both Paul and Silas
        are Roman citizens (cf. vv.22-25).
38-39   The magistrates do what Paul asks but ask the Apostles to
        go.
40   They take time to visit Lydia and to encourage 'the brethren'
        (cf. 15.32).

Paul at Thessalonica   17.1-9

1   Thessalonica, (modern Salonika), capital of the province of
        Macedonia, with a considerable Jewish population. Paul is
        able to speak in the synagogues.
2-3   For three sabbaths he shows Jesus to be Messiah: His death
        and Resurrection are God's will (cf. Luke 24.26,46; Acts
        3.18; 26.23).
4   Jews, Gentiles and some women are converted.
5   Paul arouses jealousy (cf. 5.17). 'Bring them out to the
        people' may mean to the authorities (but see v.8); they
        deliberately collect a 'rabble' from the market place. Jason
        seems to be a convert who takes Paul and Silas into his home.
6   Unable to find Paul and Silas, the mob drag out Jason and
        other Christians. 'Turned the world upside down' — they
        disturb people: these words describe very well the future of
        the Christian mission.
7   'Another king' could lead to a political charge (cf. Luke 23.2),
        a matter for the Romans: they do not understand the nature
        of Christ's Kingdom.
8   'People' — this time the people of the city in general (cf. v.5).
9   Jason has to vouch for the conduct of Paul and Silas.

PAUL AT BEROEA   17.10-15

[10] The brethren immediately sent Paul and Silas away by night to Beroe′a; and when they arrived they went into the Jewish synagogue. [11] Now these Jews were more noble than those in Thessaloni′ca, for they received the word with all eagerness, examining the scriptures daily to see if these things were so. [12] Many of them therefore believed, with not a few Greek women of high standing as well as men. [13] But when the Jews of Thessaloni′ca learned that the word of God was proclaimed by Paul at Beroe′a also, they came there too, stirring up and inciting the crowds. [14] Then the brethren immediately sent Paul off on his way to the sea, but Silas and Timothy remained there. [15] Those who conducted Paul brought him as far as Athens; and receiving a command for Silas and Timothy to come to him as soon as possible, they departed.

PAUL AT ATHENS   17.16-34

[16] Now while Paul was waiting for them at Athens, his spirit was provoked within him as he saw that the city was full of idols. [17] So he argued in the synagogue with the Jews and the devout persons, and in the market place every day with those who chanced to be there. [18] Some also of the Epicurean and Stoic philosophers met him. And some said, "What would this babbler say?" Others said, "He seems to be a preacher of foreign divinities" — because he preached Jesus and the resurrection. [19] And they took hold of him and brought him to the Are-op′agus, saying, "May we know what this new teaching is which you present? [20] For you bring some strange things to our ears; we wish to know therefore what these things mean." [21] Now all the Athenians and the foreigners who lived there spent their time in nothing except telling or hearing something new.

[22] So Paul, standing in the middle of the Are-op′agus, said: "Men of Athens, I perceive that in every way you are very religious. [23] For as I passed along, and observed the objects of your worship, I found also an altar with this inscription, 'To an unknown god.' What

Paul at Beroea   17.10-15

10   Beroea (modern Verria), south-west of Thessalonica, has
Jews among its population, and a synagogue.

11   'More noble' — high-minded and willing to listen to Paul and
the scriptural proofs he provides.

12   The result is similar to that at Thessalonica (cf. v.4).

13   Jews from Thessalonica come to stir things up.

14-15 Paul is sent away for safety. Silas and Timothy wait,
to join him later (at Corinth, 18.5).

Paul at Athens   17.16-34

16   Athens, a city that has lost much of the greatness of the days
of Socrates and Plato, yet still a beautiful place with many
learned people. Paul is angered by their idolatry.

17   He speaks first to the Jews in the synagogue, then to the
Gentiles in the market-place (the Agora), a centre where
people meet and discuss.

18   'Epicureans' (named after Epicurus, 340-270 B.C.) do not
believe in divine providence or immortality: they think that
man should look for true happiness of the mind (mental
tranquillity). 'Stoics' (after the porch or 'Stoa' where their
founder, Zeno, 340-268 B.C. taught at Athens) seek
happiness through a virtuous life: they believe in life after
death and in a divine law expressed in Nature and the
conscience. 'Babbler' = seed-picker, a man who picks up
scraps of learning as a bird picks up seeds: an abusive term.
'Foreign divinities' — Jesus and the Resurrection: a mistaken
idea that there are two divinities, male and female (common
in the ancient world), namely Jesus and Anastasis
(Resurrection).

19-20 'Areopagus' — an ancient court or council in some ways like
the Sanhedrin in Jerusalem (see note on 4.5), responsible
for culture and religion in Athens: little is known of its
powers. 'Took hold of him' sounds violent, but there is a
more friendly approach (20-21) by those who are eager to
hear more from Paul.

21   A typical description of the people of Athens.

22   'You are very religious' is not meant to be unkind, although
Paul does not share their ideas.

23   'To an unknown god' — more probably, 'To gods unknown'
(several such inscriptions have been found).

therefore you worship as unknown, this I proclaim to you. ²⁴ The God who made the world and everything in it, being Lord of heaven and earth, does not live in shrines made by man, ²⁵ nor is he served by human hands, as though he needed anything, since he himself gives to all men life and breath and everything. ²⁶ And he made from one every nation of men to live on all the face of the earth, having determined allotted periods and the boundaries of their habitation, ²⁷ that they should seek God, in the hope that they might feel after him and find him. Yet he is not far from each one of us, ²⁸ for

'In him we live and move and have our being';
as even some of your poets have said,
'For we are indeed his offspring.'

²⁹ Being then God's offspring, we ought not to think that the Deity is like gold, or silver, or stone, a representation by the art and imagination of man. ³⁰ The times of ignorance God overlooked, but now he commands all men everywhere to repent, ³¹ because he has fixed a day on which he will judge the world in righteousness by a man whom he has appointed, and of this he has given assurance to all men by raising him from the dead."

³² Now when they heard of the resurrection of the dead, some mocked; but others said, "We will hear you again about this." ³³ So Paul went out from among them. ³⁴ But some men joined him and believed, among them Dionys'ius the Are-op'agite and a woman named Dam'aris and others with them.

PAUL AT CORINTH   18.1-17

18 After this he left Athens and went to Corinth. ² And he found a Jew named Aquila, a native of Pontus, lately come from Italy with his wife Priscilla, because Claudius had commanded all the Jews to leave Rome. And he went to see them; ³ and because he was of the same trade he stayed with them, and they worked, for by trade they were tentmakers. ⁴ And he argued in the synagogue every sabbath, and persuaded Jews and Greeks.

⁵ When Silas and Timothy arrived from Macedo'nia, Paul was occupied with preaching, testifying to the Jews that the Christ was

24-25	This gives Paul an opening (cf. Isaiah 42.5). God the Creator cannot live in 'shrines made by man' (cf. 7.48-50): His Creation is evidence to the Gentiles that God exists.
26	'From one' — Adam, the common beginning of all men.
27	Through 'periods' and 'boundaries' God reveals Himself so that men should 'seek' and 'find' Him. 'Not far' — God is with men and within them.
28	Paul uses words of Greek poets to help this argument.
29	As 'God's offspring' man cannot liken God to anything made by man.
30	'The times of ignorance God overlooked' (cf. 14.16) but now the time has come for them to repent, i.e. to put away their idols and turn to God.
31	The climax to the message is short and to the point: they must look to the Second Coming of Christ and the Judgement: the Resurrection of Jesus is proof of all.
32	Talk of resurrection brings ridicule, probably from the Epicureans (see note on v.18). Some would like to hear more: they can understand immortality but not the revival of a dead body.
33-34	The last mention in the Acts of the city of Athens: no Church is referred to in the New Testament. This may suggest failure but there is some success (v.34). 'The Areopagite' is presumably a member of the Areopagus.

Paul at Corinth   18.1-17

1	Corinth, a large commercial city with considerable trade and industry, famed for its art treasures and its immorality. It has a mixture of Greek and Roman culture, the ancient Greek city having been destroyed by the Romans and later becoming a Roman colony under Julius Caesar.
2	Aquila and Priscilla are probably already Christians. The order made by Claudius is dated about A.D. 49-50, the Jews being expelled for causing disturbances in Rome.
3	All Jewish boys learn a trade and Paul is a tentmaker or leatherworker, so he can earn his keep. Goat-hair cloth is an important product of the Tarsus area (see note on 9.11).
4	Paul's usual approach is to the synagogues first. He works during the week and preaches on the sabbath, his message: Jesus is Messiah (v.5).
5	Silas and Timothy arrive (cf. 17.14-15). They have been to Thessalonica since Paul left them (cf. Thessalonica 3.1-10).

Jesus. [6] And when they opposed and reviled him, he shook out his garments and said to them, "Your blood be upon your heads! I am innocent. From now on I will go to the Gentiles." [7] And he left there and went to the house of a man named Titius[q] Justus, a worshipper of God; his house was next door to the synagogue. [8] Crispus, the ruler of the synagogue, believed in the Lord, together with all his household; and many of the Corinthians hearing Paul believed and were baptized. [9] And the Lord said to Paul one night in a vision, "Do not be afraid, but speak and do not be silent; [10] for I am with you, and no man shall attack you to harm you; for I have many people in this city." [11] And he stayed a year and six months, teaching the word of God among them.

[12] But when Gallio was proconsul of Acha'ia, the Jews made a united attack upon Paul and brought him before the tribunal, [13] saying, "This man is persuading men to worship God contrary to the law." [14] But when Paul was about to open his mouth, Gallio said to the Jews, "If it were a matter of wrongdoing or vicious crime, I should have reason to bear with you, O Jews; [15] but since it is a matter of questions about words and names and your own law, see to it yourselves; I refuse to be a judge of these things." [16] And he drove them from the tribunal. [17] And they all seized Sos'thenes, the ruler of the synagogue, and beat him in front of the tribunal. But Gallio paid no attention to this.

PAUL AT EPHESUS   18.18-28

[18] After this Paul stayed many days longer , and then took leave of the brethren and sailed for Syria, and with him Priscilla and Aquila. At Cen'chre-ae he cut his hair, for he had a vow. [19] And they came to Ephesus, and he left them there; but he himself went into the synagogue and argued with the Jews. [20] When they asked him to stay for a longer period, he declined; [21] but on taking leave of them he said, "I will return to you if God wills," and he set sail from Ephesus.

[22] When he had landed at Caesare'a, he went up and greeted the church, and then went down to Antioch. [23] After spending some time there he departed and went from place to place through the region of Galatia and Phryg'ia, strengthening all the disciples.

[24] Now a Jew named Apol'los, a native of Alexandria, came to Ephesus. He was an eloquent man, well versed in the scriptures. [25] He had been instructed in the way of the Lord; and being fervent in

q *Other early authorities read 'Titus'*

6   The Jews reject Paul: they are the reason for his turning to the Gentiles (cf. 13.46; 28.25-28). 'Shook out his garments' — now he rejects them (cf. shaking the dust from the feet, Matthew 10.14; Mark 6.11; Luke 9.5; Acts 13.51).

7-8   Justus — a God-fearer: Christian worship next door to the synagogue will hardly please the Jews. The conversion of Crispus is therefore very important. 'With all his household' (cf. 11.14; 16.15,33).

9-10   'A vision' — Paul has several (9.12; 16.9; 23.11; 27.23).

11   As a result Paul stays a long time.

12   'When Gallio was proconsul' — A.D. 51-52. The Jews try to use Roman power against Paul.

12   'Contrary to the Law' — this is the Jewish Law: there is no Roman law to stop the worship of any god, and Paul is not proselytising Roman citizens.

14-16   Gallio refuses to get involved.

17   It is not clear who beats Sosthenes, probably Romans and/or Greeks in an anti-Jewish demonstration: but if Sosthenes is the Christian convert of 1 Corinthians 1.1, then the Jews may be taking revenge (this is unlikely).

Paul at Ephesus   18.18-23

18   Cenchreae — the port of Corinth. We do not know about the vow: there are details of such vows in Numbers 6.1ff. As a Jew Paul will still follow some Jewish customs (e.g. fasts and vows): he may have completed this vow — he has his hair cut.

19   Paul's usual practice (cf. 17.2; 18.4).

20-21   There is a suggestion of haste, perhaps to keep the Feast of Pentecost in Jerusalem (cf. 20.16). He is to come back to Ephesus (19.1).

22   'He went up and greeted the church' — this must mean the Church in Jerusalem: then on to Antioch.
        N.B. This is the end of Paul's second missionary journey.

23   'Through the region of Galatia and Phrygia' — revisiting converts (cf. 16.6).
        N.B. This is the beginning of Paul's third missionary journey.

Apollos in Ephesus   18.24-28

24-25   Alexandria — a great centre of learning, with many Jews. The Jews here are broad-minded and interested in Greek culture. Apollos is well educated and knows the teaching of Jesus: he knows of the baptism of John the Baptist as a sign of repentance.

spirit, he spoke and taught accurately the things concerning Jesus, though he knew only the baptism of John. [26] He began to speak boldly in the synagogue; but when Priscilla and Aquila heard him, they took him and expounded to him the way of God more accurately. [27] And when he wished to cross to Acha'ia, the brethren encouraged him, and wrote to the disciples to receive him. When he arrived, he greatly helped those who through grace had believed, [28] for he powerfully confuted the Jews in public, showing by the scriptures that the Christ was Jesus.

PAUL'S THIRD MISSIONARY JOURNEY 19.1-41
RETURN TO EPHESUS 19.1-22

19 While Apol'los was at Corinth, Paul passed through the upper country and came to Ephesus. There he found some disciples. [2] And he said to them, "Did you receive the Holy Spirit when you believed?" And they said, "No, we have never even heard that there is a Holy Spirit." [3] And he said, "Into what then were you baptized?" They said, "Into John's baptism." [4] And Paul said, "John baptized with the baptism of repentance, telling the people to believe in the one who was to come after him, that is, Jesus." [5] On hearing this, they were baptized in the name of the Lord Jesus. [6] And when Paul had laid his hands upon them, the Holy Spirit came on them; and they spoke with tongues and prophesied. [7] There were about twelve of them in all.

[8] And he entered the synagogue and for three months spoke boldly, arguing and pleading about the kingdom of God; [9] but when some were stubborn and disbelieved, speaking evil of the Way before the congregation, he withdrew from them, taking the disciples with him, and argued daily in the hall of Tyran'nus.[r] [10] This continued for two years, so that all the residents of Asia heard the word of the Lord, both Jews and Greeks.

[11] And God did extraordinary miracles by the hands of Paul, [12] so that handkerchiefs or aprons were carried away from his body to the sick, and diseases left them and the evil spirits came out of them. [13] Then some of the itinerant Jewish exorcists undertook to pronounce the name of the Lord Jesus over those who had evil spirits, saying, "I adjure you by the Jesus whom Paul preaches." [14] Seven sons of a Jewish high priest named Sceva were doing this. [15] But the evil spirit answered them, "Jesus I know, and Paul I know; but who are you?"

r *Other ancient authorities add 'from the fifth hour to the tenth'*

26   Like Paul he speaks 'boldly' in the synagogue. Priscilla and
       Aquila fill the gaps in his learning, chiefly the fact that Jesus
       is Messiah (cf. v.28). Aquila and Priscilla do not appear again
       in Acts but their home is a Christian meeting place in
       Ephesus (cf. 1 Corinthians 16.19).
27   'The brethren' — there is a Christian Church even before Paul
       comes to Ephesus (18.19), perhaps as a result of the
       preaching of Apollos. Later Apollos is to be an important
       leader of the Church in Corinth.
28   Now he has a new message: 'the Christ was Jesus'

Paul's third missionary journey   19.1-41
Return to Ephesus   19.1-22

1   'The upper country' — inland from Ephesus. 'Disciples' are
       probably Christian converts of Apollos, and Aquila and
       Priscilla have been there.
2-3   Their baptism is that of John, in water to repentance
       (cf. 1.5; 11.16): they know nothing of the Holy Spirit of
       whom John speaks (cf. Matthew 3.11; Mark 1.8; Luke 3.16).
4-5   Paul baptizes them 'in the name of the Lord Jesus'.
6   The signs of the Spirit are present (cf. 2.4; 10.44-46). 'Laid
       his hands on them' (cf. 8.17).
8   Paul's usual tactics, speaking 'boldly' in the synagogue.
9   Again he meets with rejection. 'The Way' (cf. note on 9.2;
       11.26).
10   Paul stays a long time, using Ephesus as a centre for his work
       among Jews and Gentiles.
11   'Extraordinary miracles' (cf. Peter in 5.15).
12   Cf. Matthew 9.20-22; Mark 5.27-34; Luke 8.43-48.
13   Jewish exorcists are well known (cf. Luke 11.19): Some of
       them begin to use the Name of Jesus (cf. Luke 9.49). Casting
       out evil spirits in the Name of God or of Jesus is well known
       in the Early Church: evil spirits are believed to be the cause of
       many ills.
14   There is no high priest called Sceva, a Latin name. He may
       be a priest of some pagan cult, or just making a false claim in
       order to impress people.
15-16 The evil spirit does not know these exorcists and throws them
       out.

16 And the man in whom the evil spirit was leaped on them, mastered all of them, and overpowered them, so that they fled out of that house naked and wounded. **17** And this became known to all residents of Ephesus, both Jews and Greeks; and fear fell upon them all; and the name of the Lord Jesus was extolled. **18** Many also of those who were now believers came, confessing and divulging their practices. **19** And a number of those who practised magic arts brought their books together and burned them in the sight of all; and they counted the value of them and found it came to fifty thousand pieces of silver. **20** So the word of the Lord grew and prevailed mightily.

21 Now after these events Paul resolved in the Spirit to pass through Macedo'nia and Acha'ia and go to Jerusalem, saying, "After I have been there, I must also see Rome." **22** And having sent into Macedo'nia two of his helpers, Timothy and Eras'tus, he himself stayed in Asia for a while.

23 About that time there arose no little stir concerning the Way. **24** For a man named Deme'trius, a silversmith, who made silver shrines of Ar'temis, brought no little business to the craftsmen. **25** These he gathered together, with the workmen of like occupation, and said, "Men, you know that from this business we have our wealth. **26** And you see and hear that not only at Ephesus but almost throughout all Asia this Paul has persuaded and turned away a considerable company of people, saying that gods made with hands are not gods. **27** And there is danger not only that this trade of ours may come into disrepute but also that the temple of the great goddess Ar'temis may count for nothing, and that she may even be deposed from her magnificence, she whom all Asia and the world worship."

28 When they heard this they were enraged, and cried out, "Great is Ar'temis of the Ephesians!" **29** So the city was filled with the confusion; and they rushed together into the theatre, dragging with them Ga'ius and Aristar'chus, Macedo'nians who were Paul's companions in travel. **30** Paul wished to go in among the crowd, but the disciples would not let him; **31** some of the A'si-archs also, who were friends of his, sent to him and begged him not to venture into the theatre. **32** Now some cried one thing, some another; for the assembly was in confusion, and most of them did not know why they had come together. **33** Some of the crowd prompted Alexander, whom the Jews had put forward. And Alexander motioned with his hand, wishing to make a defence to the people. **34** But when they recognized that he was a Jew, for about two hours they all with one

17   This has a great effect on Jews and Gentiles alike.
18   Magic is a part of life in the ancient world: it is hard for
        people, even converts, to reject it completely.
19   'Books' — scrolls of magic spells. 'Pieces of silver' may be
        drachmas.
20   Success, despite the opposition of Jews and magicians (cf.
        2.41; 4.4; 5.14; 6.1; etc.).
21-22   Paul plans a collection from Gentile Churches to help the
        Church in Jerusalem (cf. 24.17 and Romans 15.24-27). He
        also plans a visit to Rome.

The riot of the silversmiths   19.23-41
23   'The Way' (cf. 9.2; 11.26; 19.9).
24-25   Artemis, Greek goddess of fertility (Roman Diana):
        Ephesus is a centre of her worship. Paul's success in
        converting pagans is a threat to the trade of the silversmiths:
        Demetrius organizes them into a union. 'Silver shrines' may
        be models of the temple of Artemis or statues of the goddess.
26   Paul preaches against idols (cf. 17.29).
27   'The temple of the great goddess Artemis' — one of the seven
        wonders of the ancient world.
28-29   'The theatre' — a large amphitheatre used for games and
        public meetings. Gaius and Aristarchus (cf. 20.4; 27.2).
30   Paul is too bold (cf. 21.39-40).
31   Asiarchs — representatives of cities of Asia, forming a
        council to look after public affairs and emperor-worship.
32   The meeting is not illegal, just a democratic gathering of
        citizens; many do not know why they are there.
33   Alexander, not known, is set up to explain that Jews are
        separate from Christians.
34   The crowd will not have this: both are unpopular.

voice cried out, "Great is Ar'temis of the Ephesians!" ³⁵ And when
the town clerk had quieted the crowd, he said, "Men of Ephesus,
what man is there who does not know that the city of the Ephesians
is temple keeper of the great Ar'temis, and of the sacred stone that
fell from the sky?[s] ³⁶ Seeing then that these things cannot be contradicted, you ought to be quiet and do nothing rash. ³⁷ For you have
brought these men here who are neither sacrilegious nor blasphemers
of our goddess. ³⁸ If therefore Deme'trius and the craftsmen with him
have a complaint against any one, the courts are open, and there are
proconsuls; let them bring charges against one another. ³⁹ But if you
seek anything further,[t] it shall be settled in the regular assembly.
⁴⁰ For we are in danger of being charged with rioting today, there
being no cause that we can give to justify this commotion." ⁴¹ And
when he had said this, he dismissed the assembly.

AT TROAS AND MILETUS   20.1-16

20 After the uproar ceased, Paul sent for the disciples and having
exhorted them took leave of them and departed for Macedo'nia.
² When he had gone through these parts and had given them much
encouragement, he came to Greece. ³ There he spent three months,
and when a plot was made against him by the Jews as he was about
to set sail for Syria, he determined to return through Macedo'nia.
⁴ Sop'ater of Beroe'a, the son of Pyrrhus, accompanied him; and of
the Thessalo'nians, Aristar'chus and Secun'dus; and Ga'ius of Derbe,
and Timothy; and the Asians, Tych'icus and Troph'imus. ⁵ These
went on and were waiting for us at Tro'as, ⁶ but we sailed away from
Philippi after the days of Unleavened Bread, and in five days we
came to them at Tro'as, where we stayed for seven days.

⁷ On the first day of the week, when we were gathered together
to break bread, Paul talked with them, intending to depart on the
morrow; and he prolonged his speech until midnight. ⁸ There were
many lights in the upper chamber where we were gathered. ⁹ And
a young man named Eu'tychus was sitting in the window. He sank
into a deep sleep as Paul talked still longer; and being overcome by
sleep, he fell down from the third story and was taken up dead.
¹⁰ But Paul went down and bent over him, and embracing him

s   *The meaning of the Greek is uncertain*
t   *Other ancient authorities read 'about other matters'*

35	'The town·clerk', secretary and president of the town assembly, a position of some importance. 'Temple keeper' is a title given to a city which has a temple (usually for emperor-worship) to a particular god. 'The sacred stone' is probably a meteorite 'that fell from the sky' and is associated with the gods.
36	The fame of Ephesus and the goddess must not be damaged.
37	The men accused have not done anything sacrilegious.
38	There is only one proconsul — his courts are there for any complaints.
40	Riots are always a cause of concern to the Roman authorities.

At Troas and Miletus   20.1-16

1-2	Paul continues the journey intended in 19.21, encouraging the disciples before he goes. He goes through Macedonia to Greece (Corinth).
3	Because of a plot to kill him on the voyage (from Corinth to Syria, bringing the collection from the Gentile Churches to the Church at Jerusalem — see note on 19.21-22; 24.17) he changes his plans: he goes overland, through Macedonia again, to Philippi (v.6).
4	These men are probably representatives of the Churches that have made gifts and are going to Jerusalem with Paul and their gifts.
5-6	They go ahead and wait at Troas (cf. 16.8). The 'we passages' begin again at Philippi where they are last used (see note on 16.9-17). Paul celebrates the Passover, which is followed immediately by 'the days of Unleavened Bread' (cf. 12.3). 'In five days' — contrast with the quicker journey in 16.11-12.
7	'The first day of the week' is already being celebrated by Christians. 'To break bread' — the meal may be the Eucharist or simply a common meal, the agape or love-feast (cf. 2.42, 46).
8-9	'The upper chamber' — cf. the Last Supper (Mark 14.15; Luke 22.12). 'Many lights' make the atmosphere heavy and smoky and this explains why Eutychus falls asleep. The helpers fear he is dead.
10	A reminder of Jairus's daughter (Matthew 9.18-26; Mark 5.35-42; Luke 8.40-56).

said, "Do not be alarmed, for his life is in him." [11] And when Paul had gone up and had broken bread and eaten, he conversed with them a long while, until daybreak, and so departed. [12] And they took the lad away alive, and were not a little comforted.

[13] But going ahead to the ship, we set sail for Assos, intending to take Paul aboard there; for so he had arranged, intending himself to go by land. [14] And when he met us at Assos, we took him on board and came to Mityle'ne. [15] And sailing from there we came the following day opposite Chi'os; the next day we touched at Samos; and[u] the day after that we came to Mile'tus. [16] For Paul had decided to sail past Ephesus, so that he might not have to spend time in Asia; for he was hastening to be at Jerusalem, if possible, on the day of Pentecost.

PAUL SPEAKS TO THE ELDERS FROM EPHESUS   20.17-38

[17] And from Mile'tus he sent to Ephesus and called to him the elders of the church. [18] And when they came to him, he said to them:

"You yourselves know how I lived among you all the time from the first day that I set foot in Asia, [19] serving the Lord with all humility and with tears and with trials which befell me through the plots of the Jews; [20] how I did not shrink from declaring to you anything that was profitable, and teaching you in public and from house to house, [21] testifying both to Jews and to Greeks of repentance to God and of faith in our Lord Jesus Christ. [22] And now, behold, I am going to Jerusalem, bound in the Spirit, not knowing what shall befall me there; [23] except that the Holy Spirit testifies to me in every city that imprisonment and afflictions await me. [24] But I do not account my life of any value nor as precious to myself, if only I may accomplish my course and the ministry which I received from the Lord Jesus, to testify to the gospel of the grace of God. [25] And now, behold, I know that all you among whom I have gone about preaching the kingdom will see my face no more. [26] Therefore I testify to you this day that I am innocent of the blood of all of you, [27] for I did not shrink from declaring to you the whole counsel of God. [28] Take heed to yourselves and to all the flock, in which the Holy Spirit has made you guardians, to feed the church of the Lord[v] which he obtained with his own blood[w]. [29] I know that after my departure

u   Other ancient authorities add 'after remaining at Trogyllium'
v   Other ancient authorities read 'of God'
w   Or 'with the blood of his Own'

11   Not very clear: 'had broken bread and eaten' may be the
        Eucharist following Paul's sermon, or simply breakfast as it
        is late (cf. v.7).

12   'Took the lad away' — to his home.

13   Paul avoids what can be a difficult journey if the wind is
        contrary.

14-15 A brief summary of the voyage to Miletus.

16   Paul is in a hurry to be in Jerusalem for Pentecost.

Paul speaks to the elders from Ephesus   20.17-38

17   To save time Paul calls the elders (cf. 14.23) from the
        Ephesus Church to Miletus.

18   This speech is Paul's last message to the great Gentile
        Church at Ephesus, a speech of farewell.

19   'Tears', 'trials', 'plots' — Paul has faced all these and will face
        more.

20   'In public and from house to house' — teaching in public
        (e.g. at Athens, 17.22-31) and in private (e.g. at Troas
        20.7-11).

21   Paul's Gospel is 'repentance to God' (cf. 17.30) and faith in
        Jesus as Messiah.

22   'Bound in the Spirit' — it is the Spirit compelling him to go
        to Jerusalem.

23   The Spirit warns Paul, through prophets in various cities,
        what to expect (e.g. Agabus, 21.11).

24   Paul's Gospel is more important than his life.

25   'Preaching the kingdom' (cf. 19.8; 28.31). 'Will see my face
        no more' continues the mood of vv.22:23.

26-27 Paul's Gospel of salvation has saved them from sin.

28   The Holy Spirit makes the elders, as 'guardians' (overseers
        or bishops), responsible for the work that Paul can no longer
        do. 'The church' is the whole Christian Church.

29-30 'My departure' may mean Paul's death. 'Fierce wolves' (cf.
        Matthew 7.15) are false teachers. Only here in Acts are
        Christians warned against false teaching (cf. the teaching of
        Jesus, Mark 13.22-23).

fierce wolves will come in among you, not sparing the flock; ³⁰ and from among your own selves will arise men speaking perverse things, to draw away the disciples after them. ³¹ Therefore be alert, remembering that for three years I did not cease night or day to admonish every one with tears. ³² And now I commend you to God and to the word of his grace, which is able to build you up and to give you the inheritance among all those who are sanctified. ³³ I coveted no one's silver or gold or apparel. ³⁴ You yourselves know that these hands ministered to my necessities, and to those who were with me. ³⁵ In all things I have shown you that by so toiling one must help the weak, remembering the words of the Lord Jesus, how he said, 'It is more blessed to give than to receive.' "

³⁶ And when he had spoken thus, he knelt down and prayed with them all. ³⁷ And they all wept and embraced Paul and kissed him, ³⁸ sorrowing most of all because of the word he had spoken, that they should see his face no more. And they brought him to the ship.

PAUL'S JOURNEY TO JERUSALEM 21.1-16

21 And when we had parted from them and set sail, we came by a straight course to Cos, and the next day to Rhodes, and from there to Pat'ara[x]. ² And having found a ship crossing to Phoeni'cia, we went aboard, and set sail. ³ When we had come in sight of Cyprus, leaving it on the left we sailed to Syria, and landed at Tyre; for there the ship was to unload its cargo. ⁴ And having sought out the disciples, we stayed there for seven days. Through the Spirit they told Paul not to go on to Jerusalem. ⁵ And when our days there were ended, we departed and went on our journey; and they all, with wives and children, brought us on our way till we were outside the city; and kneeling down on the beach we prayed and bade one another farewell. ⁶ Then we went on board the ship, and they returned home.

⁷ When we had finished the voyage from Tyre, we arrived at Ptolema'is; and we greeted the brethren and stayed with them for one day. ⁸ On the morrow we departed and came to Caesare'a; and we entered the house of Philip the evangelist, who was one of the seven, and stayed with him. ⁹ And he had four unmarried daughters, who prophesied. ¹⁰ While we were staying for some days, a prophet named Ag'abus came down from Judea. ¹¹ And coming to us he took Paul's girdle and bound his own feet and hands, and said, "Thus says

x *Other ancient authorities add 'and Myra'*

31   'Be alert' (cf. Mark 13.35,37; Luke 12.37).

33-35   Paul has worked to keep himself (cf. 18.3). These words of Jesus (v.35) are not recorded in the Gospels but may be among other sayings passed around orally.

36   'He knelt down and prayed' — a special prayer for a special occasion: the normal attitude is standing.

37-38   A very emotional scene.

Paul's journey to Jerusalem   21.1-16

1   The third 'we passage' begins (vv.1-18) -- see notes on 16.9-17; 20.5-16. Myra (see R.S.V. note) is on Paul's route to Rome.

2-3   Tyre is one of the main ports of Phoenicia.

4   'Disciples' — there is a Church here, perhaps founded in the Phoenician ministry during the persecution (cf. 11.19). Their warning reflects Paul's own words (cf. 20.22-23). 'Through the Spirit' suggests prophecy.

5   'Kneeling down' (cf. 20.36).

8   Philip the Evangelist is last mentioned at Caesarea (8.40). His daughters have the gift of prophecy (cf. 2.17).

10   Agabus, last encountered in 11.28.

11   The prophet acts out his prophecy: this verse reminds us of the fate of Jesus.

the Holy Spirit, 'So shall the Jews at Jerusalem bind the man who owns this girdle and deliver him into the hands of the Gentiles.' "
¹² When we heard this, we and the people there begged him not to go up to Jerusalem. ¹³ Then Paul answered, "What are you doing, weeping and breaking my heart? For I am ready not only to be imprisoned but even to die at Jerusalem for the name of the Lord Jesus." ¹⁴ And when he would not be persuaded, we ceased and said, "The will of the Lord be done."

¹⁵ After these days we made ready and went up to Jerusalem. ¹⁶ And some of the disciples from Caesare'a went with us, bringing us to the house of Mnason of Cyprus, an early disciple, with whom we should lodge.

12   A further plea to Paul (cf. v.4).

13   Jesus had died at Jerusalem: the same may happen to Paul.
        'The name' (cf. 5.41).

14   'The will of the Lord be done' (cf. Luke 22.42).

16   'An early disciple' — a member of the Christian Church in
        Jerusalem from its beginning.

REVISION PANEL 3

Acts 16.1-40 Paul's Second Missionary Journey

After spending some time in Antioch, Paul wanted to visit the Churches he and Barnabas had established on their first missionary journey. Barnabas wanted Mark to go with them, but Paul was reluctant to take the young man who had deserted them at Perga (**13.13**). After much argument Barnabas took Mark with him to his home island of Cyprus (**4.36**) while Paul chose Silas to accompany him. This is the last mention of Barnabas in the Acts of the Apostles but it is evident from Paul's Epistles that he and Barnabas and Mark were later reconciled (**I Corinthians 9.6; Philemon 24; Colossians 4.10; II Timothy 4.11**).

At Lystra Paul found a young man named Timothy to take the place of Mark. He may well have been a Christian, converted on Paul's earlier visits to the town (**14.6-23**). It is interesting to note Paul's attitude to circumcision, particularly after the Council of Jerusalem (**Chapter 15**) when Paul defended the position of uncircumcised Gentiles in the Early Christian Church. Timothy has a Greek father and a Jewish mother — by Jewish law he would be considered to be a Jew. His circumcision would please the Jews of the region, but in any case Paul would think that Timothy, being a Jew, ought to be circumcised. (Note: Timothy was with Paul on the journey to Jerusalem (**20.4**).)

Paul and Silas took with them the decision of the Council of Jerusalem (**15.22-35**) as they revisited the Churches of Asia Minor and 'so the churches were strengthened in the faith, and they increased in numbers daily' (**16.5**).

Luke explains the route taken by the Apostles, including their decision not to visit certain areas, as the guidance of the Holy Spirit, and so the two men arrived at the Roman colony of Troas. It was there that Paul's vision of 'a man of Macedonia' inspired him to take the Gospel into Europe.

The writer's use of the word 'we' suggests that he was one of the party — perhaps he joined them at Troas: 'We sought to go on into Macedonia' and 'We made a direct voyage to Samothrace (**16.10-11**). Other sections of Luke's book contain so-called 'we' passages (**20.5-16; 21.1-18; 27.1-28.16**).

Having landed in Macedonia, Paul and Silas went to Philippi, a Roman colony with many Jews: it was an important city named after Philip of Macedon, father of Alexander the Great. They found 'a place of prayer' (**16.13**) which may well have been a synagogue. Here a proselyte woman named Lydia received the Gospel and was baptized 'with her household': it was usual for a whole family, rather than an individual, to take on a new religion (cf. **11.14; 16.33; 18.8**). Paul and Silas were able to stay at her house.

It was on their way, one day, to 'the place of prayer' that the Apostles met 'a slave girl who had a spirit of divination' (**16.16**). Pretending to be in a trance, she probably used ventriloquism to help her fortune-telling. Paul had been annoyed by her attentions on several occasions and cast out the spirit. Her owners were naturally dismayed at the loss of income from her fortune-telling and they stirred up the crowd by asserting, 'These men are Jews and they are disturbing our city.' They achieved what they wanted: Paul and Silas were beaten and imprisoned by order of the town's magistrates.

That night there was an earthquake, and the miraculous release of the prisoners led to the conversion of the jailer. He realized that some great power lay behind the preaching of Paul and Silas and that the earthquake proved this. 'What must I do to be saved?' he cried, perhaps not knowing what he really meant by 'saved'. But Paul and Silas explained what salvation was, speaking to him 'the word of the Lord' (**16.32**). As in the case of Lydia, earlier (**16.15**), baptism included the whole of the jailer's family.

The next morning the magistrates were prepared to release the Apostles: perhaps they connected the earthquake with the remarkable power evident in Paul and Silas. The authorities would be considerably disturbed to find out that they had beaten and imprisoned Roman citizens, without fair trial 'They have beaten us publicly, uncondemned, men who are Roman citizens' (**16.37**). An apology was required and this was duly given, but the magistrates were only too pleased to see the back of the Apostles.

Acts 17.16-18.22 At Athens and Corinth
Thessalonica 17.1-9: Paul and Silas left Philippi and moved on to Thessalonica. Wherever there was a Jewish synagogue — and there were many in Macedonia and Greece — the Apostles took advantage of the opportunity to preach and worship. Their preaching invariably led to much discussion among the Jews,

and often to jealousy and hostility among the Jewish leaders. This happened at Thessalonica. For three sabbaths the Apostles preached in the synagogue, proclaiming the fact that Christ's death and Resurrection were part of God's plan and 'This Jesus, whom I proclaim to you, is the Christ' (17.3). A number of Jews and Greeks came to believe in Christ.

Eventually, jealous Jews roused a mob to attack the house of Jason, where Paul and Silas were staying. The two Apostles were not in at the time, but the mob seized Jason and some friends and hauled them before the magistrates, making rather vague charges against them: 'These men who have turned the world upside down . . . are all acting against the decrees of Caesar, saying that there is another king, Jesus' (17.6-7). The authorities had to listen to any charge concerning a rival to Caesar, but they did not take this too seriously. They took a security from Jason and his friends for the good behaviour of Paul and Silas and the Apostles decided that it was best for them to move on.

Beroea 17.10-13: When they reached the synagogue at Beroea they were very well received. The people listened carefully and then searched the Scriptures in order to satisfy themselves that Paul's preaching agreed with the Old Testament writings. Old Testament 'proof texts' were important in the teaching of the Early Christian Church (cf. **9.22; 17.2-3**). Once more, many Jews and Greeks believed. But it was not long before the news spread back to Thessalonica and Jews arrived from that city to stir up trouble for the Apostles. His friends sent Paul off to Athens: Silas and Timothy stayed behind to follow him later.

Athens 17.16-34: Athens was a great centure of culture and philosophy. There were two main groups of philosophers who had great influence in the city where their founders had taught: the Epicureans, followers of Epicurus, and the Stoics, followers of Zeno and named after the Stoa or porch where Zeno spoke to the people. Both men lived some four centuries before the time of Paul. The Epicureans refuted the idea that people's lives were controlled by the gods: when death came there could be no punishment, for the body was done away with. The greatest good lay in finding happiness through developing the mind. The Stoics believed in life after death and that the ideal human life was one lived according to Nature: man cannot alter the evil in the world and he must learn to live with it.

In his travels through Athens, Paul was impressed by the

number of idols. He spoke in the synagogue and in the Agora, or market-place: 'he preached Jesus and the resurrection' (**17.18**). Many of the people were interested in what he had to say: the Athenians were always ready to hear and talk about anything new. So Paul was taken to the Areopagus to tell them more: the Areopagus may have been the ancient and sacred meeting-place on Mars Hill or the court of elders which judged certain matters such as education and religion.

Paul and Barnabas had spoken to Gentiles who knew little or nothing about Judaism (**14.15-17**). Now, because he was speaking to a well-educated Greek audience, Paul did not use the proof texts he used with the Jews. Instead he began with what he had seen for himself in Athens, 'an altar with this inscription, "To an unknown God". What therefore you worship as unknown, this I proclaim to you' (**17.23**). He went on to tell them about the one, true, Creator, 'God who made the world and everything in it'. He even used quotations from their own Greek poets to help his argument: 'In him we live and move and have our being' (Epimenides) and 'For we are indeed his offspring' (Aratus) (**17.28**).

Finally Paul spoke of the fact that, in the past, God had been very patient with man's sin, but now that time had gone and God demanded repentance. God had raised up Jesus Christ from the dead and He would come again to 'judge the world in righteousness' (**17.31**).

Resurrection and life after death would have meant nothing to the Epicureans, and even the Stoics would have found such matters difficult to understand. It is hard to assess the result of Paul's work in Athens: 'Some mocked . . . others said, "We will hear you again about this" . . . some men joined him and believed, among them Dionysius the Areopagite and a woman named Damaris and others with them' (**17.34**). There was obviously some success, but this is the last mention of Athens in the Acts of the Apostles and there is no reference in the New Testament to any Christian Church there.

Corinth 18.1-17: From Athens Paul moved on to Corinth, chief city of Achaia (southern Greece), a great trading centre, rich in art treasures and noted for its immorality. All Jewish boys, even those who, like Paul, had trained to be a rabbi, had to learn a trade: Paul's trade was tentmaking (or leather-working), and he joined others of the same trade, Aquila and Priscilla, to provide himself with a living. Aquila and Priscilla had left Rome when the Emperor Claudius issued a decree in A.D. 49 expelling all Jews from the city: this was believed to be the result of riots in the city supposed to have involved Jews and Christians.

As usual Paul attended the Jewish synagogue each sabbath. He was joined by Silas and Timothy whom he had left behind at Beroea (17.14). As a result of his preaching, 'testifying to the Jews that the Christ was Jesus' (18.5), many Jews angrily refused to accept his message. Paul 'shook out his garments' as a sign that he would have no more to do with them and made his great decision, 'from now on I will go to the Gentiles' (18.6).

Paul left the synagogue and set up a place of worship in the nearby house of a God-fearer named Justus, thus emphasizing his break with the Jews. Many who came to hear him there believed and were baptized. For many months Paul remained in Corinth.

At length the Jews, determined to put a stop to Paul's work, brought him before Gallio, Proconsul of Achaia, on a vague charge: 'This man is persuading men to worship God contrary to the law' (18.13). By 'the law' the Jews were presumably referring to Jewish law: at least the Proconsul decided this and was not interested in their case; 'since it is a matter of questions about words and names and your own law, see to it yourselves; I refuse to be a judge of these things' (18.15).

The incident ended as 'they all seized Sosthenes, the ruler of the synagogue, and beat him in front of the tribunal' (18.17). Who 'they' were is not clear: perhaps it refers to the Jews who did this because Sosthenes had failed to plead their cause successfully, or maybe the Greeks or Romans for bringing such a trivial case before the proconsul. However, if this is the same Sosthenes as Paul's companion later (**I Corinthians 1.1**) he must have been a convert, and the Jews may have beaten him in anger over this.

At length Paul decided to return to Antioch and he sailed for Syria, with Aquila and Priscilla, from Cenchreae, the port of Corinth. 'At Cenchreae he cut his hair, for he had a vow' (18.18). This is far from clear: usually, during a vow the hair remained uncut and was cut at the end of the vow. However, Paul may have undertaken the vow when he cut his hair, intending to discharge it in the Temple at Jerusalem; this is where he went (18.22) before returning to Antioch.

When he reached Ephesus Paul stayed for a short time, visiting the synagogue as usual and discussing with the Jews. He made a promise to return 'if God wills', a promise to be fulfilled on his third missionary journey (**19.1-41**). On his return to Caesarea 'he went up and greeted the church' (**18.22**), almost certainly meaning that Paul went up to Jerusalem and to the Temple, where he could discharge his vow. His return to Antioch marks the completion of his second missionary journey.

Paul's Second Missionary Journey: a Summary (15.40-18.22)

Country	Town	Bible Reference	Incidents
Syria & Cilicia		Acts 15.41	Paul and Silas visited and strengthened the Churches.
Galatia	Derbe & Lystra	16.1	Paul chose Timothy to accompany them and circumcised him. They delivered to the Churches the decisions of the Council of Jerusalem, strengthened the Churches and added new converts.
Phrygia & Galatia		16.6	Paul and Silas were forbidden by the Holy Spirit to preach in Asia and Bithynia.
Asia	Troas	16.8-11	Paul had a vision of a man of Macedonia calling for help.
Macedonia	Philippi	16.12-40	Paul and Silas preached at the riverside. Conversion and baptism of Lydia. Paul cast out spirit of divination from slave girl: Apostles beaten and put in prison. Miraculous escape from prison. Conversion and baptism of jailer and family.
	Thessalonica	17.1-9	Paul spent three sabbaths in

Country	Town	Bible Reference	Incidents
			the synagogue discussing with the Jews. Opposition of Jews and arrest of Jason.
	Beroea	17.10-15	Successful preaching in the synagogue. Jews arrived from Thessalonica: Paul sent off to Athens: Silas and Timothy remained behind.
Achaia	Athens	17.16-34	Paul noticed many idols. He preached in the synagogue and market place, discussing with Epicureans and Stoics. Preached about the 'unknown God' in the Areopagus.
	Corinth	18.1-17	Joined Aquila and Priscilla and worked with them. Silas and Timothy arrived from Macedonia. Preached in the synagogues each sabbath that 'the Christ was Jesus' — had some converts and much opposition. Paul decided to 'go to the Gentiles', and set up place of worship next to synagogue. Many converts baptized. Paul brought before Gallio who refused to judge him on a matter of Jewish law. Sosthenes, ruler of the synagogue, was beaten.
	Cenchreae	18.18	Paul's vow: he cut his hair. Sailed for Syria.
Asia	Ephesus	18.19-21	Paul went to the synagogue. He promised to come back 'if God wills'.
Palestine	Caesarea	18.22	Paul left ship.

Acts 19.1-41 Paul's Third Missionary Journey

After staying for a time at Antioch Paul revisited the region of Galatia and Phrygia, 'strengthening all the disciples' (**18.23**) — this would probably mean the Churches at Lystra, Iconium and Pisidian Antioch. Meanwhile a Jew named Apollos was busy in Ephesus: he came from Alexandria, a great centre of learning, and was eloquent, well educated and well versed in Old Testament Scriptures. The position is not clear: he may have been a Christian not yet baptized, yet he knew the baptism of John. He was able to preach about Jesus, but not until he had been instructed by Aquila and Priscilla was he able to preach that 'the Christ was Jesus' (**18.28**). This is the last mention in the Acts of Aquila and Priscilla, although they appear in Paul's Epistles (**Romans 16.3; II Timothy 4.19; I Corinthians 16.19**).

It was while Apollos was doing good work in Corinth (Achaia) that Paul came to Ephesus, fulfilling his promise (**18.21**), and he was to stay in this large city, capital of the Roman province of Asia, for some time. He used it as a centre for his missionary activities.

Paul met twelve Christian men who were much like Apollos: they seemed to have accepted John's baptism but they had not received the Holy Spirit. Paul spoke to them of Jesus, baptized them in His Name, and laid his hands on them, and 'the Holy Spirit came on them; and they spoke with tongues and prophesied' (**19.6**).

For three months Paul spoke in the synagogue trying to win over the Jews, but those who heard refused to accept his word and even spoke evil of 'the Way', as early Christianity was called. As he had done before, in Corinth (**18.6-7**), Paul withdrew from the synagogue with his disciples and used 'the hall of Tyrannus' (**19.9**) for his discussions and arguments. This is the only mention of Tyrannus, probably a philosopher or teacher of some kind, and Paul may have used his lecture hall at times when Tyrannus was not using it for teaching, for example in the lunch or siesta period (see R.S.V. note suggesting 11 a.m. to 4 p.m.).

The news of Paul's activities spread far and wide, people tried many ways to bring healing to their sick, and many miracles took place: 'handkerchiefs or aprons were carried away from his body to the sick, and diseases left them and the evil spirits came out of them' (**19.12**).

Ephesus was a centre of magical practices, and some of the workers of magic began to use the name of Jesus in trying to heal and to cast out evil spirits. Some of these were Jews, despite the strong laws which prohibited such practices: other non-Jews used the name of Jesus for this purpose. We must note that there was no Jewish high priest by the name of Sceva (**v.14**), but he may have been a pagan priest. His sons were harshly dealt with by the man they were trying to cure, and this incident would be sure to help Paul's cause: 'fear fell upon them all; and the name of the Lord Jesus was extolled' (**19.17**). Many believed, including some who had practised magic, and these proved their good intentions by publicly burning their books of magic (scrolls of spells, etc.).

Paul was now thinking of revisiting Macedonia and Achaia before returning to Jerusalem. His object was to arrange for a collection from the Gentile Churches to help the poor Christian Church in Jerusalem. He looked forward, too, to visiting the hub of the Roman Empire, Rome itself: he was indeed to visit the great city, but not in the way he expected (**25.11-28.30**). Meanwhile there was work for him in Ephesus, so he sent off Timothy and Erastus to Macedonia.

Riot of the silversmiths (19.23-41): Ephesus was noted for the worship of the Greek goddess Artemis (Roman Diana), and her temple there was one of the seven wonders of the ancient world. One of the silversmiths, a man named Demetrius, saw in Paul's preaching a threat, not only to the worship of Artemis, but also to the livelihood of the silversmiths of the city. These men are described as making 'silver shrines of Artemis' which may mean small shrines or statues of the goddess, or these men may have been concerned with the maintenance of the temple itself.

The complaint made by Demetrius was that in Ephesus and other towns Paul's teaching was turning the people away from the worship of 'gods made with hands' (**19.26** — see also **17.29**): he was a danger, not only to the silversmiths, but also to the temple itself. With cries of 'Great is Artemis of the Ephesians!' the silversmiths rushed to a public meeting place known as 'the theatre' dragging with them two friends of Paul, Gaius and Aristarchus from Macedonia. Paul wished to go with them but he was restrained by friends. (Both Gaius and Aristarchus are mentioned again in **20.4** and the latter also in **27.2**).

The mob seemed to be confused, many not understanding why they were there. A Jew named Alexander tried to speak to them, probably to explain that the Christians and not the Jews were to blame for what was happening: he was shouted down. At length they were quietened by the town clerk, a man of great influence in the city council, who was concerned lest the riot should get out of hand. He advised them to keep within the law: the Romans could step in if they feared a riot. After all, Paul and his friends were 'neither sacrilegious nor blasphemers of our goddess' (**19.37**). If the people had any complaint it should be made to the courts. The people were dismissed and went their way.

Here Luke ends his account of Paul's stay at Ephesus, although it is evident from Paul's letters that there was much more to tell.

Acts 20.1-38 Paul at Troas and Miletus

After the riot of the silversmiths in Ephesus Paul crossed to Macedonia and Greece, encouraging the young Churches. Also he was presumably collecting their gifts for the poor Church in Jerusalem: this would explain the number of companions mentioned in **verse 4.** He was ready to sail back to Syria when a plot by the Jews was discovered and he went back overland to Philippi. Here the 'we passage' begin again (**20.5**): we last met them in Philippi (**16.17**). While his companions crossed to Troas Paul sailed from Philippi to meet them there.

Troas 20.7-12: The Church members at Troas met together on either Saturday or Sunday night 'to break bread': there was a meal and a sermon by Paul. This meal may have been a Eucharist or simply the formal breaking of bread followed by an ordinary meal (the agape). Paul spoke for a long time, and numerous oil lamps made the room hot and smoky. A young man named Eutychus, sitting in the third-storey window (there was no glass), was overcome by sleep and fell to the ground where he lay still: everyone thought he was dead. But Paul bent over him: 'Do not be alarmed, for his life is in him' (**20.10**). Paul continued his discussion and the lad was taken home.

Miletus 20.17-38: While his companions went by ship to Assos Paul preferred to go overland. He joined them there and they sailed together to Miletus. Paul was anxious to reach Jerusalem before the Feast of Pentecost, and this may explain why, rather than go to Ephesus, he sent to the city asking the Church elders to meet him at Miletus. He was also probably doubtful about the reception he would receive at Ephesus after his previous visit.

Paul's Speech to the Ephesians: This speech was different from those previously made by Paul: it was addressed to Christians rather than to Jews or Gentiles. It was a farewell speech in which Paul began by reminding his hearers of all he had said and done and of all the things that had happened to him. He went on to speak of his coming journey to Jerusalem and suggested the kind of treatment that awaited him there. He then drew the attention of 'the elders' (**20.17**) or 'guardians' (**20.28**) to their responsibilities and warned them of dangers within the Church. The words of Jesus with which he ended, 'It is more blessed to give than to receive' (**20.35**) are not found in any of the Gospels, but may well have been spoken by Jesus.

After Paul had spoken he joined in prayer with the elders of Ephesus. Prayers were normally said standing: 'he knelt down and prayed with them all' (**20.36**) emphasizes the seriousness of the moment and the sorrow over the fact 'that they should see his face no more' (**20.38**).

Luke gives a short account of Paul's return from Miletus to Caesarea. There was a stop at Tyre for seven days, where Paul met Christians who warned him of the dangers awaiting him in Jerusalem, and another farewell scene of sorrow and of kneeling in prayer (**21.5** cf. **20.36**). At Caesarea, Paul stayed with Philip the Evangelist (last heard of in **8.4-40**) and he also met the prophet Agabus (cf. **11.28**). Agabus enacted a parable with Paul's own girdle, warning Paul what would happen if he went to Jerusalem: 'So shall the Jews at Jerusalem bind the man who owns this girdle and deliver him into the hands of the Gentiles' (**21.11**). Paul was greatly impressed by the appeals of his friends, but he knew that he must go on, 'For I am ready not only to be imprisoned but even to die at Jerusalem for the name of the Lord Jesus' (**21.13**).

So with the words of his friends, 'The will of the Lord be done', Paul and those with him set off for Jerusalem, where they were to stay with a disciple named Mnason of Cyprus.

Paul's Third Missionary Journey: a Summary (18.23-21.16)

Country	Town	Bible Reference	Incidents
Galatia & Phrygia		Acts 18.23	Paul revisited and strengthened the Churches.
Asia:	Ephesus	19.1-41	Paul baptized disciples. For three months he carried on discussions in the synagogue, but because of the disbelief of the Jews he spoke daily, for two years, in the hall of Tyrannus. Many miracles were performed and many believed: many gave up their magical practices and burnt their magic books. Paul sent Timothy and Erastus to Macedonia. The silversmiths rioted because of Paul's threat to 'Artemis of the Ephesians'.
Macedonia & Greece		20.1-6	Paul encouraged the disciples. He spent three months in Greece. Jews plotted against him as he prepared to sail for Syria. He returned to Philippi while his companions sailed to Troas to wait for him.
Asia:	Troas	20.6-12	Paul here for seven days. He spoke to the disciples there: Eutychus fell from an upper window, but survived.
	Assos	20.13-15	Paul came here overland while his friends went by ship. They left via Mitylene, Chios and Samos.
	Miletus	20.15-38	Paul sent for the elders of

Country	Town	Bible Reference	Incidents
			the Church at Ephesus and made his farewell speech, telling of his plans and reminding them of their responsibilities.
Palestine:	Tyre	21.1-6	Paul arrived here from Miletus via Cos, Rhodes, Patara, Myra. Stayed for seven days and bade the disciples there farewell.
	Ptomelais	21.7	Stayed one day with the brethren there.
	Caesarea	21.8-14	Stayed with Philip the Evangelist. Agabus enacted a parable warning Paul of the dangers awaiting him in Jerusalem.
	Jerusalem	21.15-16	Disciples from Caesarea brought Paul and his friends to lodge at the house of Mnason of Cyprus.

See map on
page 134

QUESTIONS

1 Describe how the Holy Spirit led Paul to Troas. **Acts 16.8**
What happened at Troas, and what did Paul do as a result?

2 They threw them (**Paul and Silas**) into prison, charging the jailer to keep them safely. **Acts 16.23**
Why were Paul and Silas imprisoned? Describe what happened that night.

3 To an unknown god. **Acts 17.23**
What part did this inscription play in the preaching of Paul?

4 Who were Demetrius and Artemis? **Acts 19.24**
Describe how they played an important part in the story of Paul and his friends.

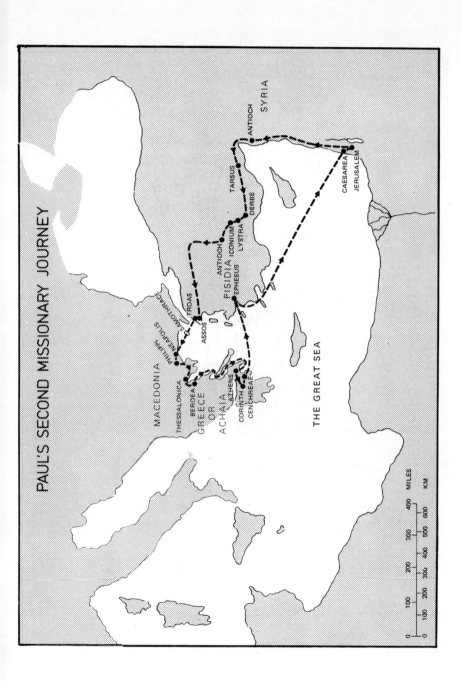

PAUL'S SECOND MISSIONARY JOURNEY

SYRIA

ANTIOCH

TARSUS

DERBE

CAESAREA

JERUSALEM

ANTIOCH
PISIDIA
ICONIUM
LYSTRA
EPHESUS

TROAS

SAMOTHRACE

ASSOS

NEAPOLIS

PHILIPPI

MACEDONIA

THESSALONICA

BEROEA

GREECE
OR
ACHAIA

ATHENS

CORINTH

CENCHREAE

THE GREAT SEA

MILES

KM

0   100   200   300   400

0   100   200   300   400   500   600

133

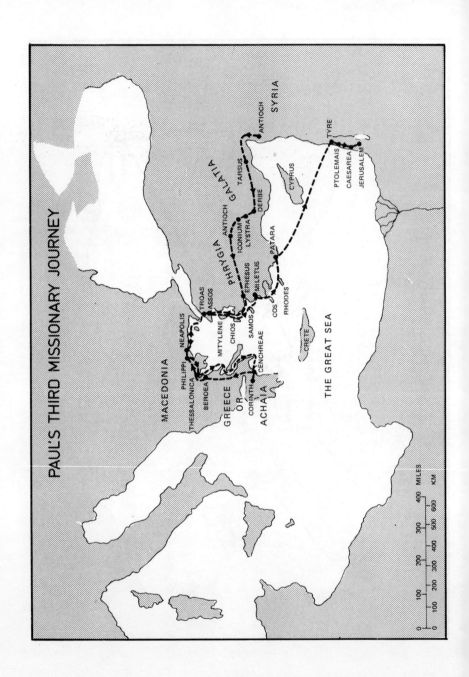

PAUL'S THIRD MISSIONARY JOURNEY

PAUL IN JERUSALEM (21.17-40)

17 When we had come to Jerusalem, the brethren received us gladly. 18 On the following day Paul went in with us to James; and all the elders were present. 19 After greeting them, he related

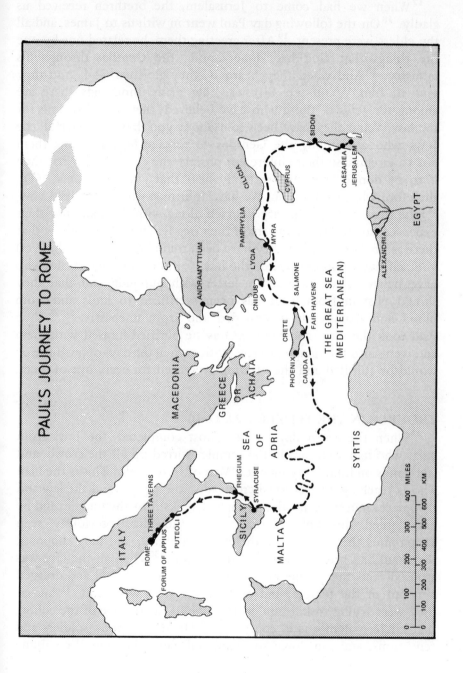

PAUL'S JOURNEY TO ROME

135

PAUL IN JERUSALEM 21.17-26

[17] When we had come to Jerusalem, the brethren received us gladly. [18] On the following day Paul went in with us to James; and all the elders were present. [19] After greeting them, he related one by one the things that God had done among the Gentiles through his ministry. [20] And when they heard it, they glorified God. And they said to him, "You see, brother, how many thousands there are among the Jews of those who have believed; they are all zealous for the law, [21] and they have been told about you that you teach all the Jews who are among the Gentiles to forsake Moses, telling them not to circumcise their children or observe the customs. [22] What then is to be done? They will certainly hear that you have come. [23] Do therefore what we tell you. We have four men who are under a vow; [24] take these men and purify yourself along with them and pay their expenses, so that they may shave their heads. Thus all will know that there is nothing in what they have been told about you but that you yourself live in observance of the law. [25] But as for the Gentiles who have believed, we have sent a letter with our judgment that they should abstain from what has been sacrificed to idols and from blood and from what is strangled[y] and from unchastity." [26] Then Paul took the men, and the next day he purified himself with them and went into the temple, to give notice when the days of purification would be fulfilled and the offering presented for every one of them.

TROUBLE IN THE TEMPLE 21.27-40

[27] When the seven days were almost completed, the Jews from Asia, who had seen him in the temple, stirred up all the crowd, and laid hands on him, [28] crying out, "Men of Israel, help! This is the man who is teaching men everywhere against the people and the law and this place; moreover he also brought Greeks into the temple, and he has defiled this holy place." [29] For they had previously seen Troph'imus the Ephesian with him in the city, and they supposed that Paul had brought him into the temple. [30] Then all the city was aroused, and the people ran together; they seized Paul and dragged him out of the temple, and at once the gates were shut. [31] And as they were trying to kill him, word came to the tribune of the cohort that all Jerusalem was in confusion. [32] He at once took soldiers and centurions, and ran down to them; and when they saw the tribune

y Other early authorities omit 'and from what is strangled'

Paul in Jerusalem, 21.17-26

18   James (cf. 12.17) the brother of Jesus and head of the
        Jerusalem Church. 'Elders' (cf. 11.30; 15.4,6). This is the end
        of the 'we' passage.

19   Paul tells of the Gentile ministry.

20   He is reminded that there are many Jewish Christians, too:
        'they are all zealous for the law.'

21   There appears to be no truth in the charge, e.g. the
        circumcision of Timothy (16.3).

22   The leaders of the Jerusalem Church foresee trouble.

23-24 The 'four men' are Christians who have taken a vow: at the
        end they are to shave their heads and offer sacrifices. Paul is
        asked to pay for these sacrifices and, at the same time,
        'purify' himself for his uncleanness, having been living with
        unclean people in unclean lands.

25   The decree made by the Council (cf. 15.20,29).

26   Paul does what he is asked (vv.23-24), trying to avoid any
        trouble by satisfying the 'zealous' Jews (v.20).

Trouble in the Temple   21.27-40

27   'Jews from Asia' and other Jews spread throughout the
        Roman world are very keen on keeping the Jewish Law.
        They know Paul, having seen him in Ephesus, and seize him.

28-29 The charge is similar to that brought against Stephen
        (6.11-13). Trophimus (cf. 20.4) is not a Jew. The Court
        of Gentiles is separated by a low wall from the Courts of
        Women and Israel: for a Gentile to pass this wall is
        punishable by death.

31   An attempt is made to kill Paul.

32-33 The riot is seen from the Fort of Antonia with its
        Roman garrison. 'The tribune', Claudius Lysias (cf. 23.26),
        takes men to stop the riot and rescue Paul. 'Ran down' —
        down the steps leading from the fort to the Court of Gentiles
        (cf. v.35). 'Two chains' — probably to a soldier on each side
        (cf. 12.6).

and the soldiers, they stopped beating Paul. [33] Then the tribune came up and arrested him, and ordered him to be bound with two chains. He inquired who he was and what he had done. [34] Some in the crowd shouted one thing, some another; and as he could not learn the facts because of the uproar, he ordered him to be brought into the barracks. [35] And when he came to the steps, he was actually carried by the soldiers because of the violence of the crowd; [36] for the mob of the people followed, crying, "Away with him!"

[37] As Paul was about to be brought into the barracks, he said to the tribune, "May I say something to you?" And he said, "Do you know Greek? [38] Are you not the Egyptian, then, who recently stirred up a revolt and led the four thousand men of the Assassins out into the wilderness?" [39] Paul replied, "I am a Jew, from Tarsus in Cili'cia, a citizen of no mean city; I beg you, let me speak to the people." [40] And when he had given him leave, Paul, standing on the steps, motioned with his hand to the people; and when there was a great hush, he spoke to them in the Hebrew language, saying:

PAUL SPEAKS TO THE PEOPLE OF JERUSALEM   22.1-21

22 "Brethren and fathers, hear the defence which I now make before you."

[2] And when they heard that he addressed them in the Hebrew language, they were the more quiet. And he said:

[3] "I am a Jew, born at Tarsus in Cili'cia, but brought up in this city at the feet of Gama'li-el, educated according to the strict manner of the law of our fathers, being zealous for God as you all are this day. [4] I persecuted this Way to the death, binding and delivering to prison both men and women, [5] as the high priest and the whole council of elders bear me witness. From them I received letters to the brethren, and I journeyed to Damascus to take those also who were there and bring them in bonds to Jerusalem to be punished.

[6] "As I made my journey and drew near to Damascus, about noon a great light from heaven suddenly shone about me. [7] And I fell to the ground and heard a voice saying to me, 'Saul, Saul, why do you persecute me?' [8] And I answered, 'Who are you, Lord?' And he said to me, 'I am Jesus of Nazareth whom you are persecuting.' [9] Now those who were with me saw the light but did not hear the voice of the one who was speaking to me. [10] And I said, 'What shall I do, Lord?' And the Lord said to me, 'Rise, and go into Damascus, and there you will be told all that is appointed for you to do.' [11] And when I could not see because of the brightness of that light, I was

34-36   The rescue is not easy. 'Away with him!' (cf. Jesus, Luke
        23.18) — meaning to kill him.
37   'Greek' — the language of commerce, known by educated
        people.
38   'The Egyptian' — some years earlier an Egyptian had led a
        force against Jerusalem, only to be defeated by the
        procurator, Felix. His followers are known as 'Assassins'
        (Sicarii or dagger men).
39   Paul reveals his pride in being a Jew and a citizen of Tarsus:
        he claims Roman citizenship, too, when he thinks it
        necessary (cf. 16.37; 22.25-28).
40   Paul is allowed to speak to the mob, in Aramaic, the language
        of Syria: Hebrew is the written language of the Scriptures.

Paul speaks to the people of Jerusalem   22.1-21

1   Cf. Stephen's speech (7.2ff.)
2   Their own language commands their attention for a time.
        N.B. Paul does not defend himself against the charges of
        violating the Temple or of teaching against the people, Law
        and Temple (21.28). His aim is to show himself to be a
        good Jew, sent by God to the Gentiles.
3   It seems that he has known Jerusalem from boyhood, and
        has been educated by the rabbi Gamaliel (cf. 5.34)..
        'Zealous for God' — in persecuting the Christians (cf. 8.1-3;
        9.1-2).
4   'This Way' — (cf. 9.2; 11.26; 24.14).
5   'The high priest and the whole council of elders' — the
        Sanhedrin (cf. note on 4.5).
        N.B. Verses 6-16 are a repeat of the story of Paul's
        conversion (cf. 9.1-9. See also 26.12-18).
6   'Noon' — giving the time of day shows that Paul's vision
        is not a dream in the night (cf. 26.13).
9   Cf. 9.7 where the men hear the voice, and 26.13-14
        where nothing is said of what the men see or hear.

led by the hand by those who were with me, and came into Damascus.

[12] "And one Anani'as, a devout man according to the law, well spoken of by all the Jews who lived there, [13] came to me, and standing by me said to me, 'Brother Saul, receive your sight.' And in that very hour I received my sight and saw him. [14] And he said, 'The God of our fathers appointed you to know his will, to see the Just One and to hear a voice from his mouth; [15] for you will be a witness for him to all men of what you have seen and heard. [16] And now why do you wait? Rise and be baptized, and wash away your sins, calling on his name.'

[17] "When I had returned to Jerusalem and was praying in the temple, I fell into a trance [18] and saw him saying to me, 'Make haste and get quickly out of Jerusalem, because they will not accept your testimony about me.' [19] And I said, 'Lord, they themselves know that in every synagogue I imprisoned and beat those who believed in thee. [20] And when the blood of Stephen thy witness was shed, I also was standing by and approving, and keeping the garments of those who killed him.' [21] And he said to me, 'Depart; for I will send you far away to the Gentiles.' "

THE REACTION OF THE MOB   22.22-30

[22] Up to this word they listened to him; then they lifted up their voices and said, "Away with such a fellow from the earth! For he ought not to live." [23] And as they cried out and waved their garments and threw dust into the air, [24] the tribune commanded him to be brought into the barracks, and ordered him to be examined by scourging, to find out why they shouted thus against him. [25] But when they had tied him up with the thongs, Paul said to the centurion who was standing by, "Is it lawful for you to scourge a man who is a Roman citizen, and uncondemned?" [26] When the centurion heard that, he went to the tribune and said to him, "What are you about to do? For this man is a Roman citizen." [27] So the tribune came and said to him, "Tell me, are you a Roman citizen?" And he said, "Yes." [28] The tribune answered, "I bought this citizenship for a large sum." Paul said, "But I was born a citizen." [29] So those who were about to examine him withdrew from him instantly; and the tribune also was afraid, for he realized that Paul was a Roman citizen and that he had bound him.

[30] But on the morrow, desiring to know the real reason why the Jews accused him, he unbound him, and commanded the chief

12	Much is made of the character of Ananias, 'a devout man according to the law' — but he is also a Christian.
14	'The God of our fathers' — the traditional God of Israel. 'The Just One' (cf. the 'Righteous One' of 3.14; 7.52).
15	'A witness' like the Apostles (cf. 1.8). 'To all men' including the Gentiles.
16	Baptism in the Name of Jesus, for forgiveness of sins.
17	A vision not mentioned in chapter 9: Paul still goes to the Temple for prayer (as Peter and John in 3.1). 'Trance' (cf. Peter in 10.10; 11.5).
18	'Him' = Jesus, who commands Paul to leave Jerusalem.
20	Paul at Stephen's death (cf. 7.58; 8.1).
21	The command to go to the Gentiles follows rejection by the Jews (cf. 13.46; 18.6; 22.18).

The reaction of the Mob   22.22-30

22-23	There is fury at any suggestion of equality between Jew and Gentile. 'Away with such a fellow' (cf. 21.36). They show disgust with garments and dust.
24	The tribune decides to flog Paul, not as punishment, but to get at the truth: he is plainly not satisfied at what he has learnt in 21.37-39.
25-26	To flog a Roman citizen 'uncondemned' is not legal.
28	Citizenship can be bought, particularly during the rule of Claudius, A.D. 41-54, often by bribing officials: hence the 'large sum'. Paul's father being a citizen, Paul is born one.
29	'He had bound him' (cf. 21.33; 22.25).
30	The tribune probably cannot understand Paul's speech (in Aramaic): he wants to know the reason for the riot. He cannot order the Sanhedrin to investigate, but the chief priests and council are keen to lay the blame on Paul: rioting is a serious offence.

priests and all the council to meet, and he brought Paul down and set him before them.

PAUL BEFORE THE SANHEDRIN   23.1-11

23 And Paul, looking intently at the council, said, "Brethren, I have lived before God in all good conscience up to this day." ²And the high priest Anani'as commanded those who stood by him to strike him on the mouth. ³Then Paul said to him, "God shall strike you, you whitewashed wall! Are you sitting to judge me according to the law, and yet contrary to the law you order me to be struck?" ⁴Those who stood by said, "Would you revile God's high priest?" ⁵And Paul said, "I did not know, brethren, that he was the high priest; for it is written, 'You shall not speak evil of a ruler of your people.' "

⁶But when Paul perceived that one part were Sad'ducees and the other Pharisees, he cried out in the council, "Brethren, I am a Pharisee, a son of Pharisees; with respect to the hope and the resurrection of the dead I am on trial." ⁷And when he had said this, a dissension arose between the Pharisees and the Sad'ducees; and the assembly was divided. ⁸For the Sad'ducees say that there is no resurrection, nor angel, nor spirit; but the Pharisees acknowledge them all. ⁹Then a great clamor arose; and some of the scribes of the Pharisees' party stood up and contended, "We find nothing wrong in this man. What if a spirit or an angel spoke to him?" ¹⁰And when the dissension became violent, the tribune, afraid that Paul would be torn in pieces by them, commanded the soldiers to go down and take him by force from among them and bring him into the barracks.

¹¹The following night the Lord stood by him and said, "Take courage, for as you have testified about me at Jerusalem, so you must bear witness also at Rome."

THE PLOT AGAINST PAUL   23.12-35

¹²When it was day, the Jews made a plot and bound themselves by an oath neither to eat nor drink till they had killed Paul. ¹³There were more than forty who made this conspiracy. ¹⁴And they went to the chief priests and elders, and said, "We have strictly bound ourselves by an oath to taste no food till we have killed Paul. ¹⁵You therefore, along with the council, give notice now to the tribune to bring him down to you, as though you were going to determine his case more exactly. And we are ready to kill him before he comes near."

Paul before the Sanhedrin   23.1-11
See note on the Sanhedrin (4.1-6).

1   Paul claims that his conversion to Christianity does not stop
     him from being a good Pharisee.

2   Ananias, High Priest A.D. 47-58. Perhaps Paul is struck for
     speaking out of turn.

3   'Whitewashed wall' — an insult (cf. Matthew 23.27): the
     outside contradicts what is within. 'God shall strike you' —
     he is to be murdered by terrorists in A.D. 66.

5   Perhaps this is irony: if Ananias were a high priest in the true
     sense then Paul would not insult him. In the Sanhedrin at
     that time few will remember the persecuting Saul of twenty
     years earlier and Paul will know few of them.

6   Paul makes use of the differences between Sadducees and
     Pharisees: the latter expect a Messiah and believe in
     resurrection. 'The resurrection' — Paul is thinking of the
     Resurrection of Jesus, but the Pharisees take it generally.

7-9 Paul's approach brings the desired result.

10   There is danger of a lynching and Paul has to be rescued once
     more.

11   Jerusalem has rejected Paul — he will 'bear witness also at
     Rome'.

The plot against Paul   23.12-35
12-13 Paul's enemies are obviously fanatical.

14-15 The plotters invite the help of the Sanhedrin in getting Paul
      out of the Fort of Antonia.

¹⁶ Now the son of Paul's sister heard of their ambush; so he went and entered the barracks and told Paul. ¹⁷ And Paul called one of the centurions and said, "Bring this young man to the tribune; for he has something to tell him." ¹⁸ So he took him and brought him to the tribune and said, "Paul the prisoner called me and asked me to bring this young man to you, as he has something to say to you." ¹⁹ The tribune took him by the hand, and going aside asked him privately, "What is it that you have to tell me?" ²⁰ And he said, "The Jews have agreed to ask you to bring Paul down to the council tomorrow, as though they were going to inquire somewhat more closely about him. ²¹ But do not yield to them; for more than forty of their men lie in ambush for him, having bound themselves by an oath neither to eat nor drink till they have killed him; and now they are ready, waiting for the promise from you." ²² So the tribune dismissed the young man, charging him, "Tell no one that you have informed me of this."

²³ Then he called two of the centurions and said, "At the third hour of the night get ready two hundred soldiers with seventy horsemen and two hundred spearmen to go as far as Caesare'a. ²⁴ Also provide mounts for Paul to ride, and bring him safely to Felix the governor." ²⁵ And he wrote a letter to this effect:

²⁶ "Claudius Lys'ias to his Excellency the governor Felix, greeting. ²⁷ This man was seized by the Jews, and was about to be killed by them, when I came upon them with the soldiers and rescued him, having learned that he was a Roman citizen. ²⁸ And desiring to know the charge on which they accused him, I brought him down to their council. ²⁹ I found that he was accused about questions of their law, but charged with nothing deserving death or imprisonment. ³⁰ And when it was disclosed to me that there would be a plot against the man, I sent him to you at once, ordering his accusers also to state before you what they have against him."

³¹ So the soldiers, according to their instructions, took Paul and brought him by night to Antip'atris. ³² And on the morrow they returned to the barracks, leaving the horsemen to go on with him. ³³ When they came to Caesare'a and delivered the letter to the governor, they presented Paul also before him. ³⁴ On reading the letter, he asked to what province he belonged. When he learned that he was from Cili'cia ³⁵ he said, "I will hear you when your accusers arrive." And he commanded him to be guarded in Herod's praetorium.

16-17 Paul is allowed visitors. We are not told how his nephew discovered the plot.

18-22 The plot is told to the tribune.

23 'The third hour of the night' — 9 p.m. The large force shows that the tribune takes the plot seriously. The plotters number 'more than forty' and the general unrest in the country must be considered.

24 Felix, Procurator A.D. 52.

25 The letter shows that Paul is innocent so far as Rome is concerned.

27 In fact the letter blames the Jews.

28-29 'Their law' — not Roman law (cf. Gallio, 18.15).

30 It seems that the tribune has told Paul's accusers to make their case before 'the governor'.

31-33 Antipatris is halfway to Caesarea, Roman headquarters in Palestine and residence of the Procurator in Judea. It is a long journey for one night, even for cavalry. Once there they are in Gentile country: the Jewish threat is reduced and the main body of soldiers can return to Jerusalem.

34 'From Cilicia' — i.e. from Tarsus (see note on 9.30).

35 'Herod's praetorium' — the palace of Herod the Great, now the Governor's headquarters.

24 And after five days the high priest Anani'as came down with some elders and a spokesman, one Tertul'lus. They laid before the governor their case against Paul; ²and when he was called, Tertul'lus began to accuse him, saying:

"Since through you we enjoy much peace, and since by your provision, most excellent Felix, reforms are introduced on behalf of this nation, ³in every way and everywhere we accept this with all gratitude. ⁴But, to detain you no further, I beg you in your kindness to hear us briefly. ⁵For we have found this man a pestilent fellow, an agitator among all the Jews throughout the world, and a ringleader of the sect of the Nazarenes. ⁶He even tried to profane the temple, but we seized him.ᶻ ⁸By examining him yourself you will be able to learn from him about everything of which we accuse him."

⁹The Jews also joined in the charge, affirming that all this was so.

¹⁰And when the governor had motioned to him to speak, Paul replied:

"Realizing that for many years you have been judge over this nation, I cheerfully make my defence. ¹¹As you may ascertain, it is not more than twelve days since I went up to worship at Jerusalem; ¹²and they did not find me disputing with any one or stirring up a crowd, either in the temple or in the synagogues, or in the city. ¹³Neither can they prove to you what they now bring up against me. ¹⁴But this I admit to you, that according to the Way, which they call a sect, I worship the God of our fathers, believing everything laid down by the law or written in the prophets, ¹⁵having a hope in God which these themselves accept, that there will be a resurrection of both the just and unjust. ¹⁶So I always take pains to have a clear conscience toward God and toward men. ¹⁷Now after some years I came to bring to my nation alms and offerings. ¹⁸As I was doing this, they found me purified in the temple, without any crowd or tumult. But some Jews from Asia — ¹⁹they ought to be here before you and to make an accusation, if they have anything against me. ²⁰Or else let these men themselves say what wrongdoing they found when I stood before the council, ²¹except this one thing which I cried out while standing among them, 'With

z   Other ancient authorities add 'and we would have judged him
    according to our law. ⁷But the chief captain Lysias came and with
    great violence took him out of our hands, ⁸commanding his accusers
    to come before you.'

Paul appears before Felix   24.1-9

1   The presence of the High Priest himself shows the importance
of this case to the Jews. They have a professional counsel,
Tertullus.

2-3   'Most excellent' (cf. Luke 1.3) — a complimentary opening.

5   These charges show little offence against Jewish Law but
may alarm the Roman procurator: Paul may appear to be a
danger to the peace.

6-7   See R.S.V. note: this is an offence against Jewish Law
(cf. 21.29): they are more likely to have lynched Paul than
to have 'judged him' if the Romans had not interfered.

Paul makes his defence   24.10-27

11   His visit to Jerusalem is to worship, as a good Jew.

12-13   He has not spoken in public or stirred up the people: he has
hardly had time.

14   'The Way' (cf. 9.2; 11.26) has no quarrel with the Law or
the prophets (cf. Luke 24.44), whose fulfilment is in Christ.

15-16   Paul and the Pharisees believe in resurrection. To follow
'the Way' leaves him with a clear conscience as a Jew.

17   'Alms and offerings' — see notes on 19.21-22; 20.4).

18-19   See note on 21.23-24. The 'Jews from Asia', his real accusers,
are not there — they are the ones who stirred up the crowd
(21.27-31).

20   The Council has not found him guilty on any charge (23.9).

21   His offence is his belief in the resurrection — a matter of
division among the Jews (cf. 23.8).

respect to the resurrection of the dead I am on trial before you this day.' "

²² But Felix, having a rather accurate knowledge of the Way, put them off, saying, "When Lys'ias the tribune comes down, I will decide your case." ²³ Then he gave orders to the centurion that he should be kept in custody but should have some liberty, and that none of his friends should be prevented from attending to his needs.

²⁴ After some days Felix came with his wife Drusil'la, who was a Jewess; and he sent for Paul and heard him speak upon faith in Christ Jesus. ²⁵ And as he argued about justice and self-control and future judgment, Felix was alarmed and said, "Go away for the present; when I have an opportunity I will summon you." ²⁶ At the same time he hoped that money would be given him by Paul. So he sent for him often and conversed with him. ²⁷ But when two years had elapsed, Felix was succeeded by Porcius Festus; and desiring to do the Jews a favour, Felix left Paul in prison.

PAUL'S APPEAL TO CAESAR   25.1-12

25 Now when Festus had come into his province, after three days he went up to Jerusalem from Caesare'a. ² And the chief priests and the principal men of the Jews informed him against Paul; and they urged him, ³ asking as a favour to have the man sent to Jerusalem, planning an ambush to kill him on the way. ⁴ Festus replied that Paul was being kept at Caesare'a, and that he himself intended to go there shortly. ⁵ "So," said he, "let the men of authority among you go down with me, and if there is anything wrong about the man, let them accuse him."

⁶ When he had stayed among them not more than eight or ten days, he went down to Caesare'a; and the next day he took his seat on the tribunal and ordered Paul to be brought. ⁷ And when he had come, the Jews who had gone down from Jerusalem stood about him, bringing against him many serious charges which they could not prove. ⁸ Paul said in his defence, "Neither against the law of the Jews, nor against the temple, nor against Caesar have I offended at all." ⁹ But Festus, wishing to do the Jews a favour, said to Paul, "Do you wish to go up to Jerusalem, and there be tried on these charges before me?" ¹⁰ But Paul said, "I am standing before Caesar's tribunal, where I ought to be tried; to the Jews I have done no wrong, as you know very well. ¹¹ If then I am a wrongdoer, and have committed

22-23 'A rather accurate knowledge of the Way' — partly from
what Paul has said, partly because Felix is married to a
Jewess (v.24). Felix puts off his decision so as to hear Lysias.
He does not regard Paul as a criminal and treats him well.

24 Drusilla, daughter of Herod Agrippa I and sister of Herod
Agrippa II (Agrippa the King in 25.13ff).

25 Paul's arguments disturb Felix (cf. Herod Antipas and John
the baptizer's preaching in Mark 6.20), but he again delays.

26 He even hopes for a bribe.

27 He does not wish to offend the Jews.

Paul's appeal to Caesar   25.1-12
1 Very little is known of the new Procurator (c. A.D. 55-56).
His early visit to Jerusalem gives the Jewish leaders a fresh
chance to make their case against Paul.

3 A journey to Jerusalem by Paul will give a fresh chance, too,
to kill him (cf. 23.12ff).

4-5 Festus insists on a trial at Caesarea.

6 He acts quickly.

7 'Many serious charges' (cf. 21.28-29; 24.5-6).

9 Festus offers Paul a trial in Jerusalem, probably to please the
Jews. 'Before me' means before Festus' own court, not
before the Sanhedrin.

10-11 Paul has not offended against Jewish or Roman law (cf. v.8).
As a Roman citizen he has the right of appeal to the Imperial
Court in Rome.

anything for which I deserve to die, I do not seek to escape death; but if there is nothing in their charges against me, no one can give me up to them. I appeal to Caesar." [12] Then Festus, when he had conferred with his council, answered, "You have appealed to Caesar; to Caesar you shall go."

PAUL APPEARS BEFORE FESTUS AND KING AGRIPPA
25.13-27

[13] Now when some days had passed, Agrippa the king and Berni'ce arrived at Caesare'a to welcome Festus. [14] And as they stayed there many days, Festus laid Paul's case before the king, saying, "There is a man left prisoner by Felix; [15] and when I was at Jerusalem, the chief priests and the elders of the Jews gave information about him, asking for sentence against him. [16] I answered them that it was not the custom of the Romans to give up any one before the accused met the accusers face to face, and had opportunity to make his defence concerning the charge laid against him. [17] When therefore they came together here, I made no delay, but on the next day took my seat on the tribunal and ordered the man to be brought in. [18] When the accusers stood up, they brought no charge in his case of such evils as I supposed; [19] but they had certain points of dispute with him about their own superstition and about one Jesus, who was dead, but whom Paul asserted to be alive. [20] Being at a loss how to investigate these questions, I asked whether he wished to go to Jerusalem and be tried there regarding them. [21] But when Paul had appealed to be kept in custody for the decision of the emperor, I commanded him to be held until I could send him to Caesar." [22] And Agrippa said to Festus, "I should like to hear the man myself." "Tomorrow," said he, "you shall hear him."

[23] So on the morrow Agrippa and Berni'ce came with great pomp, and they entered the audience hall with the military tribunes and the prominent men of the city. Then by command of Festus Paul was brought in. [24] And Festus said, "King Agrippa and all who are present with us, you see this man about whom the whole Jewish people petitioned me, both at Jerusalem and here, shouting that he ought not to live any longer. [25] But I found that he had done nothing deserving death; and as he himself appealed to the emperor, I decided to send him. [26] But I have nothing definite to write to my lord about him. Therefore I have brought him before you, and, especially before you, King Agrippa, that, after we have examined him, I may have something to write. [27] For it seems to me unreasonable, in sending a prisoner, not to indicate the charges against him."

12   'When he had conferred' — as a new procurator, Festus is
         perhaps seeking legal advice.

Paul appears before Festus and King Agrippa   25.13-27
13   Agrippa II, son of Herod Agrippa I (cf. 12.1-23) and brother
         of Drusilla (24.24), last king of the Jews, the Romans
         destroying Palestine in A.D.70. Bernice is his sister and theirs
         is a courtesy visit to the new Procurator.

14   Perhaps the King can help Festus with his problem.

15-18   Luke makes a point of Roman impartiality in justice.

19   'Their own superstition' — in the Greek the same word is
         used for 'very religious' (17.22). Festus sees that the question
         seems to be: is Jesus alive or dead?

20   Festus justifies himself; he does not understand. Perhaps the
         Jewish authorities in Jerusalem will help to explain.

22   Agrippa wishes to hear Paul (cf. Herod Antipas and Jesus in
         (Luke 9.9; 23.8).

Paul and King Agrippa   25.23-26.32
23   Fulfils 9.15. 'The audience hall' is probably Herod's
         praetorium (cf. 23.35). The officers and 'prominent men' are
         there to greet Agrippa and Bernice.

24-25   A reminder that the Jews have asked for the death penalty
         on Paul (cf. 22.22; 23.29).

26-27   'My lord' is the Roman Emperor. Festus hopes for advice
         from the King because he is a Jew and familiar with Jewish
         affairs and religion (cf. 26.3).

26 Agrippa said to Paul, "You have permission to speak for yourself." Then Paul stretched out his hand and made his defence:

2 "I think myself fortunate that it is before you, King Agrippa, I am to make my defence today against all the accusations of the Jews, 3 because you are especially familiar with all customs and controversies of the Jews; therefore I beg you to listen to me patiently.

4 "My manner of life from my youth, spent from the beginning among my own nation and at Jerusalem, is known by all the Jews. 5 They have known for a long time, if they are willing to testify, that according to the strictest party of our religion I have lived as a Pharisee. 6 And now I stand here on trial for hope in the promise made by God to our fathers, 7 to which our twelve tribes hope to attain, as they earnestly worship night and day. And for this hope I am accused by Jews, O king! 8 Why is it thought incredible by any of you that God raises the dead?

9 "I myself was convinced that I ought to do many things in opposing the name of Jesus of Nazareth. 10 And I did so in Jerusalem; I not only shut up many of the saints in prison, by authority from the chief priests, but when they were put to death I cast my vote against them. 11 And I punished them often in all the synagogues and tried to make them blaspheme; and in raging fury against them, I persecuted them even to foreign cities.

12 "Thus I journeyed to Damascus with the authority and commission of the chief priests. 13 At midday, O king, I saw on the way a light from heaven, brighter than the sun, shining round me and those who journeyed with me. 14 And when we had all fallen to the ground, I heard a voice saying to me in the Hebrew language, 'Saul, Saul, why do you persecute me? It hurts you to kick against the goads.' 15 And I said, 'Who are you, Lord?' And the Lord said, 'I am Jesus whom you are persecuting. 16 But rise and stand upon your feet; for I have appeared to you for this purpose, to appoint you to serve and bear witness to the things in which you have seen me and to those in which I will appear to you, 17 delivering you from the people and from the Gentiles — to whom I send you 18 to open thier eyes, that they may turn from darkness to light and from the power of Satan to God, that they may receive forgiveness of sins and a place among those who are sanctified by faith in me.'

19 "Wherefore, O King Agrippa, I was not disobedient to the heavenly vision, 20 but declared first to those at Damascus, then at

Paul's defence to King Agrippa   26.1-32

1   'Stretched out his hand' — the orator's gesture (cf. 13.16; 19.33; 21.40).

2-3   Perhaps there is some irony here: the Herods are not very religious Jews.

4   'My own nation' — probably the Jews rather than Cilicia (cf. 21.39; 22.3).

5   Cf. 22.3 — 'the strict manner of the law.'

6-8   His crime — as a loyal Pharisee he believes in the Messiah ('the promise') and the Resurrection (of Jesus). The Jews await the Messiah and believe in a general resurrection: why should they accuse him? 'Our twelve tribes' — the whole nation of the Jews.

9-11   Paul describes his part in the persecution of Christians in Jerusalem and in 'foreign cities' (cf. 8.3). 'Put to death' — Acts records the deaths only of Stephen (7.59-60) and James (12.1-2).

12-18   Another account of the journey to Damascus (cf. 9.1-22; 22.1-16).

13   'At midday' (cf. 22.6). 'Brighter than the sun' is an addition to previous accounts.

14   'All fallen to the ground', not Paul alone (cf. 9.4; 22.7). 'Hebrew' = Aramaic, using the Aramaic name Saul. 'To kick against the goads' — a Greek proverb about the sharp sticks used to prod the ox pulling the plough: to resent or kick against the goad only hurts more.

15-18   No mention of Ananias. Here it appears that Jesus directly sends Paul to the Jews ('people') and Gentiles, to convert Gentiles 'from the power of Satan to God' and then to lead them to 'forgiveness of sins'.

19-20   A very brief account of Paul's work: there is no record in Acts or Paul's Letters of his activities in Judea.

Jerusalem and throughout all the country of Judea, and also to the Gentiles, that they should repent and turn to God and perform deeds worthy of their repentance. ²¹ For this reason the Jews seized me in the temple and tried to kill me. ²² To this day I have had the help that comes from God, and so I stand here testifying both to small and great, saying nothing but what the prophets and Moses said would come to pass: ²³ that the Christ must suffer, and that, by being the first to rise from the dead, he would proclaim light both to the people and to the Gentiles."

²⁴ And as he thus made his defence, Festus said with a loud voice, "Paul, you are mad; your great learning is turning you mad." ²⁵ But Paul said, "I am not mad, most excellent Festus, but I am speaking the sober truth. ²⁶ For the king knows about these things, and to him I speak freely; for I am persuaded that none of these things has escaped his notice, for this was not done in a corner. ²⁷ King Agrippa, do you believe the prophets? I know that you believe." ²⁸ And Agrippa said to Paul, "In a short time you think to make me a Christian!" ²⁹ And Paul said, "Whether short or long, I would to God that not only you but also all who hear me this day might become such as I am — except for these chains."

³⁰ Then the king rose, and the governor and Berni′ce and those who were sitting with them; ³¹ and when they had withdrawn, they said to one another, "This man is doing nothing to deserve death or imprisonment." ³² And Agrippa said to Festus, "This man could have been set free if he had not appealed to Caesar."

PAUL'S JOURNEY TO ROME   27.1-28.16

27 And when it was decided that we should sail for Italy, they delivered Paul and some other prisoners to a centurion of the Augustan Cohort, named Julius. ² And embarking in a ship of Adramyt′tium, which was about to sail to the ports along the coast of Asia, we put to sea, accompanied by Aristar′chus, a Macedo′nian from Thessaloni′ca. ³ The next day we put in at Sidon; and Julius treated Paul kindly, and gave him leave to go to his friends and be cared for. ⁴ And putting to sea from there we sailed under the lee of Cyprus, because the winds were against us. ⁵ And when we had sailed across the sea which is off Cili′cia and Pamphyl′ia, we came to Myra in Ly′cia. ⁶ There the centurion found a ship of Alexandria sailing for Italy, and put us on board. ⁷ We sailed slowly for a number of days, and arrived with difficulty off Cni′dus, and as the wind did

21	For this the Jews have tried to kill him.

21   For this the Jews have tried to kill him.
22-23   Paul continually receives God's help to testify to Messiah's suffering, death and resurrection (cf. 2.23).
24-25   Festus cannot understand the idea of resurrection (cf. the Athenians, 17.32) and thinks Paul's great learning has turned his mind.
26   'The king knows about these things' i.e. the resurrection of Jesus and the Christian mission. 'Not done in a corner' — a Greek proverb = not happening in secret.
27   Paul's question reminds the King that he is a Jew.
28   The King is not pleased and replies with a sneer — Paul is quickly trying to make him 'a Christian' (cf. 11.26).
29   Paul's wish is that all may become Christians. 'These chains' — Roman prisoners are fettered on their way to court, but not necessarily in court.
30-31   All are agreed that Paul is innocent. He must go to Rome, not because of any guilt, but because he has appealed to the Emperor.

Paul's journey to Rome   27.1-28.16

1   The 'we passages' begin again, 27.1-28.16 (cf. 16.9-17; 20.5-16; 21.1-18). 'The Augustan Cohort' is an honorary title, after the first Roman emperor. Adramyttium is south-east of Troas. The ship is a trading vessel, the only means of sea travel at that time (also v.6). Aristarchus (cf. 19.29; 20.4).
3   The centurion is friendly towards Paul (cf. 27.31-32, 43).
4   'Under the lee of Cyprus' — to the east and north, as the wind is in the west.
5   Myra (see note on 21.1).
6   'A ship of Alexandria', carrying corn on its regular route.
7   Because of the west winds it is a slow, difficult voyage south to Crete and along the south coast of the island.

not allow us to go on, we sailed under the lee of Crete off Salmo'ne. [8] Coasting along it with difficulty, we came to a place called Fair Havens, near which was the city of Lase'a.

[9] As much time had been lost, and the voyage was already dangerous because the fast had already gone by, Paul advised them, [10] saying, "Sirs, I perceive that the voyage will be with injury and much loss, not only of the cargo and the ship, but also of our lives." [11] But the centurion paid more attention to the captain and to the owner of the ship than to what Paul said, [12] And because the harbour was not suitable to winter in, the majority advised to put to sea from there, on the chance that somehow they could reach Phoenix, a harbour of Crete, looking northeast and southeast[a] and winter there.

THE STORM   27.13-26

[13] And when the south wind blew gently, supposing that they had obtained their purpose, they weighed anchor and sailed along Crete, close inshore. [14] But soon a tempestuous wind, called the northeaster, struck down from the land; [15] and when the ship was caught and could not face the wind, we gave way to it and were driven. [16] And running under the lee of a small island called Cauda,[b] we managed with difficulty to secure the boat; [17] after hoisting it up, they took measures[c] to undergird the ship; then, fearing that they should run on the Syr'tis, they lowered the gear, and so were driven. [18] As we were violently storm-tossed, they began next day to throw the cargo overboard; [19] and the third day they cast out with their own hands the tackle of the ship. [20] And when neither sun nor stars appeared for many a day, and no small tempest lay on us, all hope of our being saved was at last abandoned.

[21] As they had been long without food, Paul then came forward among them and said, "Men, you should have listened to me, and should not have set sail from Crete and incurred this injury and loss. [22] I now bid you take heart; for there will be no loss of life among you, but only of the ship. [23] For this very night there stood by me an angel of the God to whom I belong and whom I worship, [24] and he said, 'Do not be afraid, Paul; you must stand before Caesar; and lo, God has granted you all those who sail with you.' [25] So take heart,

a Or 'southwest and northwest'
b Other ancient authorities read 'Clauda'
c Greek 'helps'

8   Fair Havens, an open bay, of no use for a long stay.

9-10   'The fast' — the Day of Atonement, in September/October.
       Sailing after mid-September is dangerous and Paul gives
       warning: he has already had experience of shipwreck (cf.
       2 Corinthians 11.25).

12   'The majority' — perhaps of the sailors. Phoenix is on the
       south coast of Crete, west of Fair Havens (see. R.S.V. note).

The storm   27.13-26

13   'The south wind' makes the voyage easy at first.

14   'The northeaster' blows from the mountains and forces the
       ship out to sea.

15   Unable to head into the wind, the ship runs before it.

16   The shelter of the island of Cauda, as they sail south of it,
       helps them to get the ship's dinghy aboard.

17   'Undergird' — probably pass ropes right round the hull by
       lowering them over the bows and tightening them as the
       ship's forward movement carries the ropes underneath.
       'Lowered the gear' is not clear, but may mean using storm
       sails or letting out a sea-anchor. 'The Syrtis' is a sandbank off
       the coast of North Africa, to the west of Cyrene: the north-
       east wind drives the ship towards it.

18   Perhaps the deck 'cargo', as the main cargo is thrown out
       later (v.38).

19   'Tackle' — including spare sails.

20   'Neither sun nor stars' — nothing by which to navigate.

21   'Long without food' — because of sickness and fear.
       Paul reminds them of what he has told them (v.10).

22-24 God intends Paul to reach Rome and this is in his vision: his
       fellow passengers will be saved with him.

men, for I have faith in God that it will be exactly as I have been told. ²⁶ But we shall have to run on some island."

THE SHIPWRECK   27.27-44

²⁷ When the fourteenth night had come, as we were drifting across the sea of A'dria, about midnight the sailors suspected that they were nearing land. ²⁸ So they sounded and found twenty fathoms; a little farther on they sounded again and found fifteen fathoms. ²⁹ And fearing that we might run on the rocks, they let out four anchors from the stern, and prayed for day to come. ³⁰ And as the sailors were seeking to escape from the ship, and had lowered the boat into the sea, under pretence of laying out anchors from the bow, ³¹ Paul said to the centurion and the soldiers, "Unless these men stay in the ship, you cannot be saved." ³² Then the soldiers cut away the ropes of the boat, and let it go.

³³ As day was about to dawn, Paul urged them all to take some food, saying, "Today is the fourteenth day that you have continued in suspense and without food, having taken nothing. ³⁴ Therefore I urge you to take some food; it will give you strength, since not a hair is to perish from the head of any of you." ³⁵ And when he had said this, he took bread, and giving thanks to God in the presence of all he broke it and began to eat. ³⁶ Then they all were encouraged and ate some food themselves. ³⁷ (We were in all two hundred and seventy-six^d persons in the ship.) ³⁸ And when they had eaten enough, they lightened the ship, throwing out the wheat into the sea.

³⁹ Now when it was day, they did not recognize the land, but they noticed a bay with a beach, on which they planned if possible to bring the ship ashore. ⁴⁰ So they cast off the anchors and left them in the sea, at the same time loosening the ropes that tied the rudders; then hoisting the foresail to the wind they made for the beach. ⁴¹ But striking a shoal^e they ran the vessel aground; the bow stuck and remained immovable, and the stern was broken up by the surf. ⁴² The soldiers' plan was to kill the prisoners, lest any should swim away and escape; ⁴³ but the centurion, wishing to save Paul, kept them from carrying out their purpose. He ordered those who could swim to throw themselves overboard first and make for the land, ⁴⁴ and the rest on planks or on pieces of the ship. And so it was that all escaped to land.

d   *Other ancient authorities read 'seventy-six' or 'about seventy-six'*
e   *Greek 'place of two seas'*

26   All is part of God's purpose.

The shipwreck   27.27-44

27   'The sea of Adria' includes the sea between Sicily and Crete. The sailors sense land is near, perhaps hearing breakers.

28   A fathom = six feet, nearly two metres.

29   The anchors are to keep the ship off the rocks.

30   'Seeking to escape' — at least this is what Paul thinks they are doing.

31-32   The sailors will be needed for the final acts (vv.40-41): the boat would have been useful in reaching shore the next day.

33-34   Paul encourages his fellows and repeats his certainty about their safety (cf. v.24).

35-36   His grace, said by Jews and Christians alike, reminds us of the Eucharist; the others follow Paul's example.

37   The number is uncertain.

38   The rest of the cargo (cf. v.18). is thrown overboard so that they can run the ship into shallow water.

40   They cut the anchor ropes and free the rudders — large oars used for steering. 'The foresail' at the bows of the ship will help the wind to drive the ship up on to the beach.

39   'A bay' — now known as St. Paul's Bay, to the north of Valletta.

41   'A shoal' — a sandbank with deeper water on each side: the ship begins to break up.

42-43   The centurion saves Paul's life (cf. v.3).

44   All escape safely, fulfilling Paul's prophecy (v.24).

PAUL IN MALTA   28.1-10

28 After we had escaped, we then learned that the island was called Malta. [2] And the natives showed us unusual kindness, for they kindled a fire and welcomed us all, because it had begun to rain and was cold. [3] Paul had gathered a bundle of sticks and put them on the fire, when a viper came out because of the heat and fastened on his hand. [4] When the natives saw the creature hanging from his hand, they said to one another, "No doubt this man is a murderer. Though he has escaped from the sea, justice has not allowed him to live." [5] He, however, shook off the creature into the fire and suffered no harm. [6] They waited, expecting him to swell up or suddenly fall down dead; but when they had waited a long time and saw no misfortune come to him, they changed their minds and said that he was a god.

[7] Now in the neighborhood of that place were lands belonging to the chief man of the island, named Publius, who received us and entertained us hospitably for three days. [8] It happened that the father of Publius lay sick with fever and dysentery; and Paul visited him and prayed, and putting his hands on him healed him. [9] And when this had taken place, the rest of the people on the island who had diseases also came and were cured. [10] They presented many gifts to us;*f* and when we sailed, they put on board whatever we needed.

PAUL IN ROME   28.11-31

[11] After three months we set sail in a ship which had wintered in the island, a ship of Alexandria, with the Twin Brothers as figurehead. [12] Putting in at Syracuse, we stayed there for three days. [13] And from there we made a circuit and arrived at Rhe'gium; and after one day a south wind sprang up, and on the second day we came to Pute'oli. [14] There we found brethren, and were invited to stay with them for seven days. And so we came to Rome. [15] And the brethren there, when they heard of us, came as far as the Forum of Ap'pius and Three Taverns to meet us. On seeing them Paul thanked God and took courage. [16] And when we came into Rome, Paul was allowed to stay by himself, with the soldier that guarded him.

[17] After three days he called together the local leaders of the Jews; and when they had gathered, he said to them, "Brethren, though I had done nothing against the people or the customs of our fathers, yet I was delivered prisoner from Jerusalem into the hands of the

f   Or 'honoured us with many honours'

Paul in Malta   28.1-10

1   Malta — Roman Melita.

2   They are welcomed with kindness. 'Natives' — literally barbarians (non Greek-speaking) — they are originally Phoenicians from Carthage and speak a Punic dialect.

3-5   The people are superstitious and draw their own conclusions, that Paul is a murderer: although he has escaped the sea he cannot escape Justice.

6   He comes to no harm: they change their minds and think he is a god (cf. 14.11).

7   'The chief man of the island' — the title of the Governor. Paul seems to have a great deal of freedom — he is in favour with the centurion (see note on 27.3).

8-9   The healing of the father of Publius is followed by many other cures (cf. the story of Peter's mother-in-law etc. in Luke 4.38-41).

10   'Gifts to us' — perhaps Luke, as a doctor, has been able to help in the cures. The kindness of the natives (v.2) continues.

Paul in Rome   28.11-31

11   Another 'ship of Alexandria' (cf. 27.6), another grain ship. 'The Twin Brothers' are the gods Castor and Pollux, a favourite figurehead with sailors.

12-13 The travellers reach Puteoli (Pozzuoli near Naples), the final port for Alexandrian grain ships and an important port for Rome: they come via Syracuse (Siracusa) on the island of Sicily and Rhegium (Reggio).

14-15 There are already Christians at Puteoli and Rome. 'Seven days' — Paul is again given some freedom (cf. 27.3; 28.7-9). The Roman Christians come to meet Paul: the road to Rome is the Appian Way, parts of which are still to be seen today.

16   Paul has the privilege of open arrest. This is the end of the 'we passage'.

17   As on previous missions Paul speaks first to the Jews (cf. Pisidian Antioch, 13.46, and Corinth, 18.5-6). The Jews have to come to him and he makes his defence (cf. his speeches in Jerusalem, 22.1-21, and Caesarea, 24.10-21 and 26.2-23).

Romans. [18]When they had examined me, they wished to set me at liberty, because there was no reason for the death penalty in my case. [19]But when the Jews objected, I was compelled to appeal to Caesar — though I had no charge to bring against my nation. [20]For this reason therefore I have asked to see you and speak with you, since it is because of the hope of Israel that I am bound with this chain." [21]And they said to him, "We have received no letters from Judea about you, and none of the brethren coming here has reported or spoken any evil about you. [22]But we desire to hear from you what your views are; for with regard to this sect we know that everywhere it is spoken against."

[23]When they had appointed a day for him, they came to him at his lodging in great numbers. And he expounded the matter to them from morning till evening, testifying to the kingdom of God and trying to convince them about Jesus both from the law of Moses and from the prophets. [24]And some were convinced by what he said, while others disbelieved. [25]So, as they disagreed among themselves, they departed, after Paul had made one statement: "The Holy Spirit was right in saying to your fathers through Isaiah the prophet:

[26]'Go to this people, and say,
You shall indeed hear but never understand,
and you shall indeed see but never perceive.
[27]For this people's heart has grown dull,
and their ears are heavy of hearing,
and their eyes they have closed;
lest they should perceive with their eyes,
and hear with their ears,
and understand with their heart,
and turn for me to heal them.'

[28]Let it be known to you then that this salvation of God has been sent to the Gentiles; they will listen.'[g]

[30]And he lived there two whole years at his own expense,[h] and welcomed all who came to him, [31]preaching the kingdom of God and teaching about the Lord Jesus Christ quite openly and unhindered.

g Other ancient authorities add verse 29, 'And when he had said these
   words, the Jews departed, holding much dispute among themselves'
h Or 'in his own hired dwelling'

18	In the eyes of Rome he is innocent.
19	He is a loyal Jew and yet, because of the Jews, he has to appeal to Caesar.
20	'The hope of Israel' — the Messiah.
21-22	The Roman Jews have heard nothing about Paul from Jerusalem, but they know that Christianity 'is spoken against'. There is a Church in Rome: it may be that disturbances by Christians have led to the expulsion of Jews by Claudius (see note on 18.2).
23	Paul preaches about the Kingdom of God, which has come through Jesus as Messiah: he uses the Old Testament as his source.
24	As usual, most of the Jews are not convinced.
25-27	Such rejection by the Jews is prophesied (Isaiah 6.9-10).
28	But the Gentiles 'will listen' (cf. Psalm 67.2) and this prophecy is fulfilled.
30	'At his own expense' — perhaps by following his trade (cf. 18.3).
31	'Quite openly and unhindered' — the authorities do not interfere.

N.B. The end of the story after the 'two whole years' (v.30) is not known. Acts is the story of the beginning of the Christian Church, the spread of Christianity to the Gentiles, and the coming of Paul to Rome: perhaps this is a suitable ending to the book. There are various traditions: Paul is released and goes on further missions, later being re-arrested; he remains under arrest in Rome; after the great fire of Rome in A.D. 64, for which Nero blames the Christians, there is a great persecution of Christians in Rome, Paul probably being beheaded about A.D. 65.

REVISION PANEL 4

Acts 21.17-40 Trouble in Jerusalem

When Paul arrived in Jerusalem he went to see James and the elders of the Church: James was the brother of Jesus and leader of the Church in Jerusalem (cf. **12.17**). The 'we' passage beginning at **20.5** ends at **21.18**. The elders informed Paul that he had been greatly criticized by the Jews for telling them not to circumcise their children: this was untrue, although Paul had emphasized that circumcision should not be forced on the Gentiles.

In order to prove that Paul was a good Jew who still accepted the Jewish Law, and to show that the rumours about him were false, he was asked to join four men who were completing their vow in the Temple. By paying their expenses and by undergoing purification rites with them, a process which lasted seven days, Paul could prove himself to be a good Jew and could, at the same time, purify himself for having lived in an unclean land. Paul went along with these suggestions, probably hoping that this would please the Jews and stem some of the criticism.

However, just before the seven days were over, a serious situation developed. Some Jews from Asia accused Paul of taking Greeks into the Temple: they would have recognised Paul's companion Trophimus (cf. **20.4**) as an Ephesian. There was a barrier dividing the Court of the Gentiles from the inner courts of the Temple where only Jews could go; the penalty for any Gentile who passed this barrier was death. A cry went up, 'Men of Israel, help! This is the man who is teaching men everywhere against the people and the law and this place; moreover he also brought Greeks into the temple, and he has defiled this holy place' (**21.28**).

Paul was dragged from the inner court into the Court of the Gentiles and was in danger of being killed by the mob. Fortunately, anything that happened in this court could be seen easily by the garrison in the Roman Fort of Antonia. Soldiers ran down the steps leading from the fort to the Court of the Gentiles and stopped the people who were beating Paul. The tribune in charge ordered Paul to be chained to a soldier on either side. As the officer could not make sense of the shouted accusations he told his men to take Paul into the barracks. The soldiers had actually to carry Paul up the steps because of the violence of the mob.

Paul spoke to the tribune in Greek, the language of educated people and of commerce in the Roman Empire, and told him who he was: 'I am a Jew, from Tarsus in Cilicia, a citizen of no mean city; I beg you, let me speak to the people' (21.39). He was given permission and, standing on the steps, Paul spoke to the crowd below, this time in their own language, Aramaic.

Paul's speech 22.1-21: Paul began by speaking of his birth in Tarsus and his education 'at the feet of Gamaliel' (cf. **5.34**) – he was probably being trained as a rabbi. He went on to tell how he had persecuted 'the Way' and of his journey to Damascus in this connection. There is a detailed description of what had happened on the road to Damascus and of his conversion: this differs slightly in one or two points from other accounts of Paul's great experience (cf. **9.1-9** and **26.12-18**).

Then came an account of a vision which has not been mentioned before, when Paul came to the Temple in Jerusalem and was warned in a trance to leave the city, because of the disbelief of the Jews. Finally he went on to speak of the words of Jesus to him: 'Depart; for I will send you far away to the Gentiles' (**22.21**).

This reference to the Gentiles brought immediate anger among the listening Jews: 'Away with such a fellow from the earth! For he ought not to live' (**22.22**). So the tribune had to take Paul away from the danger, into the barracks: he would not have been able to understand what Paul had said, in Aramaic, to upset the crowd. The officer gave orders that Paul should be scourged, not as a punishment but as a recognized way of getting information from a suspect. But Paul spoke to the centurion who was nearby: 'Is it lawful for you to scourge a man who is a Roman citizen, and uncondemned?' (**22.25**).

When the tribune heard about this he was concerned about the way Paul had been chained. He asked Paul about his citizenship: Roman citizenship could be bought, at a price, and in fact the tribune had bought his. But Paul's father having been a Roman citizen, Paul himself was born one.

Acts 23.1-10 Paul before the Sanhedrin

The Roman tribune, Claudius Lysias (cf. **23.26**) determined to find out why Paul had aroused the anger and accusation of the Jews. He brought Paul before the Jewish Council, the Sanhedrin, a powerful body which met at the Temple: the Sanhedrin was composed of seventy religious leaders under the High Priest, the Sadducee priests, elders, and the scribes or lawyers who were mainly Pharisees.

Paul began to address them, to the annoyance of the High Priest who ordered that he be struck on the mouth. Paul appeared to lose his temper, describing the High Priest as a 'whitewashed wall', suggesting that underneath he was far from what he appeared to be: in **Matthew 23.27** 'white-washed tombs' are 'full of . . . uncleanness'. It is interesting to note Paul's words (or are they Luke's?) 'God shall strike you' **(23.3)**: Ananias, High Priest A.D. 48-59, was later killed by a terrorist.

Paul skilfully directed attention away from himself by declaring, 'I am a Pharisee, a son of Pharisees', knowing that the Sanhedrin was composed of Sadducees, conservative and politically minded, and Pharisees, far more devout and ready to consider new ideas. Paul caused considerable division between the two groups. 'For the Sadducees say that there is no resurrection, nor angel, nor spirit; but the Pharisees acknowledge them all' **(23.8)**. Some of the scribes of the Pharisees called out, 'We find nothing wrong in this man', and in fear of the growing violence the tribune told his soldiers to take Paul away by force and return him to the barracks.

That night Jesus spoke to Paul in a vision, 'Take courage, for as you have testified about me at Jerusalem, so you must bear witness also at Rome' **(23.11)**. Paul's wish to visit Rome **(19.21)** was already beginning to come to pass.

The Plot against Paul 23.12-22: Some of the terrorist Jews, more than forty in fact, vowed neither to eat nor to drink until they had killed Paul. The informed the Council of their intention suggesting that the tribune be asked to send Paul to them again so that they could come to a decision about his case: on his way he would be killed.

Happily for Paul the plot was discovered by his nephew --- this is the only mention of a member of Paul's family — and the young man came to tell Paul: apparently, Paul was allowed to have visitors. Paul asked the centurion to let the boy speak to the tribune and he told the officer his story. The officer obviously took the threat very seriously and told two centurions to prepare a number of footsoldiers and horsemen to take Paul to Caesarea in safety. The number of men mentioned by Luke seems far greater than necessary: perhaps the tribune feared that others, besides the forty, might be in the plot. They were to leave at 9 p.m. and take a letter from the tribune, Claudius Lysias, to the Procurator, Felix. Antonius Felix was well thought of by the Emperor Nero and was Procurator of Judea from A.D. 52-61, with his headquarters at Caesarea.

Neither Paul nor Luke could have known the contents of the letter, but Luke has told us what was probably written. It is apparent that the tribune was passing the matter of Paul to the Procurator so that Paul's accusers could appear before Felix to explain their case.

The footsoldiers accompanied Paul some forty-five miles (75 km) to Antipatris, and then returned, leaving the horsemen to take Paul the rest of the journey. When they arrived at Caesarea Felix read the letter and asked Paul where he came from. He told him that he was from the province of Cilicia, and Felix had him detained in Herod's palace to await the arrival of his accusers.

Acts 24.1-27 Paul's Defence before Felix
Five days after Paul had been brought to Caesarea, the High Priest Ananias and some of the Jewish elders arrived, bringing with them their spokesman, a professional lawyer named Tertullus. As was common in those days, Tertullus began his case with words of flattery towards Felix, and then laid the charges against Paul: 'We have found this man a pestilent fellow, an agitator among all the Jews throughout the world, and a ringleader of the sect of the Nazarenes (i.e. the Christians). He even tried to profane the Temple' (24.5-6). The procurator gave Paul leave to reply.

Paul made his defence by saying (1) he had come to Jerusalem to worship and nowhere, either in Temple or in synagogue, had he disputed or stirred up the people; after all, he had been there only twelve days: (2) his accusers could not prove their case against him: (3) he was a strict Jew, following all that was said in the law and the prophets: (4) he had come with offerings for the Church in Jerusalem: (5) the Jews from Asia, his real accusers, were not present to make their case: (6) the only thing that had offended some members of the Council was his belief in the Resurrection.

At this point Felix decided to await the arrival of the tribune, Lysias, so that he could hear his evidence. In the meantime, Paul was to be kept in custody, but he would be allowed visits by his friends.

167

Some days later Felix brought his wife, Drusilla, to hear Paul speak about his faith in Jesus Christ. Drusilla was a Jewess, youngest daughter of Herod Agrippa I (cf. **12.1 ff.**) and sister of Herod Agrippa II (cf. **25.13 ff.**) Paul spoke to them about justice, self-control and future judgment, which seemed to alarm Felix. Paul was returned to custody and we are told that Felix delayed judgment, often sending for him in the hope that he would receive bribe money — this was not uncommon in those days, although it was contrary to Roman law. There is a suggestion that Drusilla urged Felix to keep Paul in custody because she had allowed Felix to entice her away from her previous husband and Paul's words about self-control seemed to have been directed against her. Felix, too, was not known for his fairness and self-control. Luke suggests that, before his recall to Rome, 'desiring to do the Jews a favour, Felix left Paul in prison' (**24.27**).

Paul before Festus 25.1-12: When Felix was replaced by Porcius Festus, Paul was, therefore, still in custody. Soon after his arrival in Caesarea Festus visited Jerusalem, and the High Priest and leading Jews made plans to get rid of Paul. They asked the new Procurator to send Paul to Jerusalem, thinking that they could ambush and kill him on the way. But Festus insisted that Paul's accusers should lay their case before him in Caesarea.

A few days later Paul was brought before Festus at Caesarea and the Jews from Jerusalem made many charges which, as before, they were unable to prove. Paul's defence was simple: 'Neither against the law of the Jews, nor against the temple, nor against Caesar have I offended at all' (**25.8**).

At this point Paul's journey to Rome came one step nearer. Festus asked Paul if he would go to Jerusalem to be tried before him there: this was probably a compromise with the Jews, to please them, although he obviously did not intend to hand Paul over to the Sanhedrin (cf. **25.4-5**). But Paul realized the danger of going to Jerusalem: he intended to be tried 'before Caesar's tribunal, where I ought to be tried' (**25.10**). He then spoke the words which assured his presence in Rome: 'I appeal to Caesar' (**25.11**).

Festus sought the backing of his own council, probably experts in the law, before making his decision: 'You have appealed to Caesar; to Caesar you shall go' (**25.12**).

Paul before King Agrippa II 25.13-26.32: Agrippa II was

the son of Agrippa I (**12.1-23**), himself the son of Aristobulus, the son of Herod the Great. He was the brother of Drusilla, the wife of Felix (**24.24**). Bernice (or Berenice) was sister to Agrippa and Drusilla. Agrippa was friendly towards Festus and had made a visit to Caesarea in order to welcome the new Procurator.

Festus talked with the King and gave him full details of Paul and the charges brought against him, ending with Paul's appeal to Caesar. Agrippa expressed a desire to hear Paul for himself and this was arranged.

When Paul was brought before Agrippa, Bernice and Festus, the Procurator made it quite clear that he had found Paul not guilty of anything deserving death. His difficulty seemed to be that, since Paul had appealed to Caesar and Festus had no charges to make, there was nothing definite that he could write to his emperor.

Agrippa gave Paul leave to speak and make his defence. Paul began in a similar way to Tertullus (**24.2-3**) with words of flattery towards the King. His speech continued with a description of his life from his youth and his vigorous persecution of the early Christians (very much like his speech to the Jerusalem mob in **22.3ff**). A third account of his journey to Damascus follows (**vv.12-18**), the shortest of the three accounts (cf. **9.1-9** and **22.6-16**) omitting some details in order to make room for elaboration on the voice (**vv.14-18**). Paul said that he had obeyed the vision and the voice and the call to serve Christ by preaching to both Jews and Gentiles, and this had led to the Jews' attempt to kill him in the Temple.

Festus broke in: 'Paul, you are mad; your great learning is turning you mad' (**26.24**). Paul turned to Agrippa and asked about his belief in the Scriptures, a question which, to a Jew with little interest in his nation's religion, seemed to be rather embarrassing. The King's reply was somewhat ironic: 'In a short time you think to make me a Christian!' (**26.28**)

Plainly, Luke could have known nothing of what was said in private by the King Bernice and Festus, but their conclusion is simple: Paul's journey to Rome was not the result of his guilt but of his insistence in appealing to the Emperor: 'This man could have been set free if he had not appealed to Caesar' (**26.32**).

Acts 27.1-28.16 Paul's Journey to Rome
The whole of this section is a 'we passage' (cf. **16.9-17; 20.5-16; 21.1-18**) and it is clear that Luke accompanied Paul on this

journey. We remember that Paul had appealed to the Emperor and had to go to Rome, together with other prisoners, under the charge of a centurion named Julius.

The voyage began at Caesarea and the ship, a trading vessel, called at Sidon. Here the centurion treated Paul kindly and allowed him to visit Christian friends. When they set sail once more the westerly wind made progress difficult and the ship was forced to take a course to the east of Cyprus, between the island and the mainland of Asia Minor. At Myra the centurion found a grain ship of Alexandria, ready to sail for Italy: many such ships regularly carried corn from Egypt to Italy and other parts of the Empire.

The wind still made sailing difficult and the ship sailed to the east of Cyprus in order to find some protection, reaching a good harbour at Fair Havens on the south coast of the island. It seems that there was some discussion among the captain, the ship's owner, the crew, the centurion and the passengers concerning the advisability of continuing the journey. Paul advised that because the fast had already gone by it would be dangerous to go on. ('The fast' was the Day of Atonement, on the tenth day of the seventh Jewish month of Tishri — the actual date would be early October — and it was thought to be the last safe date for sailing. The Day of Atonement was a most solemn day for the Jews, on which no work of any sort must be done and a strict fast was observed. The high priest made special sacrifices and offered incense in the Holy of Holies. Two goats were chosen, one to be sacrificed and its blood to be sprinkled before the Ark, and the other, carrying the sins of the people, was driven out into the wilderness and, in New Testament times, was destroyed there.)

Paul warned all on board, 'Sirs, I perceive that the voyage will be with injury and much loss, not only of the cargo and the ship, but also of our lives' (**27.10**). But the captain and the owner decided it was better to find a safer place, such as Phoenix to the west, where they could spend the winter.

Their plans came to nothing, however, for a strong wind blowing off the island carried them far out to sea. Sails were reduced, the ship's boat was hauled on board, and ropes were used to try to strengthen the hull. As the storm continued the crew lightened the ship, first by throwing out some of the cargo, and then by getting rid of the spare sails and other tackle.

The fear of the crew was heightened by the danger of their

being driven into the shoals known as the Syrtis, off the northern coast of Africa, a well-known danger to shipping in those days: added to this was the fact that, with no sun or stars visible to aid navigation, it was impossible to set a course and 'all hope of our being saved was at last abandoned' (**27.20**). But Paul had been told in a vision that neither he nor his fellow travellers would be lost, and he was able to reassure the passengers and crew, 'But we shall have to run on some island' (**27.26**).

For fourteen days since leaving Crete the ship had been drifting in the 'Sea of Adria' (central Mediterranean). Then, because the water was becoming shallower, the sailors thought they must be nearing land, so they put out anchors to prevent the vessel from running onto rocks. Some sailors had lowered the ship's boat, probably to help with the anchors, but Paul feared that they were trying to escape. He told the centurion and the soldiers cut the boat free.

As dawn broke Paul persuaded those on board to have something to eat: they had eaten nothing for fourteen days, probably because of seasickness. Again he reassured them of their eventual safety and took bread himself, giving thanks to God. Then the ship was further lightened by throwing out more cargo.

When day came no one was able to recognize the land, but the sailors were determined to run the ship onto the beach. The anchors were cast off and the ropes tying the steering oars were loosened: hoisting a small sail, they made for the shore. But unfortunately they ran onto a shoal and the bow of the ship stuck fast; before long the waves began to break up the stern. The soldiers, in a panic, resolved that the prisoners must not escape and wanted to kill them, but the centurion prevented this. He ordered those who could swim to make for the shore: others could use planks and pieces of the ship to support them. Paul's words (cf. **27.24-26**) came true, 'And so it was that all escaped to land' (**27.44**).

On Malta (28.1-10): The natives of the island were kind to the shipwrecked voyagers, making a fire to protect them from the cold and the rain. Paul helped to gather sticks for the fire and among them was a viper which clung to his hand. The islanders looked on, thinking Paul must be a murderer who, although he had escaped the sea, was to be overtaken by justice and killed by a snake. But when Paul shook off the snake and suffered no harm the islanders changed their minds, thinking that he must be a god.

Publius, chief man of the island, entertained Paul and his friends and Paul was able to heal his father. This healing was followed by many others, and all the people were able to show their gratitude when the travellers sailed on, by presenting gifts and provisions for their journey.

It was three months before they were able to resume their voyage. Another ship of Alexandria (cf. **27.6**) had wintered in Malta and now set sail for Italy, calling at Syracuse in Sicily. It was only a short time before they reached Rhegium and then Puteoli, the chief port for Rome. Paul was allowed to stay at Puteoli for seven days with Christians before the party set off overland for Rome, along the famous road known as the Appian Way.

News spread rapidly and they were met by other Christians at the Forum of Appius, nearly seventy kilometres from Rome, and at Three Taverns, just over fifty kilometres from the city. 'And when we came into Rome, Paul was allowed to stay by himself, with the soldier that guarded him' (**28.16**) — this is the end of the 'we passages'. A prisoner awaiting trial was allowed to carry on his own trade and was often allowed, also, to hire his own lodging place.

Three days later Paul called the leaders of the Jews in Rome and explained why he was there under arrest: the Romans had wanted to free him, the Jews had objected, and Paul had appealed to the Emperor. The Roman Jews had no news from Judea concerning Paul, but they wanted to hear what he had to say about the Christian sect, 'for with regard to this sect we know that everywhere it is spoken against' (**28.22**).

Later Paul was able to speak to large numbers of Jews who came to his lodging, trying to show them how the Old Testament spoke of Jesus. Some were convinced: others disbelieved. As they left, Paul reminded them of what the prophet Isaiah had said:

'Go to this people, and say,
You shall indeed hear but never understand,
and you shall indeed see but never perceive.
For this people's heart has grown dull,
and their ears are heavy of hearing,
and their eyes they have closed;
lest they should perceive with their eyes,
and hear with their ears,
and understand with their heart,

and turn for me to heal them.' (28.26-27)

Paul's final words remind us of what he had told the Jews in many places and on many occasions: 'Let it be known to you then that this salvation of God has been sent to the Gentiles; they will listen' (28.28).

Paul stayed in Rome for two years 'at his own expense', teaching and preaching about Jesus. It is here that Luke's story ends; he may have intended to write another book. We do not know for certain what happened to Paul after this. There is a tradition that he was tried, acquitted and allowed to go free, then there were further missionary journeys before he was arrested again. Another tradition says that he was kept in house custody awaiting the arrival of his accusers from Jerusalem: they never came.

In A.D. 64 a great fire destroyed much of the city of Rome, and it was said that it had been caused by the Emperor Nero; he put the blame on the Christians and great persecution followed. It is thought that Paul was put to death during this persecution, probably about A.D. 65.

Paul's Journey to Rome: a Summary (27.1-28.16)

Country	Town	Bible Reference	Incidents
Palestine	Caesarea	Acts 27.2	Paul and other prisoners were put on board a ship bound for ports in Asia.
Phoenicia	Sidon	27.3	Paul allowed to meet Christian friends.
Lycia	Myra	27.5	Paul and company transferred to Alexandrian grain ship bound for Italy.
Crete	Fair Havens	27.7-8	Ship sailed west to Cnidus and south to Crete. Paul tried to persuade the captain and others to remain at Fair Havens, because of the danger of sailing so late in the season. They sailed for Phoenix but were driven south by the wind.
	Cauda	27.16	Ship's boat taken on board

Country	Town	Bible Reference	Incidents
			and steps taken to strengthen the ship. Cargo and tackle thrown overboard.
Sea of Adria		27.27	In the night the ship neared land: anchors were put out. Sailors tried to leave and small boat was cut adrift. Paul encouraged fellow travellers to take food. More cargo thrown overboard.
Malta		27.39- 28.10	Tried to bring the ship ashore but ran on shoal: ship began to break up. Soldiers wanted to kill prisoners, they were saved by centurion. All reached shore safely. Kindness of natives. Paul's incident with the viper. Paul cured father of Publius and others who were sick. After three months sailed for Italy.
Sicily	Syracuse	28.12	Paul and party stayed for three days.
Italy	Rhegium	28.13	Set sail for Puteoli.
	Puteoli	28.14	Paul stayed seven days with Christian brethren.
	Rome	28.15-28	Paul met by Christians on Appian Way, at Forum of Appius and Three Taverns. Paul in house custody with Roman soldier. He spoke to Jewish leaders, telling why he was there; later told how the Old Testament spoke of Jesus, and how salvation had come to the Gentiles. Stayed there two years, teaching and preaching.

See map on page 135

QUESTIONS

1 They seized Paul and dragged him out of the temple. **Acts 21.30**
   What had caused the Jews' anger, and what was the immediate result?

2 I beg you, let me speak to the people. **Acts 21.39**
   To whom did Paul say this? What was the outcome of his speech?

3 Provide mounts for Paul to ride, and bring him safely to Felix the
   governor. **Acts 23.24**
   Explain carefully why Paul was taken from Jerusalem to Caesarea.

4 They laid before the governor their case against Paul. **Acts 24.1**
   Who were 'they'? What charges were brought against Paul? What
   action did Felix take?

5 You have appealed to Caesar; to Caesar you shall go. **Acts 25.12**
   Who said this? Explain why Paul appealed to Caesar.
   Who were Agrippa and Bernice and what part did they play at this
   time?

6 What part did the following places play in the first part of Paul's
   journey to Rome: Sidon (**Acts 27.3**); Myra (**Acts 27.5**); Fair Havens
   (**Acts 27.8**); Phoenix (**Acts 27.12**); Cauda (**Acts 27.16**); the Syrtis
   (**Acts 27.17**)?

7 We shall have to run on some island. **Acts 27.26**
   How did Paul encourage his fellows on board ship?
   Give an account of the shipwreck.

8 The island was called Malta. **Acts 28.1**
   Relate carefully all that happened on the island.

9 So we came to Rome. **Acts 28.14**
   Describe how Paul and his party reached Rome and what took place
   there.

BIBLE KNOWLEDGE QUESTIONS: USEFUL HINTS AND MODEL QUESTIONS AND ANSWERS

Introduction

Bible Knowledge questions, in the WASC examination, are usually of two types. We have (1) **context questions** and (2) **essay questions**. Context questions are usually sub-questions, all of which come under one major question number. Candidates are usually required to answer some, not all, of the context questions: a practice which should help them to score high marks. Nevertheless, some examining bodies make context questions compulsory since, collectively, the sub-questions carry more marks than the single essay questions.

As with context questions, essay questions are usually more in number than the candidates are expected to attempt. This number is determined by the duration of the question paper. For example, for a 1½ hour Bible Knowledge paper, the West African Examination Council currently asks five essay questions out of which the candidates attempt two (in addition to four out of six sub-questions in the compulsory context question).

The two types of question broadly aim firstly at finding out from the candidates' answers how well they are grounded in the Biblical facts within the areas prescribed for their study — this involves a basic knowledge of contemporary history, religion, ethics and personalities — and secondly, at obtaining an elementary interpretation of significant features (words, phrases, episodes, religious rites, customs, etc.). Candidates may here be required to evaluate religious, social or historical principles within the historical circumstances that gave rise to them.

To be able to achieve these broad aims, students of Bible Knowledge must realize that there can be no substitute for the Bible in whichever text is recommended for them by the examination body. The prescribed text must be closely studied direct from the Bible. No amount of attendance at Church services or Sunday school, or listening to sermons will be sufficient; not even regular attendance at school classes will equip the candidate with enough details to make a good score at examinations. To ignore the Bible text is like a student of English Literature pretending that he has studied a play of Shakespeare, say *Macbeth*, by merely listening to lectures and film shows on *Macbeth* without studying the play itself from the prescribed text.

Apart from studying the Biblical text (whose importance cannot be over-emphasized), students can gain from consulting good commentaries, either one-volume Bible commentaries or commentaries on single books prescribed for examinations. The teacher's role here is to guide the students, to recommend good commentaries and to discourage the use of cheap editions which flood the market.

Other teaching/learning aids include maps, pictures, films, etc., which make the study of Bible Knowledge more realistic and help disprove the wrong notion, current in some quarters, that Bible Knowledge is devoid of historical truths.

Context questions

Context questions usually make strong demands on candidates' ability to come to grips with the details in a rather limited but significant episode within the prescribed chapters of the Bible. Such questions are based on specific quotations, often striking in nature, which a good student is expected not to gloss over in the course of his studies.

These questions may take several forms by way of rubric. For the West African School Certificate, the rubric currently reads thus:

'Give the context of . . . the following passages, and answer the questions which follow.'

From the above, one should observe that there are two parts, namely (1) giving the context of the quoted passage, and (2) answering any follow-up or comment question attached. Let us take the two parts separately:

(1) 'Give the context . . . '

The context of any passage is usually found in the verses immediately preceding the given quotation. For example, if the given quotation is

'Men of Galilee, why do you stand looking into heaven?' (Acts 1.11) the context will naturally be found in the verses immediately preceding, or leading to verse 11. The candidate is expected to recall that this question came about some days after the Resurrection of Jesus. His disciples one day asked Him whether He would then restore the kingdom to Israel. In answer to this question He told them that they should not bother about such things, but rather that they should expect the gift of the Holy Spirit, and thereafter proclaim the Gospel everywhere. As He was speaking to them He was lifted up into Heaven. They stood there gazing upwards when two men in white robes appeared and addressed them as quoted.

What has been said so far comes from Acts 1.6-10. Thus these five verses, immediately preceding verse 11, give us the required answer to part (1) of the context question. Since the candidate must be aware of the limited time available to him, it will be superfluous for him to go into verses 1-5. He is required to strike the nail on the head and avoid irrelevant matter.

(2) ' . . . answer the questions which follow.'

The follow-up or comment question could take many forms. From the passage already given, let us suggest the following questions:

'Why were the people spoken to called 'Men of Galilee'? What else was said by the speaker?'

In answer to the first part, the candidates' background knowledge of the call of the Apostles is required. All the disciples of Jesus, with the exception of Judas Iscariot, who was not present on this occasion, were from Galilee. (It was in Galilee that Jesus did most of His work on earth.) Therefore, the two men in white robes were right to refer to the eleven disciples as 'Men of Galilee' — they were all Galileans.

The second question follows directly on the given quotation and only a candidate who has studied this section closely will be able to recall that the disciples were told that 'this Jesus, who was taken up from you into heaven, will come in the same way as you saw him go into heaven'. Note, however, that the candidate need not quote the exact words of the Bible: a good rendition of what was said by the two men will be good enough.

It will be seen from the above that the answer to any context question depends entirely on the given passage and the nature of the comment question that follows. Below are three *model context questions* and *model answers:*

Model context questions and answers

Give the context of the following passages and answer the questions which follow.

1. 'Let his habitation become desolate, and let there be no one to live in it'; and 'His office let another take.' **Acts 1.20**
   How were these words fulfilled?

Answer

Context: **Acts 1.15-19**

Some days after the Ascension of Jesus, Peter (then the leader of the small company of disciples) proposed that they should select from among themselves somebody to replace Judas Iscariot. Peter observed that after Judas had bought a field with 'the reward of his wickedness' (that is the money he realized from his sale of Jesus, thirty pieces of silver), he 'burst open in the middle and all his bowels gushed out'.

When it became known that Judas had died, the field was called Akeldama (Field of Blood), in fulfilment of Old Testament prophecy (in the Book of Psalms, as quoted in the context).

Comment (or follow-up) question: **Acts 1.23-26.**

The words of the Psalms were fulfilled when Peter suggested the qualifications to be met by the would-be nominees: they must have accompanied Jesus all through His life and witnessed His Resurrection. Two men, Joseph Barsabbas and Matthias, were selected: after prayers, lots were cast and Matthias was chosen.

2. 'This is the stone which was rejected by you builders, but which has become the head of the corner.' **Acts 4.11**
   What great benefit would accrue to all those who do not reject the man here referred to as 'the stone'?

Answer

Context: **Acts 4.5-10.**

After healing the cripple at the Beautiful Gate of the Temple, Peter and John were teaching in the Name of Jesus Crucified: the Sanhedrin (or Council) arrested them and put them in custody for the night. The following day the Sanhedrin asked them by what power or by what name they were performing.

Peter affirmed that they had healed the cripple in the Name of Jesus Christ of Nazareth, whom they, the Sanhedrin, had crucified. This Jesus, he continued, was the stone which they had rejected.

Comment question: **Acts 4.12.**

Acceptance of Jesus of Nazareth, 'the stone' which the builders (that is the Jews) rejected, ensures salvation: there is no other name under heaven by which man must be saved.

3. 'Can any one forbid water for baptizing these people who have received the Holy Spirit just as we have?' **Acts 10.47**
   What feature in this story marks it as a new development in the history of the Early Church?

Answer

Context: **Acts 10.44-46.**

After Cornelius had told Peter why he had sent for him, Peter began to preach the Good News to all who had assembled in Cornelius's house.

But while Peter was still preaching, the Holy Spirit fell upon all his hearers: Peter's companions were amazed at this novel incident. It surprised them that the Holy Spirit had been poured upon Gentiles, and that they, the Gentiles, had spoken in tongues. Peter therefore made the statement quoted.

Comment question

Two features mark the incident of the conversion of Cornelius as a new development in the history of the Early Church: firstly, this was the first time that one of the twelve Apostles had been directed by the Holy Spirit to preach specifically to a Gentile, and secondly, the Holy Spirit was here poured out on Gentiles even before they were baptized. (Note: Philip had actually preached in Samaria to an audience which was mixed: it included Jews and proselytes. He later converted the Ethiopian eunuch. However, Philip was not one of the original Apostles, but a deacon, and therefore is not covered by the comment question given here.)

Again, when the question of the admission of Gentiles into the Church came to a head, it was this incident to which Peter referred in support of the view that it was wrong to exclude Gentiles from the Church: God had taught Peter that the walls of partition between Jew and Gentile must be broken by the Church.)

Essay questions

Essay questions, unlike context questions, are of a wider scope, and offer the candidate an opportunity to attack the question from many angles. They also give the candidate more room for self-expression.

At W.A.S.C. level, candidates are required to show a reasonable knowledge of the historical, social, economic, and religious facts within a given area: with this knowledge they will be able fully to appreciate the development and growth of the Jewish religion as something that cannot be divorced from their history as a people. They will then be able to deal from a historical perspective with the Good News of the life and work of Jesus and the growth of the Christian Church as given in the Synoptic Gospels and the Acts of the Apostles.

Essay questions are of two main types: direct or angled. In the direct type the candidate is required to answer directly on a given incident. For example, he could be asked to narrate an incident such as the conversion of Saul on the road to Damascus, or to summarize Stephen's defence before the Sanhedrin. In angled questions the candidate may be required to draw inferences or analyse given situations in the light of his experience. For instance, he may be required to show how persecution of Christians led to the success of the Early Church. In such a question no specific incident is suggested: the candidate is expected to draw from his stock of knowledge of the history of the Early Church as gleaned from the prescribed area of his study, and to give a well-considered and intelligent appraisal.

However, essay questions often combine the two types. In this case the latter serves as a comment question attached to the former and usually carries fewer marks, say between 3 and 5 marks out of a maximum of 15 in W.A.S.C. Bible Knowledge.

The following examples of essay questions and model answers to them will be helpful.

Model essay questions and answers

1. Describe the Apostles' experience on the Day of Pentecost. Briefly narrate Peter's address on this occasion, and its result.

Answer (See **Acts 2.1-47**)
When the Day of Pentecost came, the Apostles were all together in one place. Suddenly they heard a sound from heaven, like the rush of a mighty wind. There appeared, on each of the Apostles, tongues which looked like fire: they were filled with the Holy Spirit and began to speak in other tongues.

At the time of this feast, Jews and proselytes from all over the Roman Empire had assembled in Jerusalem. They were surprised when they heard the Apostles speaking in various tongues: some of them mocked and said that the Apostles were filled with new wine.

Peter stood up in their midst and refuted the charge of drunkenness: it was too early in the day, he asserted, for anybody to get drunk (it was then only 9 a.m. — 'the third hour'). He supported his stand by quoting from the prophet Joel to the effect that God's Holy Spirit would be given to all men and they would prophesy. The Day of the Lord had in fact arrived. Jesus was the Messiah and in Him the promises had been fulfilled. Jesus came from the house of David, but wicked men had conspired and crucified Him. God had, however, raised Him from the dead and made Him Lord and Christ. Therefore people should repent and be baptized and receive the Holy Spirit.

The audience was moved by Peter's address, and many asked what they should do. Peter asked them to repent and be baptized. About three thousand people accepted the Good News and were baptized. The new converts became closely attached to the Apostles and a new fellowship began, marked by communal breaking of bread and constant prayers. (Note: This is an example of a *direct* essay question. All the information required comes from the Bible (**Acts 2.1-47**). What the candidate is expected to do is to be able to given an intelligent and factual narration of the incident.)

The next two questions, although different in nature, are also of the direct type. The fourth question is of the *angled* type and is more generalized.

2. How was Saul converted to Christianity? What problems and difficulties did he pass through before he embarked upon his first missionary tour?

Answer (See **Acts 9.1-30**)

Saul was party to the martyrdom of Stephen: it was at Paul's feet that the mob laid their gowns when they were stoning Stephen. A great wave of persecution befell the Apostles. Saul himself ravaged the Church in Jerusalem, dragging men and women to jail.

In his determination to exterminate the believers, Saul obtained letters of authority from the Sanhedrin to travel to Damascus and bring down from there men and women who belonged to 'the Way'. As he was on his way to Damascus, a sudden flash of light struck him down. He heard a voice saying, 'Saul, Saul, why do you persecute me?' When Saul asked who was talking to him the voice replied, 'I am Jesus, whom you are persecuting; but rise and enter the city, and you will be told what you are to do.'

Saul's companions heard the voice but did not see the speaker. When Saul rose up, he could no longer see: his men, therefore, led him by the hand into the city. For three days he neither ate nor drank.

At this time there was a disciple in Damascus named Ananias. The Lord directed him in a vision to go and meet Saul in the house of a man named Judas, in the street called 'Straight'. Ananias was reluctant to go, because he had heard how much persecution Saul had carried out against the Church, and how he had actually come down to Damascus to arrest the disciples. The Lord, however, urged him to go, because He had chosen Saul as His own instrument to preach the Gospel to the Gentiles, to kings and to the sons of Israel, and He would show Saul how much he was to suffer for God's sake.

Ananias therefore went. He laid his hands on Saul and told him that Jesus, who had met him on his way, had sent him, Ananias, to make him regain his sight. Immediately things like scales fell from Saul's eyes, he rose and was baptized and his strength returned to him.

For several days Saul remained in Damascus and proclaimed the Good News. His hearers were amazed and wondered what change had come upon a man who had been the greatest persecutor of the Church. Not long afterwards, the Jews in Damascus plotted to have him killed, but at night the other disciples let him down over the city wall in a basket, and he escaped to Jerusalem.

In Jerusalem it was not much better for Saul. The disciples were afraid of him and would not admit him, until Barnabas intervened on his behalf. Thereafter he joined them in preaching the Gospel. He had a number of disputes with the Hellenists and, when they plotted to kill him, he was sent down to Caesarea, from where he travelled to his own city, Tarsus.

3. Write notes on any **three** of the following: the selection of the deacons; Philip the Deacon; Gamaliel; Barnabas; Elymas.
(**Note:** All five are answered here: the candidate would answer only **three** as directed).

Answers
(a) The Selection of the Seven Deacons. (See Acts 6)
When the disciples were increasing in number in Jerusalem, Hellenist disciples murmured against the Hebrews because their widows were not getting fair treatment in the distribution of Church amenities. The twelve Apostles, therefore, decided that it was not right for them to be distracted from their task of preaching the Gospel in order 'to serve tables'. They should select 'seven men of good repute, full of the Spirit and of wisdom' to take charge of all distribution. Consequently seven men were chosen and called deacons. They were Stephen, Philip, Prochorus, Nicanor, Timon, Parmenas, and Nicolaus, a proselyte. After prayers the Apostles laid their hands upon them and commissioned them to their new duties.

(b) Philip the Deacon. (See Acts 8.4-13, 26-40)
Philip was, after Stephen, the best known of the seven original deacons who were initially selected for the purpose of ensuring equitable distribution of amenities among believers. After the death of Stephen there was a wave of persecutions, and many believers

escaped from Jerusalem. Philip escaped to Samaria and there preached the Good News and made many converts. He also gave many signs: people with unclean spirits were cleansed and the lame walked. Among his converts was a magician called Simon (Magus). Later, when the Mother Church in Jerusalem heard that as a result of Philip's work in Samaria the Gospel had taken root there, they sent Peter and John to confirm the work there.

This done, the angel of the Lord directed Philip to go towards Gaza, where he met an Ethiopian eunuch who was returning home after worshipping in Jerusalem. The man was reading the prophecy of Isaiah and Philip asked him if he understood the passage he was reading. Confessing that he was unable to understand unless somebody taught him, the eunuch invited Philip into his chariot. Philip then expounded the passage to the eunuch and from there told him the Good News of Jesus. When they reached a water hole, Philip baptized the eunuch and disappeared. He was later found at Azotus, and from there he continued his preaching until he came to Caesarea, where he settled down with his family.

(c) Gamaliel. (See Acts 5.34-40)

During a renewed persecution of the Church the Sanhedrin had arrested and imprisoned the disciples. At night, however, they were miraculously released by an angel and they went back to the Temple and preached in the Name of Jesus. Later, when they were re-arrested and brought before the Council, they were asked why they had not heeded the strict warning to desist from teaching in Jesus' Name. Peter boldly answered that they must obey God rather than men. This defiant answer enraged the Sanhedrin and they wanted to kill the Apostles.

Among the members of the Sanhedrin present was a leading Pharisee named Gamaliel. He was a teacher of the Law and was greatly respected. Paul had been one of his students. Gamaliel stood up and spoke in defence of the Apostles. He warned the Council to take care in their attitude towards these men. He reminded them that a man named Theudas had once rallied men around himself claiming that he was somebody, but when he was slain his men scattered. Another, Judas, a Galilean, also rose up during the period of the census and led an insurrection: he too was put down and his followers scattered.

Gamaliel warned them to leave the Apostles alone because, if their undertaking was of men, it would fail, but if it was of God, they, the members of the Council, who thought they were fighting God's cause, would in fact be found to be opposing God, and they would inevitably fail.

The Sanhedrin accepted his 'wait and see' advice and, after they had beaten the Apostles, they let them go.

(d) **Barnabas.** (See **Acts 4.36-37; 9.27; 11.22-30; 13.1-3; 14.12**)
Barnabas (the name given by the Apostles to a man named Joseph)
means 'son of encouragement'. He was one of the earliest members
of the Church, who sold his field and surrendered the money to the
Church. He was a Levite and a native of Cyprus.

It was Barnabas who intervened on Saul's behalf and introduced
him to the Church in Jerusalem after Saul's return from Damascus.
Later, owing to the growing persecution of the Church, Barnabas was
sent by the Church in Jerusalem to Antioch, to help to consolidate
the Church which was being established there. When Barnabas
got to Antioch he saw that the grace of God was active there, and he
exhorted the new converts to remain faithful to the Lord. It was at
this point that Barnabas, in recognition of his major role in the work,
was described as 'a good man, full of the Holy Spirit, and of faith'.
Barnabas left Antioch for Tarsus and fetched Saul: the two of them
remained at Antioch for a whole year and taught a large company of
people.

It was later at Antioch that the Holy Spirit directed the Church
to set Barnabas and Saul apart for the work of ministry for which
God had selected them. After fasting and prayer the Church laid
their hands upon them and sent the two away on their first missionary
tour. During this tour Saul was the chief spokesman, but Barnabas,
perhaps the elder and more venerable of the two, did less talking.
He was, at Lystra, called Zeus by the heathen people, who thought
that the two missionaries were gods come down in the likeness of
men. Later, after they had with great difficulty persuaded the people
not to sacrifice to Zeus, they were thrown out of the city. They went
back to Derbe and then retraced their route to Antioch, on the
completion of their tour.

(e) **Elymas.** (See **Acts 13.6-11**)
During their first missionary journey Barnabas and Saul came to
Paphos on the island of Cyprus. They were invited to the house of
the Roman Proconsul, Sergius Paulus, who wanted to hear the
Gospel.

In the house of the Proconsul was a certain magician, a Jewish
false prophet, named Elymas or Bar-Jesus. This man hindered the
work of the Apostles and nearly succeeded in stopping the proconsul
from accepting the Good News. Saul, filled with the Holy Spirit,
looked intently at Elymas and said, 'You son of the devil, you enemy
of all righteousness, full of all deceit and villainy, will you not stop
making crooked the straight paths of the Lord?' Saul thereupon
cursed Elymas and immediately he was struck with blindness: he

sought people to lead him by the hand. The proconsul believed, having seen what happened.

4. 'The persecution of the Early Church led to the spread and growth of the Gospel.'
   Show, from the story of the Early Church up to the conversion of Saul, how far the above statement is true or false.

Answer
Before Jesus ascended into Heaven, His disciples asked Him, 'Will you at this time restore the kingdom to Israel? (**Acts 1.6**). His disciples still had dreams of political greatness for Israel. But, instead of giving them the direct answer they expected, Jesus made them a promise: 'You shall receive power when the Holy Spirit has come upon you; and you shall be my witnesses in Jerusalem and in all Judea and Samaria and to the end of the earth' (**Acts 1.8**).

When the promise of the Holy Spirit was fulfilled on the Day of Pentecost, the disciples were not slow in taking up the work of witnessing for Christ. They immediately preached to all who had come to Jerusalem from many parts of the Roman Empire, and whilst some mocked them, they were still able to make as many as three thousand converts.

This initial success in Jerusalem would have been a strong enough reason for the Apostles to concentrate their preaching efforts in Jerusalem and Judea: Samaria and the 'end of the earth' could wait. Every day of the week they preached in the Temple and drew to themselves a large crowd who, seeing their miracles and other signs, praised God.

It was not long before their preaching and miracles began to attract the attention of the Jewish leaders, who had earlier conspired and crucified Jesus Christ. It was, to these Jewish leaders, unthinkable that the Apostles should be preaching in the Name of Jesus Crucified, and thereby bring upon them the blood of Jesus (**Acts 5.28**). The Apostles were therefore arrested, detained, tried, often thoroughly beaten, and warned to desist from preaching and teaching in Jesus' Name, with threats of heavier punishment unless they acquiesced with the order.

At this stage the persecution was not beyond endurance: the Apostles were not dispirited. They even thanked God for giving them the strength to suffer such persecution and for making them worthy to suffer for the Gospel (**Acts 5.41**). In fact, their persecutors, the Jewish leaders, were often dumbfounded by the Apostles' sheer courage and boldness: they even confessed that such courage was possible because the Apostles 'had been with Jesus' (**Acts 4.13**).

In spite of this realization, the Jewish leaders were determined to destroy the Gospel, but the more they persecuted the Apostles, the more they made steady progress and the Church grew: the power of the Holy Spirit gave them a clear victory over their enemies.

Nevertheless, after the appointment of the seven deacons, a new phase in the persecution of the Church was reached. The Jewish leaders could not tolerate Stephen's affront and his blasphemous claims: they stoned him to death. Thus the first Christian blood was shed, and persecution of the Church took a new turn. Stephen's blood was, however, to water the field for the Gospel, which not even Saul could suppress. Following Stephen's martyrdom, a great persecution was made against the Church; Saul and others went from house to house arresting men and women. Many escaped from Jerusalem and fled for their lives to Samaria, Antioch, Damascus and other places. Only the Twelve remained in Jerusalem: they were determined to sit out the persecution in spite of Stephen's death, and to ensure that the Gospel took a firm root 'at home' before they considered pushing further afield. However, they made short trips outside Jerusalem to confirm the believers. For example, Peter and John were sent to Samaria to find out the truth about Philip's success story in Samaria and to confirm the new converts there.

Saul's determination to settle, once and for all, the threat of the Church to the power and influence of the Jewish leaders, led him to Damascus, where he was to meet Jesus face to face. It was an irony of fate that Saul, the great persecutor, was dramatically converted and became the greatest of the persecuted. The miracle of his conversion is therefore the most eloquent testimony to the statement that 'persecution led to the spread and growth of the Church.'

(Note on question 4: Only exceptionally good candidates at Ordinary Level will be able to delve into as detailed an appraisal of the situation as given here. The question is a revision one, and since it is limited to **Acts 1-9**, is a good means of testing candidates' knowledge of the growth of the Early Church.)

TEST QUESTIONS

Context questions
Give the context of the following passages and answer the questions which follow:

1. Lord, who knowest the hearts of all men, show which one of these two thou hast chosen.

   Acts 1.24

   Why was it necessary to make this choice? Who was eventually chosen, and how?

2. And they were all filled with the Holy Spirit and began to speak in other tongues, as the Spirit gave them utterance.

   Acts 2.4

   What do you understand by 'speaking in other tongues'?

3. When they heard this they were cut to the heart, and said to Peter and the rest of the Apostles, 'Brethren, what shall we do?'

   Acts 2.37

   What answer was given on this occasion?

4. I have no silver and gold, but I give you what I have.

   Acts 3.6

   Complete this statement. What was the reaction of those who saw what happened?

5. And when they had set them in the midst, they inquired, 'By what power or by what name did you do this?'

   Acts 4.7

   How did those here 'set in the midst' deal with the question?

6. Whether it is right in the sight of God to listen to you rather than to God, you must judge; for we cannot but speak of what we have seen and heard.

   Acts 4.19-20

   What was the result of the above statement?

7. And when they had prayed, the place in which they were gathered together was shaken; and they were all filled with the Holy Spirit and spoke the word of God with boldness.

   Acts 4.31

   Mention one other occasion when these people had a similar experience.

8. How is that you have contrived this deed in your heart? You have not lied to men but to God.

Acts 5.4

Why was this man condemned for his action?

9. We strictly charged you not to teach in this name, yet you have filled Jerusalem with your teaching and you intend to bring this man's blood upon us.

Acts 5.28

What do you understand by 'you intend to bring this man's blood upon us'? What answer was given by those who were being addressed?

10. So they took his advice, and when they had called in the apostles, they beat them and charged them not to speak in the name of Jesus, and let them go.

Acts 5.40

How did the Apostles react after their release? Did they heed the warning given?

11. This man never ceases to speak words against this holy place and the law.

Acts 6.13

How was this charge elaborated upon and what would be the penalty if proved?

12. Behold, I see the heavens opened, and the Son of man standing at the right hand of God.

Acts 7.56

What was the consequence of this statement?

13. Give me also this power, that any one on whom I lay my hands may receive the Holy Spirit.

Acts 8.19

What was wrong with this request? Was it granted?

14. See, here is water! What is to prevent my being baptized?

Acts 8.37

Recall what happened after this man's baptism.

15. Lord, I have heard from many about this man, how much evil he has done to thy saints at Jerusalem.

Acts 9.13

What did this man do to the saints at Jerusalem? For what vocation was he being prepared?

16. And when the brethren knew it, they brought him down to Caesarea, and sent him off to Tarsus.

Acts 9.30

How did the Church feel when this man became a convert?

17. Your prayers and your alms have ascended as a memorial before God.

Acts 10.4

What was this man before this time, a Christian, a Jew, or a God-fearer? Explain your answer.

18. If God then gave the same gift to them as he gave to us when we believed in the Lord Jesus Christ, who was I that I could withstand God?

Acts 11.17

Why was it necessary to ask the above question? What was the result?

19. And when he had seized him, he put him in prison, and delivered him to four squads of soldiers to guard him.

Acts 12.4

What did this man intend to do to the prisoner? Did he achieve his objective?

20. It was necessary that the word of God should be spoken first to you. Since you thrust it from you, and judge yourselves unworthy of eternal life, behold, we turn to the Gentiles.

Acts 13.46

Comment on the significance of this statement with regard to the course of the history of the Church from this time onwards.

21. Men, why are you doing this? We also are men, of like nature with you, and bring you good news.

Acts 14.15

What 'good news' is here brought to this people? How successful was the mission?

22. Now therefore why do you make trial of God by putting a yoke upon the neck of the disciples which neither our fathers nor we have been able to bear?

Acts 15.10

What is being referred to here as 'a yoke' and why?

23. And Barnabas wanted to take with them John called Mark.

Acts 15.37

Where were Barnabas and Paul intending to go? What was the result of Barnabas's wish to take Mark? Explain what Mark had done to displease Paul.

24. Come over to Macedonia and help us.

Acts 16.9

Give the possible identity of the man who spoke these words. What was the immediate result?

25. These men are servants of the Most High God, who proclaim to you the way of salvation.

Acts 16.17

How did Paul react to these words? Describe briefly what happened next to Paul and Silas.

26. I found also an altar with this inscription, 'To an unknown god'.

Acts 17.23

How did Paul make use of this discovery?

27. Handkerchiefs or aprons were carried away from his body to the sick.

Acts 19.12

Explain the reason for this action. What was the result?

28. Great is Artemis of the Ephesians!

Acts 19.28,34

Explain the reason for the shouts. Why were these people so upset by Paul's teaching?

29. A young man named Eutychus was sitting in the window.

Acts 20.9

What happened to the young man? Explain how Paul dealt with the situation.

30. So shall the Jews at Jerusalem bind the man who owns this girdle and deliver him into the hands of the Gentiles.

Acts 21.11

Explain how this incident was 'an acted parable'. How did the words of this prophecy come true?

31. This is the man who is teaching men everywhere against the people and the law and this place; moreover he also brought Greeks into the temple.

Acts 21.28

Explain what Paul had been doing in the Temple. What happened immediately after this?

32. Away with such a fellow from the earth! For he ought not to live.

Acts 22.22

What had Paul said to bring forth this shout? Explain how the Roman tribune acted after this.

33. I bought this citizenship for a large sum.

Acts 22.28

How could Roman citizenship be acquired in the days of Paul? What claim did Paul make about his own citizenship?

34. Bring this young man to the tribune; for he has something to tell him.

Acts 23.17

Who was the young man and what had he to tell the tribune? Say briefly what action the tribune took.

35. You have appealed to Caesar; to Caesar you shall go.

Acts 25.12

Explain why Paul made this appeal to Caesar. What effect did this appeal have on the remainder of Paul's life?

36. Sirs, I perceive that the voyage will be with injury and much loss, not only of the cargo and the ship, but also of our lives.

Acts 27.10

Why did Paul give this advice, and to whom was he speaking at the time?

37. Unless these men stay in the ship, you cannot be saved.

Acts 27.31

Explain Paul's anxiety at the situation. What action did the soldiers take?

38. A viper came out because of the heat and fastened on his hand.

Acts 28.3

What did the people think when they saw this happen? How did they then change their minds?

Essay questions

1. Why was it necessary to find a replacement for Judas Iscariot? How was the choice made?

2. Describe, as vividly as possible, what took place on the Day of Pentecost.

3. Give a detailed account of the healing of the cripple at the Beautiful Gate. How did the Apostles address the people in the portico?

4. Now, when they saw the boldness of Peter and John, and perceived that they were uneducated, common men, they wondered.
   Acts 4.13
   What led to this observation and how was the matter resolved?

5. Briefly narrate the story of Ananias and Sapphira. What internal problem of the Early Church is illustrated by this story?

6. But the high priest rose up and all who were with him, that is, the party of the Sadducees, and filled with jealousy they arrested the apostles.
   Acts 5.17
   What followed this arrest? Why were these people jealous?

7. How did the Church deal with the murmur of the Hellenists to the effect that 'their widows were neglected in the daily distributions'? Briefly relate the preaching of Stephen and show his importance in the history of the Early Church.

8. 'Stephen did not put up a defence during his trial.' Say why you agree or disagree with this statement.

9. Describe the events which led to the conversion of Saul.

10. Give an account of the missionary activities of Philip the Deacon.

11. How was Peter convinced that the Gospel must be extended to the Gentiles?

12. Narrate the experiences of Cornelius which led to his conversion. Why was his conversion a significant event in the history of the Early Church?

13. How was the Church at Antioch established and what important role was played by this Church up to the First Council at Jerusalem?

14. Trace the course of the persecution of the Church by Herod the King up to the time of his death.

15. What happened on the island of Cyprus during Paul's first missionary journey?

16. Give a detailed account of Paul's address to the people of Antioch in Pisidia. How did they receive the Apostles' teaching?

17. Write all you know about Barnabas as related in the Acts of the Apostles, up to the return after the first missionary journey.

18. Describe all that took place at Lystra during Paul's first missionary journey.

19. Unless you are circumcised according to the custom of Moses, you cannot be saved.
    Acts 15.1
    How did the Church deal with the problems posed by this statement?

20. Why was the First Christian Council at Jerusalem convened and what were the decisions reached?

21. Give a full account of what happened to Paul and Silas in Philippi as a result of their encounter with a slave girl.

22. Explain carefully Paul's activities in Athens. What did he say to the people about their altar 'To an unknown god'?

23. Give a full account of the riot at Ephesus, its causes, and how it was resolved.

24. Explain why Paul sent for the Christian elders at Ephesus to meet him at Miletus. Tell in your own words what he had to say to them.

25. Give a full account of Paul's activites in Jerusalem leading up to the attempt to kill him, and his arrest by the Roman tribune.

26. In your own words, say how Paul defended himself to the Jews as he stood on the steps leading up to the Roman fortress of Antonia. What effect did his speech have on his hearers?

27. What plot was made against Paul after his arrest by the Romans? Explain how the plot became known to Paul and describe the action taken by the Roman tribune.

28. What charges were made by the Jewish leaders against Paul in the presence of the Governor, Felix? What did Paul have to say in reply? Say briefly what action Felix took.

29. Explain carefully how and why Paul, when being tried by the new Governor, Festus, made his appeal to Caesar.

30. Describe what happened when Paul appeared before Festus and King Agrippa and Bernice. What was Agrippa's verdict?

31. Give a brief account of Paul's journey to Rome, from boarding the grain ship at Myra to the landing on Malta.

32. Describe in detail the events which took place during Paul's stay in Malta.

33. How did Paul finally reach Rome, and what happened to him there? Describe carefully his conversations with the Jews in Rome.

Essay questions (short notes)

Short notes are, strictly speaking, a form of essay question based on short and specific topics. These include personalities, incidents, place names and themes. As the name 'short notes' implies, the answers are usually short, direct, and explanatory when abstract themes are involved. Candidates are usually given a choice, say three out of five topics, on which to write. The following are examples of such questions:

1. Write short notes on **three** of the following: Matthias; Ananias and Sapphira; Gamaliel; Simon the magician; the Ethiopian Eunuch.

2. Write short notes on **three** of the following: the Mount called Olivet; Akeldama; Damascus; Antioch in Syria; Caesarea.

3. Write short notes on **three** of the following: Hellenists; Sadducees; proselyte; the Sanhedrin; Gentiles.

4. Write short notes on **three** of the following: Barnabas; Aeneas; Tabitha; Herod the King; Sergius Paulus.

5. Write short notes on **three** of the following: Iconium; Lystra; Agabus; Bar-Jesus; James the brother of Jesus.

6. Write short notes on **three** of the following: sabbath day's journey; Feast of Pentecost; God-fearer; casting of lots; speaking in tongues.

7. Write short notes on **three** of the following: John Mark; Timothy; Lydia; Jason; Aquila and Priscilla.

8. Write short notes on **three** of the following: Apollos; Gallio; Demetrius; Eutychus; Artemis.

9. Write short notes on **three** of the following: Claudius Lysias; the Areopagus; Epicureans and Stoics; the Way; the Hall of Tyrannus.

10. Write short notes on **three** of the following: Macedonia and Achaia; Felix and Drusilla; Agrippa and Bernice; Publius; Tertullus.

11. Write short notes on **three** of the following: Porcius Festus; Philip the Evangelist; Trophimus the Ephesian; Fair Havens; the Syrtis.

12. Write short notes on **three** of the following: Julius; Days of Unleavened Bread; Sea of Adria; the Twin Brothers; the Forum of Appius and Three Taverns.

SPECIMEN EXAMINATION PAPER

The West African Examinations Council School Certificate and G.C.E. Syllabus for Bible Knowledge 2 (New Testament) varies from year to year according to which Gospels are set for study. Only when St. Mark is the selected Gospel is the student required to study the whole of the Acts of the Apostles: in other years, studies end at chapter 15, verse 35.

In order to give the student a clear idea of what is required, the following specimen examination paper (a mock paper based on WASC Bible Knowledge 2 and covering the same syllabus) has been prepared. It is based on a year when St. Mark has been studied along with the whole of the Acts. Remember that there is always a choice which is clearly indicated on the paper:

Section A: **The Gospel according to Matthew** and
the **Acts of the Apostles (1-15.35)**
Section B: **The Gospel according to Mark** and
the **Acts of the Apostles**
Section C: **The Gospel according to Luke** and
the **Acts of the Apostles (1-15.35)**.

Remember, also, to read very carefully what you are asked to do at the head of the question paper.

SPECIMEN EXAMINATION PAPER

School Certificate and G.C.E.

BIBLE KNOWLEDGE 2   1½ hours

NEW TESTAMENT

Answer **three** *questions in all from* **either** *Section A* **or** *Section B. (This choice may be A or C, B or C, according to the syllabus for the year.)*

One of the questions attempted must be a context question.

SECTION B

THE GOSPEL ACCORDING TO MARK, AND THE ACTS OF THE APOSTLES

1. *Give the context of* **four** *of the following passages, and answer the questions which follow:*

(a) Is it lawful on the sabbath to do good or to do harm, to save life or to kill?   (Mark 3:4)

How did those present react to this question? What action did the Pharisees take afterwards?

(b) Talitha cumi.   (Mark 5:41)

What language is Jesus using here, and what do these words mean? Give two other examples where Mark records words in the same language.

(c) Go into the city, and a man carrying a jar of water will meet you.   (Mark 14:13)

What other instructions did Jesus give on this occasion? What is unusual about 'a man carrying a jar of water'?

(d) You have not lied to men but to God.   (Acts 5:4)

Explain how Ananias had lied to God.

(e) Rise, Peter; kill and eat.   (Acts 10:13)

Explain Peter's reaction to these words.

(f) But I was born a citizen.   (Acts 22:28)

Explain how Paul was a citizen — of where? How did the man he was speaking to acquire his citizenship?

2. Explain why Jesus 'went away to the region of Tyre and Sidon'.
                                                      (Mark 7:24)

Describe what happened there. How did the woman in the story impress Jesus?

3. While they were on the road to Jerusalem what did James and John ask Jesus to do for them? How did Jesus answer their request?

4. What charges were made against Stephen?

Explain carefully how he angered the members of the Council and recount what action they took.

5. What do you know about John Mark?

In what ways was Mark responsible for the quarrel between Paul and Barnabas?

6. Tell the story of the 'young man named Eutychus'. (Acts 20:9)

Twice in this story the writers speaks of the act of breaking bread. What do you think is meant by 'breaking bread'?